JOYCE CARY REMEMBERED

ULSTER EDITIONS AND MONOGRAPHS

General Editors
Robert Welch
John McVeagh

Joyce Cary Remembered

in letters and interviews
by his family and others

Compiled and edited by

Barbara Fisher

Ulster Editions and Monographs 1

1988

COLIN SMYTHE
Gerrards Cross, Bucks

BARNES & NOBLE BOOKS
Totowa, New Jersey

Copyright © 1988 by Barbara Fisher

First published in 1988 by Colin Smythe Limited,
Gerrards Cross, Buckinghamshire
as the first volume of
the Ulster Editions and Monograph series,
sponsored by the University of Ulster

British Library Cataloguing in Publication Data

Joyce Cary remembered : in letters and
interviews by his family and others.—
1. Fiction in English. Cary, Joyce,
1888-1957
I. Fisher, Barbara   II. Series
823'.912

ISBN 0-86140-296-0

First published in the United States of America in 1988
by Barnes & Noble Books, 81 Adams Drive, Totowa, N.J. 07512

ISBN 0-389-20812-4

Produced in Great Britain
Disc translation and photosetting by Textflow Services, N. Ireland
Printed and bound by Billing & Sons Ltd, Worcester

To
David Carrigan and Paul Wiseman

Contents

PART II – Family Man and Professional Writer

Foreword and Acknowledgements

It is appropriate to remember Joyce Cary, as we approach the centenary of his birth. He was born on 7 December 1888, and died on 29 March 1857.

I collected most of these testimonies during the 1960s, when his personality was still vividly alive to many people. As many here represented are themselves now dead, and Cary is certainly due for reappraisal, it would seem a sadly irretrievable omission if these witnesses were not heard.

What is here preserved will prove valuable for future scholars, I believe. It lies behind my own interpretation of Cary, in *Joyce Cary: The Writer and His Theme* (1980), and *The House as a Symbol: Joyce Cary and 'The Turkish House'* (1986). But no critical study could include all this material explicitly, and other students may be inspired by it to follow different lines of thought.

I hope, however, that the book will prove of equal interest to the reading public for whom Cary actually wrote. In his own lifetime, he had a wide international audience, and he always believed that the ordinary intelligent reader would recognize the deeper meanings implied in his work, notably in the religious and political spheres that chiefly inspired him. The development of ideas and the course of events since he wrote make it easier to recognize his intentions. And meeting the man in these pages, through those who knew him, should help to further appreciation of his art and thought.

I am especially grateful to have had the interest of his family in this enterprise, and trust that they too will enjoy reading something of their own history as here printed. I am equally indebted to all contributors, whose regard for Cary and his work has been the chief spur to their support. I gratefully remember here, also, a travel grant awarded to me in 1967 by the Leverhulme Trustees, which assisted me in obtaining these interviews. And my appreciation of help in research related to Joyce Cary, from the staff of the Bodleian and other libraries and institutions, extends even further in this book than it did in the previous two. Above all, I warmly acknowledge the interest and

support of Professor Robert Welch and those representatives of the
University of Ulster who have made this publication possible.

Quotations from Joyce Cary's unpublished writings are made by
kind permission of Winifred Davin, on behalf of the Joyce Cary
Estate, and from the published works by permission of Michael
Joseph Limited, Curtis Brown and Harper & Row.

Oxford   Barbara Fisher
April 1988

Concerning the Text

The contributions are ordered to follow the course of Cary's life, and so form a many-handed biography. Each appears at the point where its contents are most relevant, though inevitably there is some overlap into earlier or later years. There is also, inevitably, diversity of opinion regarding events, the man, and his work. This diversity owes as much, of course, to differences between the contributors themselves, as to Cary.

Wherever possible, the contributors or their next of kin have been consulted, to ensure that this publication gives rise to no regrets. Several people have wished to expand or revise what they said many years ago, and this is understandable, in a world where our own development must keep pace with constant change (as Cary would have been the first to agree).

The situation applies as much to me as to anyone else. The questions that I asked in the 1960s now have a fuller significance for me, though they sprang even then from the belief that Cary was an original thinker, whose 'whole view of life' (which he named as his theme) deserves to be better understood. Here they are still asked in the hope of discovering what others can contribute, for example, to an understanding of his use of symbols. But my comments arising from, and justifying, these questions are confined to endnotes, and can be ignored.

Endnotes also provide brief biographies of contributors, and evidence that what is published in their name has their approval. The setting and date of each item will be clear from the note under its heading which, with the contributor's name, is the chief clue to its contents.

Italics are used to distinguish the editor's words throughout the text. As editorial comments they are enclosed in square brackets. Square brackets are also used to indicate a doubtful reading (in Cary's letters), with a question mark preceding the word. Editorial comment being thus distinguished, roman type suffices to distinguish all quotations.

For uniformity, current English usage and practice is followed throughout for spelling and punctuation; this has been applied also to

xiii

quotations from Cary's unpublished writings, unless the variation is clearly justified.

Unless otherwise indicated, unpublished material referred to is in the Bodleian Library. Wherever page numbers of Cary's published novels are quoted, they refer to the Carfax edition.

Endnotes serve finally to link the items by contributors to the 'Outline of Cary's Life and writing, in relation to this book,' which here follows. Reading this 'Outline' before the main text, in which endnotes refer back to it, should make the general picture clear from the outset – and the particular pictures easy to fit into it.

Outline of Cary's Life and Writings in relation to this book

This outline is condensed from Bibliography I in *Joyce Cary: The Writer and His Theme*, which contains all Cary's published writings known to me, listed within the framework of his life. This outline includes only those of his writings or interviews to which reference is made in the items that follow. The numbering in the full list is, however, retained, not least because readers will then realize how many more writings by Cary there are to be considered.

As explained in the fuller list, the order of published items follows the order of first publication, as nearly as this could be ascertained. A subsequent first publication in the United Kingdom or America is also listed, but later publication elsewhere is not listed, except to show changes of title or content.

The right-hand marginal letters classify the writing thus: P (Poem), S (Story), N (Novel), T (Treatise and memoir, a monograph), E (Essay, article or review), L (Letter), Q (Interview, talk, or quoted broadcast). The numbers following these letters give the chronology within each classification.

The chronological arrangement draws attention to Cary's development and concurrent use of different literary forms, and the relation of his non-fiction to his fiction. The biographical framework gives an idea of the private and public worlds from which the writing grew. Of necessity it omits much – notably annual holidays, and the many occasions, from 1942, when Cary lectured, by invitation, to various audiences in the United Kingdom. Only overseas lectures are mentioned, to affirm his world-wide reputation.

Following the outline, the letters and numbers classifying Cary's writings are listed chronologically, beside the numbers of the items that contain a reference to them. As the Carfax edition is used for reference to novels, all prefatory essays listed can be assumed to related to items in which that novel is named.

Unless otherwise stated, the name used for authorship was *Joyce Cary*. For the pseudonym *Thomas Joyce*, see item 4.

1888   Arthur Joyce Lunel Cary, first child of Arthur and Charlotte Cary, born at the home of his maternal grandparents, James and Helen Joyce, in Londonderry, Dec. 7.

1892   His brother John born, Jan. 28.

1898   His mother dies at home, 41 Kitto Rd, London, Oct. 1.

1900   His father marries Dora Stevenson, a cousin.
       The family moves to 70 Duke's Avenue, Chiswick.
       Enters Hurstleigh prep. school, Tunbridge Wells, as a boarder, with his brother, Sept.

1902   His half-brother Anthony born, Oct. 30.

1903   Enters Clifton College, Sept.

1904   His half-sister Shiela born, Jan. 15.
       His stepmother dies, May 8.
       His brother John leaves Hurstleigh to enter the Rayal Naval College, Dartmouth.
       He spends a sketching holiday in Normandy, summer.
       Is confirmed in the Anglican faith, autumn.

1906   Leaves Clifton to study art in Paris, July.

1907   Enters School of Art (soon to become the College of Art), Edinburgh, Jan.
       His father marries Mary Agar, Jan.
       The family move to 42 Grosvenor Road, Gunnersbury, ca. March

1908   *Verse* by Arthur Cary. Edinburgh: Robert Grant, July 1908.   P.2-P.14

1909   Enters Trinity College, Oxford University, Oct.

1910   In Paris with John Middleton Murry, Dec. 27 to mid-Jan.

1912   Leaves Oxford for 10 Store St, London, to write.
       Arrives in Antivari, Montenegro, Nov. 1st.
       Joins Red Cross; writing 'Memoir of the Bobotes'.

1913   Returns to England, May.
       Receives Oxford degree in law, June.
       Joins Sir Horace Plunkett's Co-operative Society in Ireland, but finds services unwanted, Aug.

1914 Enters the Imperial Institute, Jan. 12.
Appointed Assistant District Officer, Northern Nigerian Political Service, April 29.
1915 Appointed 2nd Lieut. in the West African Field Force.
Wounded in attack on Mora Mountian, Sept. 1.
1916 Granted leave in England, March 26.
Marries Gertrude Margaret Ogilvie, June 1.
Sails from Liverpool for Lagos, Aug. 9.
1917 Returns to civilian rank, Asst. District Officer, Jan.
First son, Arthur Lucius Michael (known as Michael), born April 3.
1918 Arrives in Liverpool on leave, Feb. 1.
Commences twelve months' tour of Borgu, Aug. 24.
Second son, Peter, born Dec. 9.
1919 Returns record of his Borgu tour, Dec. 10.
1920 Medical exam. 'proceeding on leave'. Jan. 6.
Retires from Nigerian Service; buys 12 Parks Rd, Oxford, April.
'Lombrosine' by Thomas Joyce. *Saturday Evening Post* (31 Jan. 1920), 30, 32, 62; [published as] 'Experimental Love' by Thomas Joyce. *Pearson's Magazine*, L (July 1920), 41-47.   S.2
'Salute to Propriety' by Thomas Joyce. *Saturday Evening Post* (9 Oct. 1920), 40, 42, 45, 46; *Hutchinson's Magazine*, IV (Jan. 1921), 54-65.   S.11
1922 Visits Hungary with members of Oxford Univ., July.
1925 Third son, Tristram, born May 14.
1926 Works on Hays Wharf London during General Strike, May.
1927 Fourth son, George, born Aug. 12.
1932 *Aissa Saved*. London: Ernest Benn, 1932 [Jan.]; New York: Harper, 1962. [See E.26.]   N.1
1933 *An American Visitor*. London: Ernest Benn, 1933 [Aug.]; New York: Harper, 1961. [See E.31.]   N.2
1936 *The African Witch*. London: Victor Gollancz, 1936 [May: a Book Society choice]; New York: William Morrow, 1936. [See E.24.]   N.3
1937 His father dies, at Wadeford, Somerset, Nov. 23.
1938 *Castle Corner*. London: Victor Gollancz, 1938 [Jan.; a Book Society recommendation]; New York: Harper, 1963. [See E.32.]   N.4

1939   *Power in Men*. London: Nicholson & Watson, for the   T.1
        Liberal Book Club, 1939 [May]; Seattle: University
        of Washington Press, 1963.

        Mister Johnson. London: Victor Gollancz, 1939   N.5
        [July]; New York: Harper, 1951. [See E.27.]

        Serves as an air-raid warden, from Sept. to 1945.

1940   *Charley is may Darling*. London: Michael Joseph,   N.6
        1940 [April.; a Book Society recommendation];
        New York: Harper, 1960. [See E.23.]

1941   *A House of Children*. London: Michael Joseph, 1941   N.7
        [Feb.; awarded the James Tait Black Memorial
        Prize, 1941]; New York: Harper, 1956. [See E.22]

        The Case for African Freedom. London: Secker and   T.2
        Warburg, 1941 [July]; revised and enlarged
        edition, 1944 [revised text, without the introduc-
        tion written by George Orwell for the first version].

        *The Case For African Freedom and other writings on
        Africa by Joyce Cary,* University of Texas Press
        (1962), 1-136; 'Co-ops for Africa?' [condensed from
        The Case for African Freedom]. *World Digest* (May
        1945), 44-47.

        Herself Surprised. London: Michael Joseph, 1941   N.8
        [Nov.; a Book Society recommendation]; New
        York: Harper, 1948. [1st book of 1st tril.; see also
        E.15, E.78.]

1942   Attends Civil Defence Course in Bournemouth, April
        27 to May 2.

        To be a Pilgrim. London: Michael Joseph, 1942   N.9
        [Oct.]; New York: Harper, 1949. [2nd book of 1st
        tril.; see also E.16, E.78]

1943   Sails for Freetown as script writer with Thorold
        Dickinson, to make film *Men of Two Worlds*, Jan.
        17.

        Flies in stages to Dar es Salaam; home on May 20.

        'Tolstoy's Theory of Art' [from a lecture entitled   E.6†
        'Tolstoy on Art and Morals' delivered at the Univ.
        of Edinburgh on 27 Nov. 1942]. *University of Edin-
        burgh Journal*, XII (Summer 1943), 91-96.

        Process of Real Freedom. London: Michael Joseph,   T.3
        1943 [Nov.].

        Revises *The Case for African Freedom*, with a new
        introduction as first chapter.

1944   *The Horse's Mouth*. London: Michael Joseph, 1944   N.10
       [Aug.; a Book Society recommendation]; New
       York: Harper, 1950 [A Book-of-the-Month Club
       selection]. [3rd book of 1st tril.; see also E.17, E.78]

1945   *Matching Soldier*. London: Michael Joseph, 1945   P.15
       [March].

       'Bush River.' *Windmill*, 1, no. 2 (1945), 120-5;   S.16‡
       [revised for publication in] *Esquire* (US), XLII
       (July 1954), 40, 106-7 [British edn., vol. I].

       Finally revises script of *Men of Two Worlds*, June
       19.

1946   Tours India on film project with Thorold Dickinson,
       Jan. 3 to mid-April.

       The Moonlight. London: Michael Joseph, 1946 [May;   N.11
       a Book Society recommendation]; New York:
       Harper, 1947. [See E.33.]

1947   *The Drunken Sailor:* A Ballad-Epic. London: Michael   P.17
       Joseph, 1947 [Nov.].

1948   His wife has an operation for cancer, April 28.
       Spends a holiday in Switzerland with his wife, Aug.
       15 to Sept.1.

1949   *A Fearful Joy*. London: Michael Joseph, 1949 [Oct.];   N.12
       New York: Harper, 1950. [See E.28.]
       Declines the award of a CBE, Dec. 5.
       His wife dies, Dec. 13.

1950   'The Old Strife at Plant's' [a discarded chapter of *The*   S.18
       Horse's Mouth]. With an Introduction by the
       author. *Harper's Magazine*, CCI (Aug. 1950),
       80-96; *World Review* (Feb. 1951), 45-62; [the intro-
       duction appears as 'Author's Note' on pp. 43-44 of]
       100 copies with illustrations by the author, at the
       New Bodleian, Oxford, 1956 [which differs slightly
       from the first version].

       'Umaru.' *Cornhill Magazine*, CLXV (Winter 1950/   S.19‡
       1951), 50-54.

       'Three New Prefaces" [subtitled] *Herself Surprised*,   E.15
       To be a Pilgrim, The Horse's Mouth'. *Adam Inter-*   E.16
       national Review, XVIII, nos 212-13 (November-   E.17
       December 1950), 11-14. [Published separaetly as:]
       'Prefatory Essay'. *To be a Pilgrim*, Carfax ed.
       (1951), 7-8; 'Prefatory Essay'. *The Horse's Mouth*,
       Carfax ed. (1951), 7-10.

'The Novelist at Work: a Conversation between Joyce   Q.2
Cary and Lord David Cecil.' Transcribed from a
Telediphone Recording made on 7 July 1950 (by
courtesy of the BBC). *Adam International Review*,
XVIII, nos. 212-13 (November-December 1950),
15-25.

1951   Tours the United States, lecturing, Jan. 2 to April
21.

'A Talk with Joyce Cary' [conducted by Harvey   Q.3
Breit]. *New York Times Book Review* (18 Feb.
1951), 14.

'The Revolution of the Women.' *Vogue* (US), CXVII   E.18
(15 March 1951), 99, 100, 149.

'Prefatory Essay.' *A House of Children*, Carfax ed.   E.22
([Oct.] 1951), 5-8.

'Prefatory Essay.' *Charley is my Darling*, Carfax ed.   E.23
([Oct.] 1951), 5-10.

'Prefatory Essay.' *The African Witch*, Carfax ed.   E.24
([Oct.] 1951), 9-13.

1952   'Prefatory Essay.' *Aissa Saved*, Carfax ed. ([Feb.]   E.26
1952), 5-11.

'Prefatory Essay.' *Mister Johnson*, Carfax ed. ([Feb.]   E.27
1952), 5-10.

'Prefatory Essay.' *A Fearful Joy*, Carfax ed. ([Feb.]   E.28
1952), 5-8.

'The Mass Mind: Our Favourite Folly.' *Harper's*   E.29
Magazine, CCIV (March 1952), 25-27; [published
as] 'Myth of the Mass Mind: a Modern Catchword'.
Cornhill Magazine, CLXVI (Summer 1952),
138-42; [published as] 'Myth of the Mass Mind'.
Reader's Digest, LXII (Feb. 1953), 135-6; [conden-
sed and translated as] 'Le mythe de "l'homme
robot"'. *Sélection du Reader's Digest*, XIII (Sept.
1953), 150, 152, 154.

'Prefatory Essay.' *An American Visitor*, Carfax ed.   E.31
([May] 1952), 7-11.

'Prefatory Essay.' *Castle Corner*, Carfax ed. ([May]   E.32
1952), 5-8.

'Prefatory Essay.' *The Moonlight*, Carfax ed. ([May]   E.33
1952), 5-11.

'Success Story.' *Harper's Magazine*, CCIV (June   S.21‡
1952), 74-76.

Prisoner of Grace. London: Michael Joseph, 1952   N.13
[Sept.]; New York: Harper, 1952 [Oct.]. [1st book
of 2nd tril.; see also E.46.]

'Romance.' *Time* (20 Oct. 1952, 119 [Atlantic ed.,   S.22‡
p.47].

1953   His youngest son, George, dies, Jan. 9.

'The Oxford Scholar.' *Holiday*, XIII (June 1953), 96,   E.41
98, 100, 132, 134, 136, 137, 139-43.

Receives honorary degree, Doctor of Laws, Edinburgh University, July 3.

Tours the United States, lecturing Sept. 13 to Dec. 8.

Except the Lord. New York: Harper, 1953 [12 Nov.];   N.14
London: Michael Joseph, 1953 [16 Nov.] [2nd
book of 2nd tril.]

'A Child's Religion.' *Vogue* (US), CXXII (Dec.   E.43†
1953), 86-87; *Family Doctor*, IV (Aug. 1954), 440,
442.

1954   Lectures in Turin, Genoa, Milan, Rome, March
19-23.

Stays in Nice and Menton, March 25 to April 1.

'Prefatory Essay.' *Prisoner of Grace*, Carfax ed. ([22   E.46
March] 1954), 5-8.

Lectures in Cologne, Frankfurt, Marburg, Mainz,
Freiburg, Stuttgart, Tübingen, Munich, Berlin,
June 29 to July 14.

'Switzerland.' *Holiday*, XVI (Aug. 1954), 27-29,   E.49
32-33, 36-37.

[On the Censorship of Boccaccio.] *Times* (London) (2   L.4
Aug. 1954), 7.

'Catching up with History' [a review of Richard   E.52
Wright's *Black Power*]. *Nation* (16 Oct. 1954, 332,
333; *The Case for African Freedom and other writings
on Africa by Joyce Cary* (1962), 219-24.

Lectures at the British Institute, Paris, Oct. 27.

Lectures in Stockholm, Uppsala, Helsinki, Malmo,
and Copenhagen, Nov. 30-Dec. 8.

'An Interview with Joyce Cary' [conducted by John   Q.7†
Burrows and Alex Hamilton]. *Paris Review*, II, 7
(Winter 1954-5), 63-78; *Writers at Work: The Paris
Review Interviews*. Ed. Malcolm Cowley. London,
Secker & Warburg (1958), 47-62; New York,
Viking (1958), 51-67.

1955   'The Heart of England.' *Holiday*, XVII (Jan. 1955),   E.54†
        27, 28, 30, 76, 78, 79, 81; *Joyce Cary Selected
        Essays*. Ed. A. G. Bishop. London, Michael Joseph
        (1976), 189-203.

        Aboard a plane that crashes at take-off, but boards
        next flight for Athens, Jan. 16; gives 9 lectures – in
        Athens, Corfu, Salonica, Nicosia, Limassol, Fama-
        gusta; returns Feb. 4.

        Becomes a hospital out-patient, treated for paralysis
        developing in his leg, Feb. 11.

        Not Honour More. London: Michael Joseph, 1955   N.15
        [April; a Book Society recommendation]; New
        York: Harper, 1955 [May]. [3rd book of 2nd tril.]

        'Out of Hand.' *Vogue* (US), CXXVI (July 1955),   S.33‡
        60-62; *She* (Sept. 1956), 28-29.

        Learns that his illness is amyotrophic lateral sclerosis,
        a form of paralysis that will steadily extend from his
        limbs to the rest of his body; he can live for five
        years at most, and will more probably die within
        two years; Nov.

1956   'Westminster Abbey.' *Holiday*, XIX (April 1956), 62,   E.67†
        63; *Joyce Cary Selected Essays*. Ed. A. G. Bishop.
        London, Michael Joseph (1976), 204-9.

        'A Slight Case of Demolition.' *Sunday Times* (20 May   E.69†
        1956), 6.

        'If You Could Face Your Problems Today as this Man   Q.8
        Faces His ...' [Interview conducted by Merrick
        Winn] *Daily Express* (27 Aug. 1956), 4.

        'You're Only Young Once.' *Encounter* (Sept. 1956),   S.38*
        24-26.

        His six Clark Lectures read on his behalf by his
        nephew Robert Ogilvie, at Trinity College, Cam-
        bridge, between Oct. 19 and Nov. 32; by now Joyce
        Cary cannot stand, and his failing voice makes
        dictation difficult; he writes with his hand suppor-
        ted by a sling from above, and the pen fastened to
        his fingers; the paper is on a bed-desk invented by
        himself, on spools that move it automatically when
        his wrist drops on to an electrically-controlled
        button.

        'Cromwell House.' *New Yorker* (3 Nov. 1956), 45-52,
        54, 56, 61, 62, 64, 67; *Joyce Cary Selected Essays*.

Ed. A. G. Bishop. London, Michael Joseph (1976), E.72†
43-65.

1957 Realizes he cannot revise ' The Captive and the Free'
for publication, as well as the Clark lectures; so
works on the lectures, stories (S.44, 45, 47) and
letters (L.9, 10), Jan.

Sends manuscript of lectures, as 'Art and Reality', to
the publisher, and polishes his last short story, by
mid-March; can no longer write, but remains men-
tally clear and alert to the end.

'A Conversation with Joyce Cary' [interview conduc- Q.10
ted by Nathan Cohen, in Sept. 1956; broadcast on
CBC in Jan. 1957]. *Tamarack Review*, no. 3 (Spring
1957), 5-15.

'A Valedictory of a Great Writer' [based on Cary's Q.11
written answers to questions sent in Dec. 1956].
Life (25 March 1957), 105, 106, 108.

Dies in his sleep, at home, at 10 a.m., March 29.

'The Tunnel.' *Vogue* (US), CXXX (1 Oct. 1957), 186, S.43*
187, 226.

1958 'Preface.' *First Trilogy*. New York, Harper (1958), E.78
pp. ix-xv.

Art and Reality. The Clark Lectures, 1956. Cam- T.5
bridge: Cambridge University Press, 1958 [7
March]; New York: Harper, 1958.

'The Meaning of England.' *Holiday*, XXIII (April E.79†
1958), 117; *Joyce Cary Selected Essays*. Ed. A. G.
Bishop. London, Michael Joseph (1976), 71-73.

'The Sheep.' *Texas Quarterly*, 1, no. 4 (Winter 1958), S.47*
23-37.

1959 *The Captive and the Free*. New York: Harper, 1959 N.16
[Jan.]; London: Michael Joseph, 1959 [March].

1960 *Spring Song and Other Stories*. London: Michael S.49
Joseph, 1960 [Feb.]; New York: Harper, 1960. -53
[Contains all stories marked with an asterisk; a 2nd
asterisk gives the additional information that, from
the evidence of paper and handwriting used, the
story was completed in substantially its final form
between 1935 and 1940.] The last five pieces in the
volume are hitherto unpublished [so giving its
designation to the collection].

Memoir of the Bobotes. Austin: University of Texas   T.6
  Press, 1960; [also issued as a Supplement with
  Texas Quarterly III, no. I (Spring 1960)]; London:
  Michael Joseph, 1964.
1971 His brother John dies, March 23.
1976 His eldest son, now Sir Michael Cary, dies, March 6.
  Selected Essays. Ed. A. G. Bishop. London: Michael   E.80-
  Joseph, 1976. [Contains all items marked with a   82
  dagger; the following, hitherto unpublished, give
  the collection its designation.]
'Carrig Cnoc.' pp. 29-31.   E.80†

Cary's Writings (classified as above), listed beside item numbers of
contributions that contain a reference to them.

For items marked with asterisks, see entry on *Spring Song and Other
Stories* (S.49-53) on p.xxiii; for items marked with a dagger, see entry
on *Selected Essays* (E.80-82) above.

P.2-P.14	Items 9, 12, 16.
S.2-S.11	Item 47.
N.1	Items 19, 22, 65.
N.2	Items 19, 23 (n.9), 27, 47, 48.
N.3	Items 16, 22, 25 (n.1), 36 (n.1), 40, 65, 67.
N.4	Items 1, 2, 3, 14, 16, 28, 33, 39 (n.3), 54 (n.2).
T.1.	Items 16, 18, 54 (n.2), 57.
N.5	Items 3, 18, 22, 27, 28, 31, 34, 39, 44, 48, 49, 50, 65.
N.6	Items 5, 20, 29.
N.7	Items 1, 2 (n.1), 3, 4, 5, 6, 11, 16 (n.4), 22, 23, 28, 31, 32, 44, 59.
T.2	Items 18, 34, 40, 65.
N.8	Items 32, 39, 44.
N.9	Items 22, 28, 32, 38, 40, 44, 47.
E.6†	Item 33 (n.4).
T.3	Items 18, 33.
N.10	Items 3, 14, 16, 19, 22, 28, 30, 31, 32, 35, 38 (with ref. to Gulley), 39 (n.1), 41, 44, 46, 47, 49, 56, 59 (n.1), 61, 64, 65, 67.
P.15	Item 16 (n.12).
S.16**	Item 47.
N.11	Items 16, 34, 35, 38, 40, 44.

P.17   Item 48.
N.12   Item 29 (n.3).
S.18   Items 40 (n.3), 59 (n.4), 60, 67.
S.19★★   Item 47.
Q.2   Item 39.
Q.3   Item 53.
E.18   Item 52.
E.22   Item 5.
E.23   Item 5.
E.24   Item 40.
E.29   Item 51.
S.21★★   Item 47.
N.13   Items 34, 37, 38 (n.1), 39.
S.22★★   Item 47.
E.41   Item 50.
S.24★★   Item 47.
N.14   Items 5, 27.
E.43†   Items 40, 42 (n.1), 52.
S.26★★   Item 47.
L.4   Item 61 (n.6).
L.5   Item 39.
E.52   Item 47.
Q.7†   Items 19 (n.4), 38 (n.4), 57 (n.3).
E.54†   Item 50.
N.15   Items 5 (n.2), 32, 37, 48, 54, 59, 67.
S.33★★   Item 52.
E.67†   Item 50.
E.69†   Items 14 (nn.3,4), 18 (n.2).
Q.8   Item 63 (n.1).
S.38★   Item 61.
E.72†   Items 36 (n.2), 47.
Q.10   Item 61.
Q.11   Item 59.
E.76†   Items 52, 57.
S.43★   Item 61.
T.5   Items 31, 46, 54, 57, 59, 62, 67.
E.79†   Item 67 (n.7).
N.16   Items 54, 61, 64, 67.
S.49-S.53   Item 67.
T.6   Items 7 (n.4), 14, 40, 59, 67.
E.80   Item 3.

Part I

Family Background
and
Early Years

1

The Cary Family of Inishowen

Lionel Stevenson

In 1963, Professor Stevenson prepared multigraphed copies of this unpublished history as Christmas gifts for his kinsfolk; in January 1964 he kindly sent a copy to me. It begins:

The Cary family is usually assumed to be of Norman descent; but as surnames had not come into use at the time of the Conquest, the tracing of family origins at that period is possible only among the nobility. Landowning families soon began to be identified by the names of their estates, and thus the Carys derive their patronymic ultimately from the little river Cary, in southeastern Somersetshire, on the bank of which the manor of "Kari" is listed in Domesday Book as one of the many fiefs of Walter de Douai, a powerful baron of William the Conqueror. It was probably Walter who built there one of the mightiest strongholds in Somerset, and named it Castle Cary; but early in the twelfth century it came into the possession of the Lovel family. The first recorded ancestor of the Carys, appropriately named Sir Adam de Kari, of Castle Cary, is mentioned in a document of 1198. [...]

For the next five generations the de Carys prospered, marrying the daughters of neighbouring knights, acquiring knighthoods themselves, and gradually spreading through the southwest of England, especially in Devonshire. Apparently at some point a younger son of the family migrated to Bristol to follow mercantile pursuits in that thriving city; as early as 1313 one Lawrence de Cary held civic office as 'senister' and in subsequent generations others of the family served as bailiff or as mayor. These wealthy cloth-merchants habitually used the arms of the Devonshire Carys, and eventually, in 1699, three of them successfully petitioned the College of Heralds for official sanction, on the ground that it had been a constant tradition in the family, 'time out of mind,' that they were descended from a cadet of the Devonshire house.

The Bristol cloth-merchants, however, were exceptional in adopting urban and commercial life; their kinsmen remained satisfied with their country estates. By the middle of the fourteenth century Sir John de Cary, a great-great-grandson of Adam, was Lord of the Manor of Cary in the parish of St. Giles in the Heath, on the western border of Devonshire [...]. His son, another Sir John, became a figure of national importance. [...] as a result of his outspoken defence of the monarch [Richard II] he was impeached and sentenced to death, and his estates were confiscated. When the sentence was commuted to banishment in Ireland he was granted a maintenance allowance of twenty pounds per year, but was forbidden to travel more than two miles outside the town of Waterford.

After Sir John's death his estates were restored in 1404 to his elder son, Robert (the other son, John, was a priest who subsequently became Bishop of Exeter). [...]

Sir Robert Cary brought additional prestige to the family by marrying Margaret, daughter of Sir Philip Courtenay of Powderham. Sir Philip was a son of Hugh de Courtenay, second Earl of Devon, who in 1325 had married another Margaret, daughter of Humphry Bohun, Earl of Hereford and Essex, whose wife, Lady Eleanor Plantagenet, was a daughter of Edward I. Through this union all the subsequent Carys could claim royal ancestry, leading back through both the Bohuns and the Plantagenets to William the Conqueror and thence all the way to Charlemagne, and through the Bohuns also to the reigning family of Scotland in the person of King David I (St David).

A grandson of Sir Robert, Sir William, [...] had a son, Thomas, who fathered new branches of the family in other parts of England. His eldest son, Sir John, of Plashey and Fremhall Priory, Essex, was the grandfather of Henry Cary (1576-1639), who served as Lord Deputy of Ireland from 1622 to 1629 and became the first Viscount Falkland. Meanwhile even greater honours had come through Thomas Cary's younger son, William, a Gentleman of the Inner Bedchamber to Henry VIII; in 1520 he married Anne Boleyn's sister Mary, and thus his son Henry was a first cousin and close confidant of Queen Elizabeth I, who created him Baron Hundson in 1559. [...] but this illustrious line lost its influence through devotion to the Jacobite cause, and finally became extinct with the death of the last Lord Hunsdon in 1765.

Descendants of Viscount Falkland, on the other hand, survive until the present day. The second Viscount, Lucius Cary (1610–1643), the brilliant courtier of Charles I, gathered a famous intellectual coterie at Great Tew, his seat in Oxfordshire, and died heroically at the Battle of Newbury. By virtue of rank, the present (fourteenth) Viscount

Falkland may be considered the head of the Cary family; but in genealogical terms he represents a junior branch, being descended from a younger son of Sir William Cary of Cockington and Clovelly, whereas the eldest son, Robert, had inherited the Devonshire estates.

When this Robert Cary died in 1540 the properties in South and North Devon were divided, the Cockington manor going to a son of his first marriage, Thomas, while the Clovelly one went to a son of his third marriage, Robert. Both branches distinguished themselves during the spacious days of Great Elizabeth. Sir George Cary, the eldest son of Thomas of Cockington, was appointed treasurer-at-war in Ireland in March, 1599, and six months later, when the Earl of Essex suddenly returned to England, he became a lord justice; subsequently, in 1603, he was Lord Deputy of Ireland for eight months. Meanwhile the squires of Clovelly Court maintained the hospitable home which is depicted vividly by Charles Kingsley in *Westward Ho!*, though Kingsley takes liberties with history in his portrait of Will Cary as a high-spirited young son of the house who sailed to the Spanish Main in 1583 and later took part in the defeat of the Armada. In point of fact, the old squire, Sir Robert, who died in 1586, was succeeded by his son George, the eldest of six brothers, any one of whom may have performed such exploits, but none of them was named Will; and the real Will, George's son and heir, was only twelve years old at the time of the Armada.

The six brothers all fathered large families, and therefore it was essential that their sons should find opportunities in the expanding domains of England overseas. The nearest area of expansion was Ireland, where the family had the advantage of their cousin's service as Lord Deputy and also of their friendship with their Devon neighbour, Sir Arthur Chichester, who succeeded him in that office and became the chief administrator of the 'plantation' of Ulster. In 1608 Chichester defeated and captured Sir Cahir O'Dougherty, chieftain of Inishowen, the isolated peninsula of County Donegal between Lough Swilly and Lough Foyle, forming the northernmost region of Ireland. King James then granted the confiscated property to Chichester, who parceled it out among a score of his Devonshire comrades, one of whom was George Cary, eldest son of the youngest brother of George of Clovelly.

As a part of the scheme for controlling the native Irish and promoting prosperity, the little town of Derry, strategically situated on the isthmus joining Inishowen to the rest of the country, was selected by the English authorities for development into the city of Londonderry, financed by the great London guilds. When the city charter was granted by the king in 1613, George Cary was one of the first aldermen, and about the same time he was appointed as Recorder of the city. From 1615 to 1640 he was member for Derry in the Irish parliament. His property, on which he built a house that he named Redcastle, was a few miles north of the city, on the shore of Lough Foyle. In 1615 he strengthened his local status by marrying Jane Beresford, sister of Sir Tristram Beresford, baronet, who was second only to Chichester in his power and influence in Ireland. On George Cary's death in 1642 he left five sons, who extended the family holdings; when the eldest, George, inherited Redcastle, his brother Robert built Whitecastle on an adjoining tract, Edward established his home at Dungiven, south of Londonderry, and Tristram went to Coleraine, on the east side of Lough Foyle. [...]

Through the seventeenth and eighteenth centuries the Carys of Inishowen lived a peculiarly sheltered life. The whole of Ireland in those days was remote from the main currents of history, but the far northern peninsula was remote even from the rest of Ireland. Separated from their Celtic tenants by insuperable barriers of culture and religion, the plantation families found their entire social existence within their own limited ranks. During the first two or three generations the Carys sought their brides in the other English households of the region – Vaughans, Bensons, Staples, Cunninghams, Harts; but by the beginning of the eighteenth century there were so many branches of the family that Carys were marrying Carys and producing a bewildering entanglement of cousinships. For example, [... a] complicated relationship occurred about 1780 when George of Redcastle died at the age of twenty-one, leaving a pregnant young widow, who soon afterwards married his cousin, neighbour, and namesake, George Cary of Whitecastle. This event apparently aggravated an unfriendly relationship that had developed between the two branches of the family as a result of propinquity and local rivalries over many years.

The friction was a symptom of tensions that were inevitably growing up as a result of isolation and squabbles over inheritances and marriage settlements. At first glance, it may seem to have been an ideal existence in those placid days of the eighteenth century, when everyone assumed that the structure of society was immutable and that civilization had reached its permanent fulfilment. The landlords of Inishowen were untouched by the first uneasy stirrings of industrialism, of political democracy, of new inquiries and ideas on any subject. Essentially they were the last survivors of feudalism, automatically fulfilling their public duty by serving as Justices of the Peace, and supervising their tenants with paternalistic authority. Because their acreages among the rugged hills and gloomy turf-bogs of Inishowen were relatively small and infertile, they could not afford the luxury of spending much – if any – of their time in Dublin or in London, and so they did not lapse into the vice of absenteeism that devastated the relationship of landlords and tenants in the more productive parts of Ireland.

At the apogee of their prosperity, about the middle of the eighteenth century, there were at least seven branches of the Cary family flourishing on separate estates in Inishowen and adjacent territory. About five miles north of Redcastle and Whitecastle, on a hilltop with a magnificent view across the widest stretch of Lough Foyle to Benevenagh, a new house named Castlecary was built by Edward Cary, second son of Edward of Redcastle, when he married Ann Benson of Birdstown. [...]

Their lives being undisturbed by the innovations and controversies of the larger world, the Carys of Inishowen were still unable to recognize, much less to contend against, the insidious tides of change that were threatening their way of life. After the Act of Union in 1800 the economy of the whole of Ireland was rapidly undermined. Overpopulation and poverty could not be controlled by even the most conscientious of the landlords; and their extravagant habits were too innate to be surrendered even when rising prices and taxes caused their expenditures to outrun their incomes. The fatal spiral of evictions, emigration, and famine darkened the first half of the nineteenth century, in Inishowen as in the rest of the country.

Hence it is not surprising that the seven Cary branches began to diminish [through debt, and the absence of male heirs, some of whom emigrated, or adopted professional careers,] until in 1822 the [Redcastle] estate was put up for sale in the Court of Chancery, and by appropriate historical irony was acquired by a man name Doherty, descended from the original Irish chieftains from whom Inishowen had been seized two centuries before. Doherty's only grandchild, Elizabeth Frances, married Captain the Hon. Ernest Cochrane, RN, and Redcastle remains in the possession of Cochranes at the present time. [...]

For a while the Whitecastle branch seemed to be in less critical difficulties. George Cary of Whitecastle and the Casino was succeeded by his son Tristram (1786-1830), but the latter's son George left no progeny, and the property was disposed of by Tristram's daughter Caroline, Mrs Alexander Curry. Whitecastle ultimately came also into the hands of Dohertys, whose descendants still occupy the house.

Meanwhile, the younger son of George of Whitecastle, the Revd Anthony Thomas Grayson Cary (1788-1848), rector of Glendermott, Co. Donegal, inherited Castlecary when the direct line of its builder came to an end. Not long afterwards he died of famine fever incurred while ministering to his parishioneers during the hungry forties, and his widow (née Charlotte Slacke, of Slackegrove, Co. Monaghan) was left with the care of a large family – five sons and two daughters. [...]

The fourth brother, Arthur Lunel Cary, was the only one who did not prepare for a profession. He went to sea for a time, and then tried his fortune at the Australian gold diggings; but about the time of his marriage in 1859 to Jane Sproule, daughter of Andrew Sproule of Strabane, Co. Tyrone, he settled down at the family property of Castlecary, built a new house on the site of the old one, and adopted the vocation of land agent for neighbouring estates.

Arthur and Jane Cary were a handsome couple, and between 1861 and 1875 they had nine handsome children. Mr Cary was a genial host and a respected local magistrate; but like many of his neighbours he was a lenient landlord, and when all tenants' arrears of rent were canceled by the Irish land Act of 1881 the mortgage upon his fine new house was foreclosed. the family rented dilapidated old Falmore House a few miles away, and the eldest children, now grown up, went off to earn their livings as best they could. By the time Arthur Cary died, in 1885, his eldest daughter, Olive, was working as a governess in England, and two of the sons had crossed the Atlantic. Tristram Anthony Cary (1862-1931) enlisted in the American army [...]. His brother, George Lunel Cary (1866-1924), emigrated to Canada at seventeen [...].

Between Tristram and George in age, Arthur Pitt Chambers Cary (1864-1937) was aided by generous cousins to complete his education as a civil engineer, and he established himself in London with the firm of Rendell, Palmer, & Tritton. [...]

Three of the sons of Arthur and Jane Cary married, but only one of them had children. Arthur P.C. Cary in 1887 married Charlotte Joyce, daughter of a bank manager in Derry, and their eldest son, Arthur Joyce Lunel Cary, was born there the next year. [i.e. Joyce Cary, who might have inherited Castlecary. ...]

By ironical coincidence the last contact with the ancestral home occurred not long before Joyce Cary's death. The Castlecary property had gradually fallen into neglect and disrepair, and the current occupant (grandson of the business man who had foreclosed the mortgage seventy years before) offered to sell it to Joyce for an absurdly low figure. For wholly emotional reasons, he was strongly tempted. It was the house that his grandfather had built and in which his father was born; once again a Cary would be a landowner in Inishowen as his predecessors had been for nearly three centuries; the reversal of the family fortunes would be dramatically illustrated. Moreover, the happiest episodes of his childhood were associated with the summers that he had spent in that region. Whitecastle figured as 'Castle Corner' in his novel of that name; and in that book and *A House of Children* he had enshrined his love for the scenery and the way of life. Sailing across the lough to Magilligan Strand, bathing from the rocky shore, picnics at Malin Head or Shroove beach, charades and other indoor amusements, all are portrayed against the austere background of lonely hills and sea. It was his own nostalgia that he attributed to his character, Felix Corner: 'he felt that pain which belongs to the special grief of the exiled; who lose something more and nearer to them than any living kin.'[1]

Common sense, however, warned him that the proposal was ludicrous. It would cost thousands of pounds to make the house habitable, and then he would never have occasion to live in it except perhaps for holiday visits. In the future it would be only a useless burden upon his sons. Nevertheless he went through a distressing inner conflict before rejecting the offer. The sequel might have served for conclusion of the unwritten final volume of the trilogy in which he had planned to present the history of the Corner family. No other purchaser for the house appeared; the owner's death occurred about the same time as Cary's; and soon afterwards the empty building was torn down in order to avoid the payment of taxes. [...]

NOTES

Lionel Stevenson (1902-1973) was Joyce Cary's first cousin, the only child of Mabel, the youngest of Arthur Lunel Cary's daughters; she had remained in Inishowen with her mother, moving from Falmore (above) to Whitecastle for a time, and then to Clare Cottage, where Lionel was born, his mother having married her cousin, Henry Stevenson, in 1900 (soon after his sister Dora became Joyce Cary's stepmother). After Jane Cary's death, in January 1907, Mabel's brother George, on a visit from Canada, persuaded them to emigrate, and they settled in Duncan, Vancouver Island, where Lionel's father, an invalid, died within three months, and George became their supporter. In 1918 they moved to the city of Vancouver, so that Lionel could attend the University of British Columbia, and by 1924, when George died, Lionel was studying for a Ph.D. at the University of California, where he was appointed as an instructor the next year, and could support his mother, who joined him there. His story is resumed in item 16.

Regarding this history, his widow, Lillian Stevenson Pollock wrote, on 21 June 1987: '[...] of course you may quote anything you like/need from Lionel's family history, "The

Cary Family of Inishowen" – his representation of the family is accurate. Perhaps I told you that he had intended to continue that history when we came back from Vancouver – alas, that was not to be.'

1. *Castle Corner*, p. 30 (N.4); *A House of Children* is N.7.

2

At Whitecastle:
Carys and Dohertys

Frank Doherty   Elsie Doherty

In September 1963, through Mrs Gillen, proprietress of McKinney's Hotel in Moville, and especially Mr J.J. Keaveney, the schoolmaster, I met several Inishowen people who had known Joyce Cary's family. They included Miss Kane, in her shop at Castlecary, who said, as she shook her head sadly: 'It's never been the same since the gentry left!'

[**Mr Frank Doherty** of Whitecastle gave me this account of his inheritance:] George Cary was a bachelor, and my grandfather's uncle, John Doherty, got Whitecastle after him. John Doherty came here at twelve years old. He was taken on by surveyors and educated by them. Then he married a wealthy woman of Gravesend, and he came back. He knocked on the door, with that very knocker [*like a lion's head, on the front door*], and he said: 'Now it's my turn. You get out.' And George Cary moved to a small wee house.

John Doherty was landlord of the townland, but he never lived here. He lived and died at Gravesend. Whitecastle was leased to Joseph Cresswell, who went bankrupt ten years before his lease expired. So John Doherty excused Cresswell's back rent if he would forfeit his lease, and he put my grandfather, William, into Whitecastle, at a rent, in 1892. Then the Tenant's Right Act was passed, and my grandfather William got the right of occupation and a government grant for seventeen hundred pounds.

Between the time that Cresswell forfeited his lease and 1892, when my grandfather came, Mrs Cary [*Joyce Cary's grandmother*] came to live at Whitecastle. And she lived on here for about two years after that. The Dohertys lived in one part of the house, and Mrs Cary in another. Master Leo [*her youngest son*] was with her, and Miss Netta, who did the paintings on the doors. Miss Mabel was here, who married her cousin Harry Stevenson, and Mrs Bridget Tobin, their housekeeper. She moved with them from here to Clare Cottage.

11

It seems that Joyce Cary could have lived for quite a time in this house, at least until he was six years old.

[**Mrs Doherty**:] Yes. He brought his wife and boys here, because he wanted to show them where he spent his boyhood days, he said. That would have been in about 1946 or '47, soon after I came here (which was in 1943, when we were married).

Now I'll show you round the house. [...]

[*From a large bedroom on the first floor we entered a room facing south, with bay windows reaching from ceiling to floor:*]

[**Mrs Doherty**:] Mr Cary wanted to look from these windows at the trees in the front drive. The beech tree there, that he looked at when he was a boy, was much bigger now, he said. He had slept here as a small boy, I think, and his grandmother in the big bedroom.

This could be the room with waves on the ceiling, that he describes in one of his novels. [1]

[*Of the basement kitchen and outbuildings, Mr Doherty said that there had been alterations in 1922; but the plan I drew under his instruction confirms that Cary was indeed describing Whitecastle in* Castle Corner (*p. 19*), *when Bridget slid down fourteen steps to the kitchen − an act that could have been witnessed by Cleeve from a window above, if the house were Whitecastle.*]

NOTES

Frank Doherty (1911-1971) was born, lived, and died at Whitecastle House. Elsie Doherty (née Kirkland) was born in Cooley. Their four children are George (the eldest), Kenneth, Billy, and Joy (the youngest), and the youngest son, Billy, is now the owner of Whitecastle and runs the farm.

In a letter of 9 March 1988, Mrs Doherty kindly agreed to the publication of this item.

1. *A House of Children*, p. 55; that night Mrs Doherty most kindly invited me to stay, and I slept in the large bedroom, but spent some time in the other, watching what Cary described thus: 'the whole top of the room opposite the windows was flowing with a web of pearl-white ripples and their shadowy hollows like moon–spots.'

3

Chambers Family Links:
Carrig Cnoc – Flowerfield

Muriel Munro
George Bryan   Robert Pitt-Chambers

This interview with Mrs Munro took place at her home in Belfast, on 25 September 1963. In 1987 and 1988 it was developed with Mr Bryan and Mr Pitt-Chambers, as shown.

[**Mrs Munro**:] I am related to Joyce through George Cary of Whitecastle, whose daughter Matilda married my great grandfather John Chambers.[1] The Chambers family were lawyers in Derry, where my father, Robert Newman Chambers, was town clerk. He was very interested in family history, and of course knew all the Carys.   In Joyce's books, Castle Corner is Whitecastle, and the uncle is drawn I think from Joyce's Uncle Tristram, who was a doctor, and also interested in greyhounds. In *A House of Children*, I think Delia is Joyce's aunt Netta. The house is one just north of Moville – Ravenscliff, with ravens on the gate.

Joyce also stayed at our holiday house, Carrig Cnoc. It was about five miles past Moville, in Tremone Bay, at the mouth of Lough Foyle. It was a paradise for children, and he would have remembered it very well from his childhood.[2]

Is Shell Port cave, in A House of Children, *near there?*

Yes. It's drawn from Porta Doris, which you reach from Shell Bay. If you haven't a car, you can take the bus to Shrove, and get down the cliff from there.

Did you personally know the Joyce family in Londonderry?

Yes. They lived at the Belfast Bank House, where grandfather Joyce was manager. His niece, Mina Joyce, was a student at Girton, and my

13

governess for a time. I married in 1904, and Hector Munro was my brother-in-law. You may remember that he wrote under the name 'Saki'. He was killed in 1916, and never knew Joyce Cary. But I saw Joyce in Ireland after the war; he stayed with us at Flowerfield, and he visited Carrig Cnoc [see items 16, 23]. I also saw them in Oxford in about 1929-30, when our daughter Juniper was eleven years of age, and at Wychwood School, near Oxford. She often spent Sundays and weekends with the Carys. I remember her saying that one of Joyce's books was banned in their school library, but I can't tell you which one. Juniper is now Mrs George Bryan and lives here in Belfast.

I think of Joyce as a very warm-hearted person.

[On 15 November 1987 I telephoned Mr Bryan; his wife Juniper had died in 1985, but our exchange of letters and telephone conversations produced the following:]

[**Mr Bryan**:] Carrig Cnoc was acquired by Muriel Munro's father, Sir Newman Chambers, as a holiday / seaside house. He left it in equal shares to Muriel and her brother Brooke who died in 1930. After his death Muriel gave her half share to Brooke's widow Marie who lived in the house for some years.[3] It was, I think, later sold to the Roman Catholic church. My wife Juniper often spoke of the house where she stayed from time to time and mentioned especially the splendid bathing from a secluded bay in front of the house. My brother was general manager of the Londonderry Development Commission for a time and lived in a house at Greencastle – 'Portavela' – about a quarter of a mile from Carrig Cnoc.

[...] Charles and Muriel Munro came to live in Flowerfield in about 1922; Charles died in 1952. Juniper and I were married in the same year, the wedding reception being held in Flowerfield. Muriel continued to live there until around 1962, when she came to live near Juniper and me at Bristow Park, Belfast. She died in 1967, and she and Charles Munro are both buried in Agherton Cemetery, which adjoins the grounds of Flowerfield.

When our children were young we often stayed at Flowerfield. Those were enjoyable times. Although Portstewart is not a wooded area, there are some fine trees around the house. Flowerfield is now owned by the Coleraine district Council and has become a Museum and Art Centre. When my elder daughter Barbara was a student at the New University of Ulster at Coleraine she and some other students were visiting the Art Centre at Flowerfield. She surprised the party when she pointed out the room which used to be her bedroom.

There is little I can say about Joyce Cary. I never met him. [...] I came across two letters written by Joyce to Muriel Munro, which I now enclose.[4]

Both these letters stress her many burdens, and courage in facing them, and show why she thought Cary 'very warm-hearted', as when he writes, in the second: '[...] I often think of you, especially when I am annoyed or depressed because then when I think of how you tackle life and make it into something gracious and fine for yourself – chiefly in looking after other people, I feel ashamed of my own petulance. With much love, [...].' *Is there more you could tell about Muriel Munro?*

I was very fond of her. She was a most kind person. After Juniper and I were married she brought over from London her sister-in-law Ethel Munro who was a semi-invalid. Ethel lived with Muriel at Flowerfield for the rest of her life. Muriel was a painter. I have some of her pictures in the house.

Do you know the date of her marriage?

The date [...] was 1st June 1904.

She could not, therefore, have been the Miss Chambers who was a painter and invited Joyce Cary to Étaples in 1904; that Miss Chambers could only have been Muriel Munro's aunt, her father's unmarried sister Juanita, known as 'Winnie'.[5]

A source of information might be Robert Pitt-Chambers, son of Muriel's brother Brooke.

[*Mr Pitt-Chambers* writes, in a letter of 27 February 1988:]

I can produce no record of Juanita, whom I always knew as Great Aunt Winnie. At that time between 1930 and 1937 I was a school boy and she seemed incredibly ancient. I did not know of her life in France but I did know she had not long returned from Canada together with Great Uncle Harold. She must have died between 1942 and 1945.

[...] At some stage they (my father and Joyce Cary) had a flaming row and like all good Irishmen never spoke to each other again.

I met him once, some years after my father's death, when I was fifteen or sixteen at Greencastle, Co. Donegal. I remember thinking he was a pleasant fellow. [...]

Personally I prefer *Mr Johnson* and also *Castle Corner* to *The Horse's Mouth*.

NOTES

Muriel Munro, née Chambers (1881-1967) was married to Charles A. Munro, who was governor of the Londonderry Prison and later governor of Mountjoy Prison, Dublin. Their children were Felicia, who died on 6 Sept. 1985, and Juniper, wife of George Bryan.

George Arthur Pollexfen Bryan (1915-) has always been called Pat, perhaps to distinguish him from his father George Bryan, who was chief Local Government Auditor for N. Ireland when he died in 1930, as was 'Pat', from 1965. His mother was Ruby Jackson of Sligo, a cousin of Jack and W.B. Yeats (his maternal grandmother, Alice Jackson (née Pollexfen) being their mother's sister). His grandfather, Arthur Jackson, was Deputy Lieutenant for Co. Sligo – as his wife's grandfather was for Co. Donegal.

On 9 January 1988 he kindly agreed to the publication of Mrs Munro's interview and also his own account.

Robert Pitt-Chambers (1920-), born at Neuchâtel, Switzerland, lived variously in Switzerland, Burma, England, Ireland and India, until his father's death (1930); he then attended Marlborough College, Wilts. and the Camborne School of Mines, Cornwall, and after war service in the Indian army (1940-46), worked in Ghana, Co. Tipperary, and India. In 1947 he married June Richardson, had two sons, and now lives permanently in France.

He kindly agreed, on 15 March 1988, that his letters might be quoted.

1. In 1803; the George Cary here named was the grandfather of George Cary, the last Cary to own Whitecastle.

2. See 'Carrig Cnoc', *Joyce Cary Selected Essays*, 29-31 (E.80).

3. Thomas Brooke Winsley Chambers married Marie Perrenoud, a Swiss National, at Poona, India, in 1917.

4. The first, of 16 July 1933, is from his sister-in-law Elsie Carlisle's home in Heswall; the other, of 1 April 1934, is from his Oxford home.

5. Cary called her 'aunt' (see item 10), though she was a distant cousin. He mentions her thus in connexion with the prototype of Gulley Jimson's father in *The Horse's Mouth*: 'I daren't give his name – but I was in France, and I was staying with an aunt who was a good amateur painter. She'd been taught by him and I met this man who'd been a well-known painter in England and sold his pictures. He'd got a strong family there.' (It is for this reason, presumably, that Cary 'daren't give his name.') But here in France 'his family was starving. The Impressionists had knocked him right out, and he couldn't sell a picture.' Scholars have been confused because, in Cary's copy of *Adam* (in Bodley) where this conversation appears, he has circled 'him' which, in the context, can refer only to the one man here described. But beside it he has written 'Garrido'. Had Cary recognized that the situation was more complex (*or could have been?*) than his conversation showed, with the old painter having been his aunt's teacher, whom Garrido replaced? This explanation would fit 'On His Own Method', MS. Cary 237, fols. 8-10, which cast light on Cary, besides distinguishing the two men:

'My aunt was an enthusiastic amateur of painting, a pupil of the impressionist Garrido, and between bathing at Parisplage or hunting with the beagles through the woods above Le Touquet which was then under construction, I amused myself with sketching. I amused myself above all with the artists and their talk.

'They were of all ages, and one of them living in a farm near by with his wife and several children, thin starved looking children, had exhibited at the Academy.' Here follows Cary's oft-repeated account of being shown a rejected picture, on an easel in the garden, of a girl on a swing, by a man in his sixties who found himself destroyed by 'the impudent nonsense of the impressionists.'

However, J. Quigley, *Leandro Ramon Garrido* (London, Duckworth, 1913), shows that Garrido too was well-known in England, with an English mother, Elizabeth Allsop, of a strong family; he studied Art at the South Kensington Schools, then in Paris, in 1890; he admired Manet (as Gulley Jimson did); in July 1903 he married Mary Rayner (daughter of an English medical man),and until 1906 lived in Étaples, where he 'painted young girls and had a lot of pupils' (p. 97); on 3 Oct. 1904 (just after Cary met the old painter who could sell nothing), Garrido (aged 36) wrote from Étaples to an English friend: 'I find my present style of works sells readily, which makes it difficult to accumulate for a future date' (p. 112). It seems that *opposites*, as well as similarities, might have contributed to what Cary's imagination made of his encounter with painters in Étaples; for its symbolic significance, see item 35.

4

His Mother's Family

Elisabeth Cusworth

This interview took place on 13 October 1967, and was developed in discussions and letters at later dates.

We have agreed that maternal ancestors must always be as important as those on the father's side, at least genetically; and you know more about Joyce Cary's maternal ancestors than anyone else, I believe.

I can give you genealogical tables.[1] They show that William de Hackett, who went to Ireland with Prince John (later King John) in the twelfth century, was Joyce's direct ancestor as well as mine. That is because William's descendant, Thomas Hackett, had eight daughters, and two of them married brothers. Emily married my grandfather, Dr Lancaster Joyce, and Helen married Joyce's grandfather, James Joyce; so their father, William Joyce, was Joyce's great grandfather and mine too – as Thomas Hackett was also, of course.

Lancaster had a daughter Mina, who was at Girton, and a son – my father – Jim Joyce, who became a bank manager in Larne. He was shy, charming, and a good raconteur. My mother was a Grose, from army people at Melmont, Strabane. Lancaster was drowned when my father was only six years' old, and he and Mina often spent holidays with Joyce Cary's grandparents. They had two children, Charlotte and then Helen, who were quite a lot older than my father and Mina. Charlotte married Arthur Cary, and their two children were Joyce and his younger brother Jack, who became a Commander in the Royal Navy. Helen married Gerald Beasley, and they lived latterly at Limavady.

James, Joyce's grandfather, was a bank manager in Londonderry, and Joyce Cary was born in his home above the bank.[2] Joyce would have spent most of his holidays with his grandparents. He also saw a lot of his great uncle William Joyce, who lived in Omagh in Co. Tyrone, and was devoted to Joyce. Regarding him, you might learn more from the Lynams; Joc was head of Lynams after his father Hum

18

and his uncle, who was always called the Skipper.[3] All the Joyces had been in linen. The family vault is in Omagh.

Great-grandfather Joyce's daughter, Elizabeth, married Dr Agar, in Henley-in-Arden. He founded a famous nursing home there for mental private patients (who had their own servants and carriages). It was carried on by their son, Dr Samuel, and then by Samuel's nephew, Dr Willoughby Agar. Sam's sister Mary married Arthur Cary – his third wife.

Aunt Mary Cary was very interested in family history, and I can let you have her notes on the Joyce family, who were descended from the 'Joyce country' family in Co. Galway. This ring that I'm wearing was my father's, and it shows that our crest is the same as she quotes: the Wolf's head ducally gorged – that is, with a crown round the wolf's neck. And I have heard my father and my Aunt Mina (the Cambridge early Girton girl) talk of the Archbishop of Armagh who was Confessor to Edward II; he is shown in Aunt Mary's notes to be of this family.[4]

If, as you say, Joyce Cary called his Joyce ancestors 'strange mountainy men',[5] and had already decided, by 1909, to write stories under the name Thomas Joyce, I agree that the idea might have come to him through Aunt Mary. Her notes show that Thomas Joyce was the founder of the 'Joyce country' family; and, after all, it was only because he had inherited money from the Joyce family that he could think of setting himself up as a writer with a secretary in 1909, when he was only twenty.[6]

Aunt Mary was a marvellous old lady, and I believe that she and Joyce were very fond of each other. But after the break came between her and Arthur Cary I lost touch with him and his family, and can't tell you anything particular about Joyce. But Do. must have been able to tell you a lot about him as a child, because her mother spent so much time with him then [see next item].

NOTES

Elisabeth Cusworth had been an actress until her marriage. As Mrs Howard Cusworth she wrote articles and gave lectures, based mainly on her extensive travels, but also on public speaking. She lived in Devonshire Place, London, and was awarded an MBE in 1984. She died in 1986, aged eighty-one.

This interview makes understandable Mrs Cusworth's extreme distress at the false account of her father's life given by Malcolm Foster in his biography of Joyce Cary. Having named him 'Uncle Jim Joyce' beneath an unmistakable photograph, he describes him as a bachelor brother of Joyce Cary's mother (who had no brother), and attributes to him one of Joyce Cary's fictional ideas concerned with an 'Uncle Joyce' who 'Gets Drunk'. However, such notes in the Bodleian as the following (in MS. Cary

270/S.11.A, made while *A House of Children* was forming in Cary's mind), do suggest that they centred on a real uncle: 'Uncle Joyce a book of those years, close friendship. I go to school and tell him everything [...]'. A likely person would be the 'Uncle William' who was 'devoted to Joyce', according to Mrs Cusworth. Unfortunately, she died unexpectedly before I could put the suggestion to her. But the wish to discover the truth behind Foster's false assumptions led me to assemble the following record, kindly assisted by Mrs Jean Gallagher; it contains valuable facts about the Joyce family.

Their great grandfather William Joyce, of the parish of Drumcree in Portadown, and Charlotte Joynt of the same parish, were married on 8 April 1824, and their first child was christened Elizabeth on 3 April 1825. Great grandfather William's death, aged 75, on 6 July 1872, is recorded in the burial register of Mountjoy Church, Cappagh Parish, Mountjoy East, Omagh, and he is the first of the family to be buried in the family vault of which Mrs Cusworth spoke. His will mentions his wife Charlotte and then his eldest son James John (Joyce Cary's grandfather) to whom he willed his property in lands. James John must later have transferred the land to the second son, Joyce Cary's great uncle William, who farmed the family holdings at Mountjoy Forest East and left over four times the amount of money that his father did. A third and a fourth son are also named: Lancaster (Mrs Cusworth's grandfather) and Wolsley Atkinson Joyce – whose first names are those of a firm at Eden Villa, Portadown (from whom Joyce Cary received statements of rents e.g. on 5 Jan. 1921, as shown in the Bodleian MS. Cary 325, fol. 20); it seems therefore that this fourth son had been named after a friend of his father.

Though the wills have been destroyed their indexes survive (in the Public Record Office), and show that '*Wolsley Atkinson Joyce*, late of *Buncrana*, gent. died 3 July 1884', administration of his estate being granted to 'Emily Georgina Joyce of Shipquay St. Derry, the widow.' Thus it is possible that he left a son, related (as first cousin once removed) to Joyce Cary, who might conceivably have called him 'Uncle Joyce'; but I have found no trace of such a person. His great uncle Wolsley Atkinson is certainly ruled out, as he died before Cary was born; he is buried at Omagh, as is his brother William; but James John is buried in the Derry city cemetery, and Lancaster at Ballybeg.

James John died on 20 Dec. 1902 and, for his will, administration was granted at Derry to '*Wolsley R. Atkinson*, retired bank manager and Francis W. Joyce, bank clerk.'

Francis William Joyce was born in Ballybay, Co. Monaghan, being the son of Elisabeth Francis Johnston of Co. Carlow (south of Dublin), who married Lancaster Joyce in 1865, when he was practising in Shercock in Co. Cavan. As he was brought up by relatives in Buncrana, and went to boarding school at an early age, it seems probable that his mother died soon after F.W. Joyce's birth. He named his own son Lancaster, and a friend of the family has passed on the information, that he 'cannot recall drink ever being over that door'; so Francis William cannot be thought of as an uncle who drank. He was however Jim Joyce's half brother, of whom Mrs Cusworth may not have known.

Emily Hackett was in fact Lancaster Joyce's second wife, and this explains why their children, Mina and Jim Joyce, were much younger than James John's daughters. But one cannot suppose that Jim would have been called 'uncle' by his cousin's children; he might have been called 'Cousin Jim', as this was customary in their family when speaking of older cousins, Dorothy Lake has told me.

She also told me that she had known William J. Joyce, the son of Cary's great uncle William, and could not imagine that any drink problem applied to him – even if this *cousin* were called *uncle* by Joyce Cary.

His great uncle William is in fact the one and only person whom Joyce Cary could be expected to have called Uncle Joyce, and to have done so naturally, as the brother of the man whom he called Grandfather Joyce. This William Joyce died in Omagh on 30 June 1909, and his death entry states that he was a farmer, a widower, aged 78 years. He had been an executor of his father's will, but the fact that their father left his property to John James for William to farm may indicate that his father thought William unreliable. 'Willy drank' actually appears with early notes from my conversation with Mrs Cusworth, as well as the fact that he was 'devoted to Joyce'. As the grandparents with whom he had spent most holidays both died when Joyce Cary was fourteen years old, it seems likely that he would have turned to this uncle. He was evidently a boating man, and records might exist of his activities, of this or other kinds. Any information concerning him would be appreciated.

1. Headed 'The Pedigree Register (Sept. 1910)', and compiled by Alan Sarratt, grandson of the youngest Hackett sister, Thomasina.

2. It was then the Belfast Bank; in 1978 I was kindly shown over the family's home by permission of the Manager of the Bank of Northern Ireland, who then occupied the premises.

3. A family named Lynham lived in Omagh, and the name appears first in a directory of 1906; F.J. Lynham was a solicitor and the county surveyor for Co. Tyrone. But 'Joc was Head of Lynams' shows that Mrs Cusworth was referring to the famous family of the Oxford Dragon School (who spell their name as shown); Joyce Cary's friendship with Joc is recorded by Toni Thompson (item 23.), and 'The Skipper', who was a keen boating man, might well have known his Uncle Joyce in that capacity, though I have not yet established a link.

4. The notes are from 'The History of the Town and County of Galway' by James Hardiman, published in 1820 by Folds and Sons of Dublin, and reprinted by the Connacht Tribune in 1926.

5. In a letter of 7 Dec. 1916 to his wife, he attributes his temperamental 'ups and downs' to his 'Irish blood', and adds: 'The Carys are wayward and the Joyces were strange mountainy men'.

6. On 25 Sept. 1909 he told his brother that he expected to 'play any fool's games I like under it, and have Cary for the drawing-room.' 'Thomas Joyce' was his pseudonym for his first 15 stories; those omitted from the 'Outline' above were sold only to SEP (see also item 47).

5

A House of Children
Its Irish Family Background

Dorothy Lake

The following account, received on 12 December 1987, developed from interviews on 16 September 1967 and 12 November 1987.

Kathy in *A House of Children* was drawn from my mother, Helen Robertson née Beasley. She was the eldest child of Joyce Cary's aunt, Helen, who was one year and nine months younger than Joyce's mother Charlotte. My mother in her turn was fourteen months younger than Joyce. As the younger of James Joyce's two children, Helen was always known as 'Baby', in due course shortened to Bay. From all accounts, she was treated as a baby throughout her childhood and adolescence. For instance Bay's hair was always 'done' by Charlotte until Charlotte married. Both sisters appear to have had Irish charm and warmth – my grandmother certainly did – but Charlotte always comes across as competent with some spirit while Bay had less vivacity and was much less able to cope. The two sisters were sent to boarding school for the latter part of their education to a school at Bray outside Dublin. My mother always called it 'French School Bray' and they had to talk in French all the time.

Do you think that the relationship between sisters in Cary's novels might owe anything to the relationship between his mother and aunt? Georgina and Ruth in Except the Lord *come to mind, as well as Delia and Frances in* A House of Children.

I get no feel that the characters of Delia or Frances relate to Charlotte and Bay. I felt if anything that Delia, when she was hardworking, may have overtones of Mina Joyce.

The character of Kathy points to aspects of the family background that Joyce did not bring into focus in the novel, although my mother felt that he had captured the essential quality of the summer holidays

22

they shared when staying with Grandfather and Granny at Ravenscliff (Crowcliff), a house on the Donegal shore of Lough Foyle just north of Moville.

My mother, from the age of two, spent most of her time with her Joyce grandparents. At this time a brother, Harry, was born who had a severe congenital heart disorder. When my grandmother was pregnant for the third time and my mother was four years old, Grandfather and Granny Joyce took Harry to live with them and my mother too as company for Harry. Ankatel in *A House of Children* is based on Harry.[1]

My mother's reaction to leaving her own home and having a spirited but very delicate younger brother as her only playmate, except when Joyce and Jack visited, was to become very protective towards Harry, and to develop the characteristics that Joyce has depicted in Kathy. Photographs of my mother as a small child show an unhappy, lost little girl and she always gave me the feeling that she had felt responsible for looking after Harry. The two children were often looked after by servants particularly by one housemaid, Jane, who was the one person who could hold Harry to comfort him when he had painful attacks of breathlessness, which he suffered after he had done too much.

My mother was very fond of Granny Joyce, who was one of the eight Hackett sisters. She has come across to me as petite, vivacious, musical, with warmth and charm. However she also had an anxious side. She was very concerned to do the right thing, particularly to keep life running smoothly for her husband. I feel that, from the way my mother spoke of her early life, Granny Joyce behaved as though the consequences of not getting things right, for society in general and the grown ups around her in particular, were all disastrous. This way of seeing life means that adults tend to impress on children, through getting angry, or becoming worried or moralistic, that to prevent disaster they should fit in with the plans of the adults, do what they are told and keep out of the way whenever grown-ups deem it necessary. Sending children this message was seen as a way of protecting them from pain. That it might also cause pain is something the anxious adult is unable to contemplate.

I do not have as clear a picture of Grandfather Joyce as I do of Granny. I feel my mother was somewhat in awe of him. She certainly could cajole him into doing what she wanted but only when she had been good. He was upright, kind hearted, and a good businessman with financial acumen. He was helpful in adversity and gave over the years consistent support to his wife's sister Aunt Emily, and to her children Jim and Mina, after the sailing tragedy in which his brother Lancaster, Aunt Emily's husband, was drowned. Likewise he extended help to his grandchildren. He also however had his share of anxieties very similar in nature to those of his wife. To prevent disasters things had to be done properly and he could become very angry if they were not. He suffered for years from indigestion which became worse as he got older and I suspect his indigestion had a considerable psychosomatic element. It became crippling enough for surgery to be advised and undertaken about two years before he died. He retired from the bank about the time of the operation which meant a move from the Bank House, and died on 20th December 1902. Granny Joyce died three weeks later. She had cancer and had been unable to walk for some months though she could be carried down to the drawing room where she would play the piano. At this time, aged twelve, my mother did what she was told to run the house and there was no other adult in charge.

My mother's reaction to being exposed all her childhood to the anxieties of her grandparents was to adopt their beliefs, to comply with their expectations and do what she could to make them happy. However at the same time she could see that the grown-ups around were usually too busy to watch Harry sufficiently so that he lived within the narrow limits imposed by his heart. Fears for Harry's life were realistic. He did indeed die when he was nine years old, my mother eleven and Joyce twelve. Because of her fears about Harry and about the consequences of her own behaviour, my mother repressed, so far as she could, her resentment that she had, in order to achieve any kind of emotional comfort, to put Harry's welfare and the rules of her grandparents before any of her own desires. The result of having to deal with this conflict, which was inherent in her world as she saw it, made her a bossy little girl because if things were not done as she said there would be a disaster. When others did not respond as she hoped, she would appear lost and 'not there'. She would then have been very annoying.

Being 'not there' sounds very like 'gone mule', as Jim Latter applies it to Nina in the second trilogy.[2] Jim's childhood relationship with Nina, who was orphaned by the age of four, as your mother seems virtually to have been, suggests that Nina as well as Kathie owes a good deal to her. Would you agree?

I don't think I can comment on whether Nina was drawn from my mother. It is very possible but it could have been someone else. Withdrawn children have much in common.

My mother and Joyce did not meet from the time of their childhood until they were about forty. I suspect they did not meet very often, if at all, after Grandfather Joyce's operation. I well remember the first time they re-met. The occasion was one of the periodic luncheon parties exchanged between Aunt Netta Clark (née Cary and a sister of Joyce's father) of the Bungalow, Castledawson, and my Beasley relatives (my grandmother, my aunts Maude Beasley and Bunny Ritter, and my Uncle Tom) of Limavady.[3] On this occasion the party was held at Castledawson. Aunt Netta (for me a courtesy title) fascinated me. I was then a rather shy girl of about thirteen. Aunt Netta had the aura of beauty despite a rather dumpy figure, very ordinary clothes, and a permanent cigarette. She did however have a beautiful voice and a welcoming presence. She talked about ordinary things in an infectiously interesting way and her anecdotes had a sharp tang to savour.

The Bungalow was one of those Irish houses in which time was treated with gentle disdain. The hour at which lunch would appear was somewhat unpredictable but what eventually did arrive always deserved appreciation. After lunch there was sometimes tennis (in those days the drive to Castledawson was treated as an excursion for the day) or the grown-ups talked and the children were sent out to play. Usually Uncle Leo Cary, who was nearly blind and who had what my Beasley relatives would describe as 'the bad Cary eyesight', would call. He, I can remember, was quieter than Aunt Netta. He usually spoke with wit but usually above my head. His stories did not have the infectious quality that Aunt Netta gave to hers.

When Joyce and my mother re-met they began to talk at once as though it had all happened just last summer. There was much laughter and each reminiscence was immediately capped by another. Both pointed out the scar on Joyce's forehead which had apparently been caused by my mother. The vivacious side of my mother was uppermost and there was no sign of Kathy on that day. After lunch my brothers and I were sent out to play with Michael. who was about my age, and Peter.[4] I would have preferred to listen in the drawing room. These meetings were repeated once or twice when our holidays in Ireland happened to coincide with Joyce's.

It is certainly significant that Joyce Cary began A House of Children *soon after meeting your mother again, and that early plotting for Nina's story dates from around this time also. But could you fill out a little more the background of the home in which they always met?*

Joyce's reaction to the anxious side of his grandparents was very different from my mother's. I have no picture of the relationship Joyce had with Granny Joyce. I suspect he charmed her and made sure she did not know about any escapade that might worry her. I do however know about the relationship with Grandfather. They often quarrelled and Joyce was able to go ahead and do things that angered Grandfather. My mother allowed Joyce to draw her (in part very willingly) into activities she must have known were likely to come to light and upset Grandfather. I feel she regarded these exploits as worth the scolding. One story is of Joyce and my mother going off to Fahon over on the other side of the peninsula, for a trip and an adventure. Grandfather found out and was very angry.

At Ravenscliff the children were Joyce and his brother Jack, my mother and Harry and then, half a generation older, Jim and Mina, children of Lancaster Joyce who had been drowned. My mother considered that Philip in *A House of Children* was based on Jim Joyce but, like many of the other characters, had elements of Cary relatives.

The four younger children used to have lessons in the morning. As the eldest Joyce must have been rather bored. But for whatever reason he regularly played up the governess until Aunt Charlotte took to sitting with her sewing outside the window.

I have no picture of the relationship between my mother and Aunt Charlotte except that she was kind. I also have no picture of Uncle Arthur except the family character sketch. Grandfather and Granny were unhappy about the marriage. The Carys were considered to be irresponsible and given to drink. Uncle Arthur was seen as having considerable charm, as did all the Carys, but was also selfish. He was reputed to have kept Aunt Charlotte short of money. The story of her death was that she had been without domestic help and had bicycled some distance to interview a maid. On her return she developed pneumonia which ran a rapid course and she was dead before her father and mother could reach London.

Joyce was always the ringleader of all activities. He could spin compelling stories, mostly about King Arthur, and in everything the children did Joyce always took the role of king, or general. When aged about nine he organized the group to write a newspaper for which he was editor and chief copy writer. My mother spoke of labouring to compose a story and how Joyce finally finished it. The Montgomeries lived near by and I think some Montgomery children were involved in the venture.[5]

It seems significant that Arthur was Joyce Cary's own first name (as well as his father's and grandfather's); and also that he mentions the Montgomeries in his prefatory essay to Charley Is My Darling, *which seems intended as a companion book to* A House of Children. *He describes himself as a seven-year-old delinquent, who once enjoyed tearing several doorbells* 'clean from their sockets', *until warned of the police, he says, by* 'some larger boy (I have an idea it was one of the Montgomeries, perhaps the present commander-in Chief)' *(pp. 5-6). The Field Marshal, a year older than Cary, lived in Tasmania until he was fourteen. Have you any other suggestions?*

Beyond this incident, my mother had no memories of the Montgomery children. She always said they were so much older. I suspect Joyce may have played with them on his own, and this may have been a sore point to my mother. I am not surprised that Joyce considered himself a seven-year-old delinquent. I feel that Joyce must often have been bored by the group at Ravenscliff and thrown back on his own initiatives. He did not have anyone in the family group who was his peer. My mother was over a year younger and when she was able to be adventurous I am sure could be an interesting companion. When she was being like Kathy (in the way we have discussed), they would fight or she would withdraw. Harry was over three years younger and hampered in his activities. Jack again was younger, and Jim and Mina Joyce were adolescents.

I feel also that Joyce may have been brought up to fulfil parental expectations of being a special person with qualities of a much older child. There is a photograph of Joyce as an infant labelled 'The Man'. Perhaps he gained special approbation from his parents when he was precocious, which is a difficult role to maintain. Again the uncomfortable relationship he had with Grandfather Joyce must have made him feel cramped and resentful. Joyce reacted to the family anxieties in a completely different way than did my mother.

Grandfather Joyce seems a likely prototype for Uncle Herbert in A House of Children, *where Aunt Hersey, as his* 'slave', *answers your description of Granny Joyce. Lesson time at Ravenscliff, as you describe it, supports my belief that, except during these visits, Joyce Cary was taught at home by his mother, whose expectations of him as* 'The Man', *would fit your suggestions.*

You would presumably agree that the major event in A House of Children *is the mother's death, which occurs around the narrator's tenth birthday, as it did for Joyce Cary. Yet he says elsewhere that she died when he was eight. And the escapade with the doorbells, which he attributes to himself at the age of seven, ends with him rushing to meet his mother; but an early, unfinished story, centred on that escapade, ends instead with the child*

*returning home to learn from his father that his mother has gone away with
another man, and will never be seen by her son again.*[6] *How would you
relate these fictional accounts to Cary's own life?*

I am unhappy about speculating very much further about the
relationship between Joyce and his parents, and how it affected his
makeup. His mother's death must, without doubt, have made a
significant impact on him, and so must the loss of his much loved
step-mother during his adolescence. The impression I have from *A
House of Children* and my mother's reminiscences is that Joyce, like
many people, had stored up and had ready access to memories of
episodes in his childhood which he had enjoyed and which served to
enhance his sense of competence. And that he had let slip out of
awareness the memory of episodes linked to a sense of demoralisation.
I see Joyce and my mother having (to use the language of psychoanaly-
tic Object Relations Theory) very different defences against the pain
and distress engendered by close relationships that are conflict-ridden
and involve loss. Joyce shows that he could block off such pain,
certainly for the events of his childhood. He thus reacted to reminders
of those losses and episodes of demoralisation without suffering a
sense of depression. My mother could also block off episodes associated with suffering, but much less completely than did Joyce. My
mother's experiences led her to respond to reminders of certain kinds
of loss and of conflict-ridden relationships with despairing resentment
and the sense that she was unable to be effective. As a consequence she
became, during periods of her life, severely depressed.[7]

Joyce Cary is reported as saying that all women are masochists.[8]

That belief could have been derived from his relationship with his
mother. I have been told how hard working and selfless she was. A
view borne out by the circumstances of her death.

*Do you think that the conflict in Joyce Cary's makeup might have owed
most to the fact that neither side had really approved of his parents'
marriage? You have implied that the Joyces feared his father might prove
'wayward'.*[9] *Might the Carys, as gentry, have objected that the Joyces
were not, strictly, gentry? If so, the need to reconcile the two sides of his own
make-up becomes, understandably and very subtly, the key to Joyce Cary's
writing.*

Again it is anybody's guess whether the supposition in this question is correct. I feel it is likely that, like many novelists, Joyce is, through his writing, speaking for his inner self and his characters are working out aspects of his life he cannot reconcile with the front he feels comfortable about presenting to the world. I regret I do not know his novels sufficiently to have enough evidence with which to explore the hypothesis you put forward.

The conflict in his nature would presumably explain his reaction to rules. He insisted repeatedly that one cannot make judgements 'by rule of thumb', but must judge each case on its merits.[10]

I feel Joyce is likely to have had more than one conflict to resolve. Perhaps the steadfast belief that one must judge each case on its merits rather than make judgements by 'rule of thumb' was born of his own integrity and experience of the consequences of so doing. A reaction to rule could stem in part from a reaction to his family upbringing, where they lived to a large extent by the rules of social conventions: 'You must do so-and-so', 'it is not done'. He could also be regretting the awe of learning which ran through the Joyce family and possibly the Cary family too. They liked beautiful objects, their houses had a pleasing style, but learning was something to which one should not aspire. Learned people were remote and odd.

That would explain why Joyce showed diffidence about his own scholarship, though it was (in the end) considerable, and something he had clearly aspired to, for himself and certainly his sons. Have you any personal memories of him?

I got to know him when I lived in Cambridge. He called on us fairly often and continued to visit after my husband died in 1952. I remember his coming in the middle of a child's birthday party. I never suspected that he had a sense of diffidence about his own scholarship. He always came across as a well-read and witty don [*though not a don, in academic terms*]. Unfortunately at the time my own diffidence about discussing literature held me back from the conversations I would have had now.

He visited Cambridge mainly, no doubt, because his son George was at Cambridge University. But then George died, in 1953. Facing death is indeed a continuing, tragic, theme, in both life and writing, for Cary. So finally, since this discussion has centred on A House of Children, *it would be most valuable to have your reaction to the preface Cary wrote in 1951 for the Carfax edition, but then replaced with another. It reads:*

'This book, *A House of Children*, is about my own childhood. I've changed names and descriptions so as not to hurt feelings, but the book is true to the feelings of my childhood, which was a very happy one.

I want to say this because it is so often said that I became a writer because of some neurosis – because my mother died when I was eight [sic] and after that, I was so much away from home at boarding school or with relations. Or because I was born in Ireland which was then full of trouble, the kind of tensions and neuroses which lie behind the work of the Russians, Dostoevsky, Tolstoy and Tchekov.

But my childhood was very happy, especially in Ireland where I was usually with a crowd of cousins, and where we did pretty much what we liked and where the country people spoilt us.

Of course it's true that Ireland then was full of tensions and neuroses, of secret societies and secret pressures. That always happens in agrarian and religious war. But I doubt if it worried me. As a child I was outside it.

I remember once in Derry coming to Shipquay Gate, in Derry walls. These walls are twenty feet thick and the gate was like a tunnel. I had been out shopping with a Joyce cousin, a girl called Helen. Helen was a good-looking girl with long yellow hair down to her waist and we had agreed to marry. At ten we were devoted. In town we were always together.

We came to the gate, which was on our way home to our grandfather Joyce's house just inside the walls. But we found the tunnel full of men fighting – there was a terrible noise of yelling and cursing. We stopped in perplexity. But after a moment one of the men recognized us and began to yell, 'Hi – stop – stop – it's Miss Helen and Master Joyce, they want to get through.' And the men did stop and we walked through – they only started again when we had passed safely.

They say I have made such a thing of family life because I didn't have it myself. But even if I didn't have a very settled home I had a very happy childhood. After all, family life is the natural thing – it's the natural place for happiness. And all my children, who did have a settled home, are family people now – I have seven grandchildren already and expect a good many more.'[11]

This preface contains Joyce's own judgement and conscious understanding of his life and is a valid statement. My own sense of life in the

Joyce family – and in the Cary family too – is that there was the potentiality for considerable unhappiness. I can understand how Joyce might find a way 'to be outside it'.

By the way the story about the fracas by the Shipquay Gate is very familiar. My mother recounted it in the same words.

NOTES

Dorothy Lake (née Robertson) is known professionally as Dr Dorothy Heard, her name from her first marriage. She is a psychiatrist who has specialized in psychotherapy and child psychiatry. She held coincidental appointments as a consultant child psychiatrist at the Tavistock Clinic, and as a consultant psychotherapist at Addenbrookes Hospital, Cambridge.

On 6 January 1988 she kindly agreed to the publication of the above account.

1. Cary's son Tristram also contributed; see item 22, n. 3.

2. See *Not Honour More* (N.15): 'She looked as calm and cool as a waxwork – and I knew she had gone mule as I called it. / And this had always driven me mad. She had played it that day at Lilmouth [...] spoiling the first great moment of our love [...] by her mulish tricks' (p. 58; also pp. 59, 70).

3. Apart from a brief sojourn in Liverpool (1894-5), the Beasleys lived until 1903 in Buncrana, when they moved to Limavady because of the beauty of the setting, and rented first an 18th century house on Main Street owned by the Tyler family, who wanted it themselves in 1918; so the Beasleys moved across the road to a house owned by the Proctors.

4. This memory dates the meeting as shortly after 7 April 1933, when Peter visited (see item 23).

5. The home of the family made famous by Field Marshal Montgomery of W.W.II is very near Ravenscliff, just north of Moville.

6. 'Whick Macarthur' is the name of the child in the story, which is MS. Cary 252/S.3.D. in the Bodleian; 'Whick' seems a likely contraction for 'Whiskey', the narrator's nickname in *A House of Children* (p. 157) which, with its Irish spelling, might well have been Cary's own – as *Macarthur*, 'son of Arthur', might have been his surname.

7. For Joyce Cary's frequent depression, see Isabel Cary, item 35.

8. See Cecilia Dick, item 37.

9. Joyce Cary's word for 'The Carys'; see item 4, n.5.

10. MS. Cary 258/S.5.K. exemplifies this.

11. From MS. Cary 244.

6

My Mother and Joyce

Cary Clark

This interview took place at Mr Clark's home, the Bungalow, Castledawson, in August 1966, and was expanded by a letter he wrote on 13 September 1966; it is continued in item 17.

My mother was Joyce Cary's Aunt Netta, who went to live with his father (her brother Arthur) when his mother died. Joyce rather resented her in place of his mother, she said. She married in 1906 – when Joyce was eighteen – and from then on her home here – the Bungalow – could have seemed like a home in Ireland for Joyce. My father was her second cousin, Jackson Clark (always called Peter), and he had lived here at Castledawson all his life. I carried on the family linen works here too.

Would you describe Joyce's father?

He had a very commanding personality. He could shrivel you with a look. He was not a big man, but surprisingly strong. There's a story of him accepting the challenge of some performer of feats of strength – and coming off best. He was a good golfer, too. And really a very affectionate man. Joyce was a good swimmer, and he played football and did boxing at school. But Clifton was a rough school, I think.

Was your mother the 'very pretty' aunt mentioned in Cary's preface to A House of Children, *whom King Edward VII reproved for smoking?*

Yes. One of her jobs was secretary to Lady Warwick, who was a friend of King Edward – a favourite of his. Netta smoked, and Lady Warwick objected, and the King backed her up.

Did your mother stop smoking?

No. That wasn't the Cary way. Their way of arguing was: 'As a matter of fact, you're quite wrong.'

32

Where did she live, when she wasn't with her brother Arthur?

She shared a flat in London with her sisters and youngest brother Leo. They called it 'Poker Flat' (from the Bret Harte story). Hessie was there, until she went to the United States. She painted animals very well, and illustrated magazines. Jim Joyce had a fancy for Netta. And Joyce admired Bunny at Roe Park.[1]

Did your mother take a special interest in Joyce's life, having looked after him as a child?

She loved both Joyce and Jack and regarded them as older sons. In fact, if I had been of a jealous nature I might have been upset. On the other hand I have an idea that at one time they rather resented the way I teased my mother.

Do you remember anything she told you about them as children?

She had a story about Joyce being very upset when Jack broke a window; and when she asked Jack what had happened, he said: 'I was just throwing a knife at Joyce.' Another story she thought typical was about them as small boys, when they got pennies which Joyce saved and Jack spent. Their father thought Joyce was wrong. But he was saving for a toy to give Jack.

Joyce came here after the Montenegrin campaign, and worked on his drawings. That was in the summer of 1913.

NOTES

Jackson Anthony Cary Clark (1906-1980) was the only son of Jackson and Netta Clark; he had five daughters, and his widow Agnes, in March 1988, kindly gave final details and agreed to the publication of this item, and item 17.

1. 'Bunny' Ritter, née Noel Pullyne Beasley (1898-1951), was the sixth child and fourth daughter of Cary's Aunt Bay, the eldest being Helen (see item 5); in 1922 she married John Alexander Ritter of Roe Park, outside Limavady, which she inherited on his death in 1929; in 1950 she married George Buchanan, who inherited Roe Park on her death, and sold the house and land.

7

At His Brother's Home

John Cary   Shiela Cary   Mimi Wakeham

This conversation took place in April 1966 at Commander Cary's home, Burnside, at Wadeford, near Chard, in Somerset.

[*Jack*:] I was three years younger than Joyce, and born in Nunhead.[1] I went to Mrs Borden's kindergarten and then I was at Aske's with Joyce for two terms.[2] We were day-boys, and Joyce was having such a good influence that the headmaster said, 'Please don't take him away.' But we went to Hurstleigh prep. school that year (September 1900), and when I was twelve I went to Osborne. Joyce had gone to Clifton the year before (1903).

I remember holidays with the Joyces in Buncrana. We stayed at the Tower House. Jim Beasley was one year younger than I was.[3]

Do you remember your Cary aunts?

[*Jack*:] Of course. Aunt Netta looked after us when our mother died, and after she married Jackson Clark, we stayed with her at the Bungalow, at Castledawson. Olive married Hall, in the merchant world; Mab married Harry Stevenson, and went to America; so did Hessie (Bulsterbaum), who was an expert on dogs and horses; Agnes married a doctor, George Hayden. They all bristled at the name of Gladstone, who was responsible for the loss of their land. The whole Cary family did.

Was your brother interested in genealogy?

Yes. I remember that at one time he wrote up a pedigree, and I saw a genealogy copied by him.

I left England at the end of 1913. But I saw Joyce at Store Street, in London, before I left. He was broke, and hoping to pay his debts with the book he was writing.[4] There were heaps of papers everywhere, held down by old shoes, books etc.

He had affected the dandy at Oxford. He wore a monocle, and an opera cape. He was keen on dancing.

Did you see much of him after he married?

[*Jack*:] Yes, I stayed with them quite often during the twenties. Gertie was a great planner. She had an alert brain, but her plans were too involved, and then fell flat. She was devoted, and worked, typing for him, in a room they called 'Piggers'. But she interrupted him all the time. Ask Shiela and Mimi – Miss Wakeham.[5]

[*Shiela*:] I think Gertie was spoilt by her mother, and rather selfish. When Joyce was at home she was always calling him, and he always came. He was completely devoted, and never complained.

[*Jack*:] When Gertie's brother Fred became Trustee of her money, he wouldn't let Joyce get at it, and therefore Joyce ran up against him. They had dreadful arguments. I think the Ogilvies would have liked Gertie to marry someone with money.

[*Shiela*:] Gertie was pretty.

[*Mimi*:] No, but she had a charming manner. She had pretty blue eyes, and light brown hair. I thought Joyce and Gertie very critical. It was always a relief when they left.

[*Jack*:] I hated visiting the Glade (the Ogilvies' home). They had about ten servants, morning prayers, etc. But I think Joyce liked it. Gertie sang. She was a musician, and played the cello. Her mother was German. I always thought of her as the Great White Queen. Mr Ogilvie was a fine old Scot.

When did you come to live here, in Somerset?

[*Jack*:] I got this house, Burnside, in 1929, and father came and lived here then, until he died, in 1937. Shiela came then too, and Miss Wakeham.

[*Shiela*:] Gertie was always organizing complicated plans that never came off. Peter was devoted to her. But Gertie would say, 'No, Michael will do it better.'

[*Mimi*:] The house seethed till they left.

What would you say were your brother's special qualities, which he could draw on as a writer?

[*Jack*:] He had a terrific memory; remarkable. And he had an intense interest in accurate detail. I remember when he came to inspect my ship. He asked so many questions about the height of the mast and so on that I had to send for the ship's book.

NOTES

Commander John Pitt Cary (1892-1971) retired from the sea in 1931 and finally retired in 1935; but he was recalled for the war in 1939, first as Duty Officer at the Admiralty and then sent out to Ceylon. These details (with those in n.5) were kindly supplied, and the record of this interview approved, on 9 Oct. 1987 by Miss Shiela Cary, who lives still at Burnside – not far from Castle Cary, where the family fortunes began in Britain (see item 1.)

1. In south-east London, the house being 11 Ivydale Road.
2. Haberdashers' Aske's Hatcham Boys' School is in Pepys Road, within a hundred yards of 41 Kitto Road, New Cross, where the Carys lived from c. 23 Sept. 1897 until a date between 28 April and 21 Oct. 1900. The Archives and Local History Dept of the London Borough of Lewisham (whose staff kindly supplied this information) holds a register of admissions to Aske's (reference A73/14/1), which shows Joyce Cary's registration number as 3887, in Sept. 1898, on a page where the date of admission for most boys is entered as 12 Sept. '98, but left blank for Joyce Cary – a fact probably indicating that he was admitted later, and likely to be linked to his mother's illness and death on 1 Oct. 1898. Jack's registration, number 4015 in Sept. 1899, also shows no date of admission; but both are shown to have left in July 1900. Nobody named 'Borden' appears in New Cross directories for the 1890s, but there were many private schools and kindergartens in the area at that period (the Archivist, C.W. Harrison, writes).
3. A younger brother of Harry Beasley (see item 5); he was born in 1894, studied medicine at Trinity College Dublin; killed in action at Gallipoli in 1915.
4. He had returned from the Balkans in May, and was writing *Memoir of the Bobotes* (T.6).
5. Shiela Cary was their half-sister, born in 1904, who writes, in a letter of 9 Oct. 1987, that Phyllis Carrie Wakeham, 'mostly known as "Mimi"', was a friend who came to them in 1909, 'to help, and looked after Dad when I was away. She died in March 1977 aged 91.'

8

Of Clifton, and Cary's Sons

Stephen McWatters

This item is compiled from correspondence in 1964, resumed through telephone conversations in 1987.

In 1964, when you were the Headmaster of Clifton College, you kindly sent me the following information about Joyce Cary.[1]

He entered what is now known permanently as Oakeley's House in September 1903. At that time it was called Tait's House, but in 1904 it became Rintoul's House, so as Cary did not leave until July 1906 he had 2 years or so of Rintoul's House. (It was not finally and permanently labelled Oakeley's House until early in the 20s.)

I have made some enquiries, and unfortunately Joyce Cary was not in close touch with Clifton, though my predecessor but one (H.D.P. Lee) did succeed in persuading him to come and talk to the VI Forms in the 'Current Affairs' series on 18th October 1952. His talk was labelled 'The Novel as History' so this confirms the note you have found. As far as I can discover he did not come here on any other occasion.[2]

In a postscript to your letter, you added that you were a close friend of Michael Cary. Would you tell me what you can remember about the family?

Joyce Cary had a very talented family, but Michael is the only son whom I knew well. Peter I remember at the Dragon School as an excellent singer. He took the title part of Patience, while I, two years younger, played a minor role, the Duke of Dunstable. But the age-gap and his departure to Rugby meant that I never became a close friend.

George was younger than me, and gained a scholarship to Eton after I had left. Like Michael, he was an excellent scholar, and I believe very highly thought of in academic fields.

Tristram I remember slightly as a very good long-jumper for his age, breaking some youthful record at the Dragon.

37

I could tell you much about Michael. He was a man of immense talent and enormous charm. An actor – at the Dragon and at Eton. Good at games – he was in College Wall side for at least two years. An excellent musician, singer chiefly (I expect he played too) and in recent times a maker of harpsicords, rushing between one Cabinet meeting and the next to tune one of his instruments for a concert. A goodish scholar at Eton and University (1st in Greats, at Trinity Oxon) and a high-powered civil servant – a real mandarin, who wore his ability very lightly, with great humour and charm.[3]

Do you recall whether he ever spoke of his father, or did you ever encounter Joyce Cary in any circumstances?

I remember meeting Joyce Cary quite often when walking with my father in the Parks at Oxford. My father knew him slightly and was more or less his contemporary. We exchanged news about the family. He was on his own, I remember, and usually affable and friendly, occasionally a little distant (shy perhaps) in manner.

The reason was, I am sure, that he was 'stuck' with a problem in his writing. On such occasions, 'he would go out for a rapid walk in the University Parks' and 'His concentration was so intense as to be almost trancelike', according to Dan Davin.[4]

NOTES

Stephen McWatters was a Kings Scholar at Eton (1934-40), and read classics at Trinity College, Oxford (1940-41, 1945-46, being on Active Service in between). He became a Master in College and Housemaster at Eton (1947-63); Headmaster of Clifton (1963-75); Headmaster of the Pilgrims School, Winchester (1976-84); now retired, he teaches part-time at Winchester College.
He has kindly agreed to the publication of these letters.

1. The main purpose of my enquiry was to date two of Cary's notebooks in the Bodleian.
2. From a letter of 24 Feb.1964.
3. From a letter of 29 Nov. 1897, to B. Fisher.
4. See *Closing Times*, p. 100 (item 67, n.1).

9

A Friend at Clifton

Margaret Fisher

This interview took place at Mrs Fisher's home in Edinburgh on 22 August 1968.

My husband Matthew was at Clifton with Joyce Cary, and they both left in July 1906. But Matthew was nine months older, and went on to the sixth form, whereas Joyce did not. They were both in Tait's House, and Matthew was keen on football. I remember his story of coaching Joyce by kicking about a hairbrush case in the dormitory. He was always amazed that Joyce had written poetry so easily. He thought Joyce *spoke* poetry. And he thought him a complete mixture of the philosophical and the practical.

Matthew was reading classics at Edinburgh when Joyce was an art student here. He gave Matthew a book of poems that he had published. Would you like to see it?

Yes indeed. It is very rare. Neither the British Library nor the Bodleian has a copy.[1] What was your own impression of Cary?

I thought of him as a quixotic character – in going to the Balkan war, for example. I did not meet him until 1953, when he came to Edinburgh to receive an honorary degree – Doctor of Laws. My husband was then Dean of the Faculty of Laws, and in this capacity he laureated various candidates, such as Eisenhower and the present Queen, though not on this occasion. With Cary were S.L.A. Manuwa, Professor H.W. Garrod, and Professor Emeritus Charles McNeil. Matthew learned to write these speeches through doing classics, but nevertheless he spent hours on them. He had read all Joyce Cary's novels, but I think he thought Joyce might have made his characters *nicer* – as I do too!

The graduation ceremony was on the morning of July 3rd, and Joyce arrived on July 2nd to stay with us for two nights. He arrived in time for tea, and had scarcely got in the door when he was ordering flowers for me; in almost the same breath he looked at the clock and observed that it was off level. (It had never kept good time, and Matthew worried about its level from then on.) My immediate reaction to Joyce was that he was absolutely charming. He had natural manners.

NOTES

Margaret Fisher (née Thomas) was born in Cramond, Midlothian, and there were three daughters of her marriage to Matthew George Fisher, Professor Emeritus, Q.C. (Scotland), born in Shelmorlie, Ayrshire, who died in 1965. My last letter from her is dated 3 February 1980, after which I lost touch, but I should be glad to know where I may reach any of her family.

1. *Verse* by Arthur Cary, 1908 (P.2-P.14) became an anathema to its author, who did not own a copy; Margaret Fisher kindly agreed to let the Bodleian have her copy at a very modest price.

10

'He was a Queer Fish'

Donald M. Mackie

This item draws on two letters of 1968, from Westfield House, Balmoral Road, Blairgowrie, Perthshire, answering enquiries.

[...] Joyce Cary was in Étaples round about the years you mention [1904-7] staying with his Aunt, a Miss Chambers, an Artist who had a studio Apartment in Étaples, Irish young Pretty and Charming.[1] He later came to Edinburgh and went to the Art College and we saw quite a lot of him.

I was quite a young boy in those days about eight or nine years old and had little to do with Cary personally but remember a lot of these times.

He met most of the well known Artists writers musicians and others at our house at our Friday nights at Homes, some of whom I have no doubt had some influence on his later life. A 'Queer Fish' in many ways on looking back on those now so far away times.[2]

[...] My father just met Joyce Cary in Étaples when Cary was staying with his Aunt. As I said he subsequently went to Edinburgh to study Art at the Art College, whether on my father's advice I simply don't know, very probably and I daresay on his Aunt's advice as well.

How long Cary stayed in Edinburgh I don't remember, not very long I think. I remember he had digs in Torphicen Street but never visited him there.[3] [...]

When I said 'he was a Queer Fish' he seemed so to me being rather a moody person and you must remember I was just a young boy at the time, about eight or nine years old. [...] When Cary was in Étaples he used to go off by himself for the day and spend hours lying on the Sands about Le Touquet or Paris-Plage.

[...] Cary had a great friend I believe called Eric Robertson also an Art Student who died a good many years ago, in I believe somewhat tragic circumstances not known by me.[4]

41

NOTES

Donald Mackie has died since I received these letters, and I have not succeeded in tracing his relatives – from whom I should like to hear. There are two letters from his father, Charles Mackie, in the Bodleian, which show his friendliness towards Cary.
1. See item 3. n.5.
2. From a letter to B. Fisher of 2 Nov. 1968.
3. The address on Cary's letters home was 16 St. Bernard's Crescent.
4. From a letter to B. Fisher dated 11 Nov. 1968.
   An exhibition of oils, pastels, and drawings by Robertson was held at the Piccadilly Gallery London from 25 Nov. '87 to 15 Jan. '88, and biographical notes in its catalogue include: 'accredited as one of the most brilliant art students of his period [...]. When his years as a student were almost complete he was already at odds with the establishment, and on one occasion the director of the Edinburgh College of Art removed his drawings from an exhibition of work by the students' sketching club, because he thought the drawings would damage the reputation of the College. Robertson's open involvement with a number of the women art students did nothing to enhance this reputation, and when he became involved with Cecile, the elder daughter of the distinguished Scottish artist, E.A. Walton, the Waltons did everything possible, including sending their daughter to Florence for a year, to deter him. [*His marriage to her in 1914 ended in 1923, when he moved to Liverpool, but he failed to get commissions as a portrait painter, and also as a commercial artist. By 1927, when he re-married, he was dependent on his wife's small earnings from nursing and financial help from a sister.*] In the late nineteen-thirties he contracted tuberculosis and died in 1941 on the Wirral, Cheshire.
   Perhaps it was Cecil Gray who had the insight to the problem that beset Robertson the artist: 'as a painter he was too much influenced by the Pre-Raphaelites, Gustave Moreau and William Blake, to appeal to contemporary taste.'
   Might he have contributed to Gulley Jimson, whom Cary was creating in 1941 – when he made one of his frequent visits to the Wirral, to visit the Carlisles (see items 21, 22)?

11

The Edinburgh School of Art

Adam Bruce Thomson

This interview took place at Mr Thomson's home in Edinburgh on 25 August 1968.
Three letters, dated as shown, are also quoted.

Do you have clear memories of Joyce Cary?

My clearest memory is of 1942, when he got the James Tait Black
prize. Dr Arthur Melville Clark, a lecturer in English, was on the
platform. I was late for the lecture, and got in at the back. But I went
down and spoke to him at the end, and he remembered me in an
extraordinary way. He knew me at once, and said, 'Do you remember
when I took you and threw you down outside? You took it awfully
well!' He had rushed at me without warning and taken me in a rugby
tackle. It was just Irish high spirits. He was high-spirited, but not
particularly Irish. I remember him as rather good-looking, with an
aquiline nose, and soft brown eyes; he wore glasses for art class.

Did you ever wrestle at the School of Art at other times?

We used to wrestle sometimes in the life class. Women and men had
separate life classes then. Henry Lintott was teacher of anatomy (he
died about three years ago). He was quite a character, and a very good
draughtsman and teacher. He came to see me in 1942 a day or two
after Cary, but I don't think they had met. I met Mrs Cary at the
lecture and had to admit that I hadn't read Cary's novels, and she said,
'Oh you should – they're awfully good' (or something to that effect). I
remember seeing them on to a train and arranging to see him next day.
He came alone and we talked about old times, and about his family. It
was a Saturday morning.

What can you tell me about those 'old times'?

The School of Art was then in the Royal Institution, where the Royal
Scottish Academy now is, on the Mound. Cary came because he had

43

met Charles Mackie, an Academician, at Pas de Calais, where Mackie was painting, and Mackie had suggested studying art in Edinburgh. Cary came at the beginning of 1907. Part of the College of Art had still to be built, and after it opened in 1908 I don't think Cary was there. But I think that classes continued to be held at the Mound, and it is possible that Cary was only at the Institution. On certain afternoons there were no classes, and then we practised cricket at the nets. I remember the way Cary called, 'I say, we have all the style, haven't we?' He looked stylish bowling, too.

We had very small classes at the School of Art – about twelve in a class. Eric Robertson was Cary's great friend. He was a talented man who died some years ago.[1] Alexander Sturrock was a friend too, but particularly Eric Robertson. I remember going alone to Paris in the spring of 1910 and meeting Eric Robertson and John Duncan, and then we met Cary, by accident. He was there again in July 1910 [*what followed here is also in a letter, quoted below*].

Was Cary ever sketching or painting when you saw him in Paris?

No, I never saw him painting. He was not very good at drawing from the model. But he had an aesthetic sense and great taste. He was very discriminating. And he was interested in classics.

How did he dress?

As a student he was not dressed in Bohemian style – *not* the dress of art students of the Latin quarter. In art classes we wore overalls – I can show you a photograph.[2]

How would you sum Cary up?

He was a rather good-looking, earnest man, who early on showed an interest in intellectual pursuits. He was always an interesting talker, and was liked by fellow-students.

Who could tell me about André Raffalovich? He had a profound influence on Cary, his notebooks show.

Arthur Melville Clark could, I am sure.[3]

[*Next quoted is Mr Thomson's letter of 16 September 1968:*]

[...] I delayed writing because my old friend D.M. Sutherland was due to spend last weekend with me and when I might discuss 'Cary' with him. Although he had previously told me that he didn't remember Joyce Cary as a student he could recall meeting Cary in Eric Robertson's studio in Albany St. D.M.S. mentioned that Cary had a 'room' above Robertson's studio.[4] He didn't remember details about this meeting except that during tea Eric and Joyce had a lively talk.

Raffalovich – D.M.S. lunched with him about 1913 when Raffy lived in Whitehouse Terrace.

John Duncan was an older artist who had been an exhibitor in the RSA and who travelled to Paris with Eric Robertson in 1910 to work there for a period. I met them there and they decided to stay where I was – at 9 Rue de Sommerard *[see above]*. Duncan's age at the time was about 40. It will be apparent that Duncan didn't study in the life class with us. [...]

My daughter leaves today for Oxford and hopes to deliver the life class photograph to you in a day or two. [...]

[*Next quoted is Mr Thomson's letter of 16 February 1969:*]

[...] Mary brought the photo and your letter at mid-December.[5] I am interested to know that the Bodleian have made a copy of the photo. May I say that you are welcome to use it but don't in the least feel obliged to do that, however. Referring to your diagram which I am sending with this, in general I should say it was a mixed class and as one might expect,the young men went their diverse ways. I shall make a few further identifications[6] [...]. (6) Walter B. Hislop, killed in action Gallipoli 28.5.1915 a most promising painter whose sister I married;. (4) A.C. Dodds, a water colour painter, elected RSW (Royal Scottish Society of Painters in Water Colour). He remembered Joyce and later sometimes spoke of him. (8) Eric Robertson. Painted in Edinburgh after School of Art days and subsequently continued to paint in England. (10) Adam Scott. I remember his facility as an oil painter. Emigrated to Canada approx. 1910 or earlier. (12) A. Stuart Hill. Continued to paint in London from say 1910 until the fifties when he died. (13) Blacklock. Painter in oils – trained at Royal College of Art – Our teacher. (14) A.R. Sturrock RSA. Died in late fifties. Knew Joyce quite well. (15) D.M. Sutherland MC, RSA, LL.D.

About the time of this photograph became a student of the RSA life class.

I can't recall just what I told you about Eric Robertson except that I have an impression that I conveyed the essentials. Eric was friendly with Joyce and continued to meet outside School of Art classes – for instance in Eric's studio in Albany St. They had much in common in their literary interests and were both fond of discussion.

[*Next quoted is Mr Thomson's letter of 25 March 1971:*]

[...] John Duncan took me to visit J.D. Fergusson in his Paris studio in 1910.[7] I think the month was March. I was much the junior member of the three. At this distance of time I can't recall much of the conversation. My memory of Fergusson was that he was very forthright; decided in his opinions and that his views on painting were very contemporary 1910. Matisse was much spoken of then and if Fergusson wasn't one of several (and I think he was) who familiarised me with the name of Matisse he would certainly have been in the van as an admirer.

Fergusson said he couldn't get colours – tubes of paint bright enough; the Louvre seemed to have no interest for him. In dress he had none of the Bohemian about him. The Latin quarter of that time might typify the kind of young men, if not the young women, of whom we see so much in 1971. His studio seemed very orderly and his clothes were not at all Frenchy. He was just like a well dressed Scotsman, far removed of course from the business man. Memory plays tricks so I must be careful. I know that Fergusson was acquainted with Peploe, a Scottish colourist who spent some time in Paris in 1910 and who had been acquainted with Fergusson here in Scotland and who shared the then contemporary interest and admiration for Cézanne and some of those artists who became known as the Post Impressionists. Yes! I think that Fergusson had a very forceful personality [...].

I had met Joyce about that time very briefly (March 1910) [...] I remember more clearly meeting Cary with a man who I think was Middleton Murry. They were seated in the Luxembourg Gardens. I had returned from Spain in early July. I'm sorry that I have nothing of consequence to tell you about, for our conversation was very general and probably was mostly about my travels in Spain and about art.[8] [...] I have no knowledge whatsoever of Cary's friendships and way of life at that time.

NOTES

Adam Bruce Thomson, OBE, RSA, HRSW (1885-1976) was a Scottish artist. He taught at Edinburgh College of Art from the years before the First World War (in which he served) until 1950. He was President of the Society of Scottish Artists (1936), Treasurer of the Royal Scottish Academy (1949-56) and President of the Royal Scottish Society of Painters in Watercolour (1956-63). His work is represented in public and private collections. A centenary exhibition was held in Edinburgh in 1985.

He is survived by two daughters, who have kindly agreed to the publication of extracts from letters as well as the interview.

1. See item 10, n.4.
2. This he did, and sent it to me to have a copy made by the Bodleian, where it was shown in an exhibition from their Joyce Cary Collection, between Jan. and April 1988.
3. See item 33.
4. See item 10, n.3.
5. That is, the original was returned at this date; see also n. 2.
6. The numbers refer to the position of the figures in the photograph.
7. Fergusson was Cary's original inspiration for Gulley Jimson, as M.K. Joseph of Auckland N.Z. heard him say (confirmed on 2 March 1976). Cary met him with John Middleton Murry (if not before) between 27 Dec. 1910 and 12 Jan. 1911, as he recorded in his 'Paris Diary' (now MS. Cary 253/ N.9 in the Bodleian); the spelling *Fergusson* is a correction of *Ferguson* in this letter. See item 13.
8. John Middleton Murry, *Between Two Worlds* (London: Jonathan Cape, 1935), pp. 126, 161, indicates that his first and second visits to Paris were in the winter of 1910 and spring 1911; but conceivably he failed to mention a visit with Cary in July 1910.

12

In Edinburgh Art Circles

Constance Kirkwood

This item combines two letters, written from Lyme Regis, Dorset.

[*The first letter, dated 13 September 1968, includes:*]

[...] He was just one of the nice boys we knew before the 1914 war. I cannot remember how we first met him, but he did not know many people in Edinburgh. He came to our house very often and met our friends. At that time John Duncan RSA had a studio in Torphicen Street – he was a bachelor at the time – and knew a lot of interesting people, including Father Gray and Raffalovich. Nearly every Thursday a number of all sorts might be met with there – J.D. made tea and one of us poured out and it was all very friendly and Joyce would meet people there. He gradually came less frequently to our house as he was invited by other people. He went over to Étaples for a holiday and wrote amusing letters. I kept a few for a time but there was nothing in them of importance or indication of genius!

Joyce gave my older sister and me each a copy of his first poems and I spoke to a man I knew on 'The Scotsman' and asked him to put a word in for Joyce. Rather reluctantly he said he would if I would give him my copy. As far as I remember the notice was quite nice but criticising the style in some way.[1]

Joyce used to talk a lot about Ireland and his brother and stepmother, both of whom he seemed very fond of. He must have been about seventeen I think when we saw so much of him. He was very easy to get on with and our friends liked him.

Father Gray and Raffalovich and a Miss Gribbell (I met them all at the studio) were all connected with a new church at Morningside – I heard them irreverently referred to as 'The Trinity'. They had a professional non-R.C. quartet of vocalists who sang parts of the evening service. My oldest sister was one of them.

I don't know if you have heard of the 'Outlook Tower' in Edinburgh – it was a centre of great and varied interests, the chief power there being Professor Geddes. I do not know if the Tower still functions but if so there might be some one there young enough to remember Joyce.

In those old days Edinburgh was full of keen, clever interesting people of all ages so Joyce would not stand out as exceptional. I don't think he can have stayed in Edinburgh very long. I remember him very clearly as himself – nice-looking and amusing and unaffected. He enjoyed life and we found him easy, like one of the family – keen about doing anything, going for a picnic or meeting people. But I have forgotten the talks and discussions we had – it is so long ago.

The friendly social meetings among artists and students and cultured people seemed to fade out with the advent of cars and wireless and organized entertainments.[...]

[Next quoted is Miss Kirkwood's letter of 29 September 1968:]

[...] He told me he had published his first poems 'to get rid of the desire to publish.' I told this to the late Ian Colvin – father of the present writer L.C. – and he said it was the silliest reason he had ever heard! I don't think he, or any of my other friends, was greatly impressed by the verses – but we all liked Joyce.

I wrote to an old friend – one of the studio group, to ask if she had any memories of Joyce that I could tell you about and I have just heard. She says 'He had beautiful manners.' She had destroyed some letters he wrote to her late sister that were good but I think she would have kept them if they had been illuminating – She does not remember anything definite about Joyce's talks and ends her letter, 'Wasn't he related to the Duke of Norfolk?'

NOTES

Constance Kirkwood was an artist who painted pictures and pottery, and died on 3 May 1975; she was the third in a family of eleven, of whom Miss Olive Kirkwood, of 20 Roseburn Place was tenth; she had been only a child when Cary visited them, though she remembered him vividly as a person at our meeting on 24 Aug. 1968. In a letter of 17 Dec. 1987, she kindly agreed to the publication of this item.

1. *Verse* by Arthur Cary is reviewed in *The Scotsman*, October 15 1908, p. 3: 'An Affectation of archaism [...] occasionally mars Mr Cary's verses. However they have enough sunshine in them successfully to carry off these blemishes. There is one longish piece in the volume which in a convincing way pokes poetical disdain at the scientific spirit; but most of the pieces in the pamphlet are brief lyrics [...] perhaps the best about them is that they promise more substantial things.'

13

J.D. Fergusson and Cary

Margaret Morris Fergusson

The letter here quoted was written by Margaret Morris Fergusson on 29 August 1971, on notepaper of the J.D. Fergusson Art Foundation, of which she was Hon. Secretary.

[...] Fergusson certainly knew Joyce Cary, and *admired* him very much – he often talked of him to me and wished he could meet him again. But as you say it was in the *early* Paris period – I only came on that scene in *1913*! And *I* never met him.

It is just possible there might be letters – in Glasgow – where we lived from 1939. I am working on a biography of my husband, and hope to be in Glasgow in September – looking through papers etc, and will *certainly* let you know should I find anything. [...]

NOTE

Margaret Morris Fergusson (1891-1980) was founder of the Margaret Morris Movement, in Dance, which has continued to grow, internationally, since her death. Her biography, *The Art of J.D. Fergusson* (Glasgow and London: Blackie, 1974), contains no reference to Cary, about whom she evidently found nothing when she looked (as promised, above) in Glasgow. (See also item 11, n.7.)

14

At Oxford University

Thomas Higham

This item and item 18 are compiled from two interviews, both in Oxford, on 11 October 1967 and 30 April 1986.

As you were both at Clifton before Oxford, could you tell me something about Joyce Cary's career there?

I knew Joyce only slightly at Clifton, as I was in a different House. But he told me that he regretted being in Tait's House, which was renowned for sport, but not academically, and that it had taken him a long time to outgrow that tradition. He thought it had done him a great deal of harm to be in Tait's House.

There was a House for Jews founded at Clifton, mainly to get in some money, but also because the Jewish sabbath and kosha food made a separate House a sensible arrangement. To get to school the Jewish boys had to pass Tait's House, where boys pelted them with cheese and the like, in good-humoured scorn – the scorn being due mainly to the fact that Jews were the wrong shape to do well at football. Hore-Belisha[1] went to Clifton, presumably to the Jews' House, and he once told me that he had been surprised, on coming to England, after being educated in France or Germany, to find so much anti-Semitism here – stronger than he had known previously. I think Joyce probably had to outgrow that sort of schoolboy anti-Semitism.

What you say supports my belief, that Gulley's treatment of Hickson in The Horse's Mouth *is meant to be anti-Semitic in just that way, and adds to his sense of kinship with 'Artist Hitler' (as he calls him); Hickson's name is derived from Isaacson, and his character from Nussbaum and Benskin in* Castle Corner.

I agree that Nussbaum and Benskin sound like Jewish names.

Why do you think Joyce Cary read law, when letters show that he planned to read English literature?

English literature was then regarded as a soft option, mostly taken by women. But I don't think he was interested in academic work. He spent a lot of time editing *Rhythm* for Middleton Murry. Murry was always hard up and borrowed a lot from Joyce too.[2]

Did Murry regard Cary as a lightweight?

We all regarded him as a lightweight. Prichard made mincemeat of him;[3] he'd never got his teeth into philosophy, and never with a tutor. His friends reading Greats all had.

So his article 'A Slight Case of Demolition' makes clear.[4] Do you have any photographs of these friends?

Yes, I can show you several. Here is one of the Trinity College Gryphon Club, which we all joined; and there, on the left of the back row, is Percy Horsfall, from South Africa, whom Joyce referred to (though not by name) in 'A Slight Case of Demolition'. He got first class honours in both parts of the *Litterae Humaniores* – a double first as Joyce said – and he did enter the world of high finance.[5] Joyce and I both came up to Trinity in 1909, and so did Philip Mitchell and Duncan MacGregor.

Duncan, like Joyce, was two years older than most of us [...]. He was better read than any of us and had the keenest intellect, though lacking the training in Greek and Latin Composition (especially in Verse, which was common in English but rare in Scottish schools). He knew more of the world and more of literature than we did; and we all learnt a great deal from him. He 'loved his glass' – but that did not prevent him from gaining first class honours in both parts of the *Litterae Humaniores* course, and proceeding to a Fellowship at Balliol as tutor in Ancient History.[6]

He became one of Cary's close friends when he returned to Oxford in the twenties, I believe. What of Mitchell?

Philip Mitchell, educated at a London school (St. Paul's) and with a home in Gibraltar, was more worldly-wise than most of us and inclined to be wild, often in adventurous ways which involved risking encounters with the Police or with the University Proctors or with the dean (that is, the disciplinary officer of the College). He was physically strong, good at most games, especially golf, and also good-looking; and he never to my knowledge drank more than he could hold. Nor did Joyce. A keen sense of humour was also part of this make up: and he was apt to exercise it at the expense of Authority. He kept fairly clear of trouble during his first five terms, gaining at the end of them 2nd class honours in the first part of the *Litterae Humaniores* course – that is, in Classical Honour Moderations. After that he seems to have decided that systematic study was not his métier. His work fell below the standard required of a Scholar or Minor Scholar of the College; his improbable adventures became more frequent and some escapades which became known to the dons counted against him. I can't remember what they were, if I ever knew. The final one, which sealed his fate, included the abstraction from Balliol, the neighbouring College, of academic caps ('squares') and gowns belonging to four dons. Laden with these and with an oblong banner inscribed 'Votes for Women' abstracted from some depot of the militant suffragettes he and possibly some friends climbed the Chapel tower of Trinity, which has at the four corners female figures emblematic of Geometry, Astronomy, Theology and Medicine. On these figures the caps and gowns were set and between the two of them that face the outward world the suffragettes' banner was suspended. Philip, sent down [*expelled*] though he was, remained a loyal member of the College, subscribing generously to its War Memorial and sometimes visiting Oxford on behalf of the Colonial Office to lecture candidates selected for the Colonial Service. He would come to see me and also, I think, Joyce, on these occasions, and in 1939 invited my daughter to stay with him and his wife at Government House, Uganda, in the course of her visits to friends or relations in South Africa and Tanganyika. But the outbreak of war prevented that tour. His final style, by the way, was Major-General Sir Philip Euen Mitchell, GCMG, MC.

Here is a College group photograph taken in the summer of 1910, I think. Mitchell is in the doorway, under the 'T' of Trinity that has been chalked above; and under the first 'E' of College is Duncan MacGregor (with a 'morning-after' look about him). I am in the back row, last but one on the left as you look at the photo, and beside me (third from the left) is Count Albrecht Theodor Andreas Bernstorff, a German Rhodes Scholar of our year (1909), from Charlottenburg, with whom we were all on very friendly terms. He hated having to go to war against England in 1914-18, but of course he had to serve. Between the wars he held a high post in the German Embassy in London until the Nazis became powerful, when he retired to his home and banking interests in Schleswig-Holstein. Eventually he was executed by the Nazis for participation (real or supposed) in the bomb plot against Hitler.

One begins to understand what Cary meant when he said that the most important part of his Oxford education came from his friendships.

He himself, of course, seemed more worldly-wise than most of us, having been in Paris. I recall him discussing Rimbaud with us. Then he went to Montenegro. I remember his story of being in charge of rations there, and being given a live sheep to kill before cooking it. He was not permitted to waste ammunition by shooting it, and I think he ended by hitting it on the head. I saw him after he came back from Montenegro, in a very ramshackle place in Store Street, in London. He was writing *Memoir of the Bobotes* then.

Only to abandon it when he went to Nigeria, and war again in the Cameroons. Would you lend me some of these photographs, to make copies from? I would give them to the Bodleian later, if you agreed.

Certainly. You may copy letters too, and give them to the Bodleian when you have finished with them.[7]

NOTES

Thomas Farrant Higham (1890-1975), was educated at Clifton and Trinity College, Oxford, of which he was elected a Fellow in 1914 after gaining a first Class in Honour Moderations, and the Gaisford Prize for Greek Verse. In 1915 he married Mary Elizabeth Rogers and had one son and one daughter. He served with the British Forces in Salonika (1916-19), and was attached to the Foreign Office (1940-45). From 1939 to 1958 he was Public Orator of Oxford University.

1. Hore-Belisha was responsible for the Belisha beacons at pedestrian crossings, introduced when he was Minister of Transport during the 30s; he served in W.W.I, and was a member of the War Cabinet during W.W.II.

2. See Michael Cary on Murry, item 20.

3. Harold Arthur Prichard (1871-1947), fellow of Trinity College, Oxford (1898-1924) and White's professor of moral philosophy (1928-1937), published one book, *Kant's Theory of Knowledge*, in 1909 – the year of his 'demolition' of Cary, who could not explain his aesthetic judgements (see n. 4).

4. See E.69; in the series 'A Turning-Point in Life' – as Cary shows it was indeed for him; since Murry and these other 'friends' had already spent a year at Oxford being trained in philosophical discourse, it was scarcely fair, much less kind, to enjoy his humiliation by Prichard who, as a fellow-Cliftonian entertaining a new undergraduate, was not treating his guest in the way Cary had been brought up to expect.

5. In the article Cary wrote: 'I only once again, in Oxford, raised the question of aesthetic judgement. [...] The only one who bothered to answer used words like "depth", "richness of conception", which, as even I could perceive, were analogues of *[what he had said to Prichard, such as]* "It means something all over." But I didn't go any further. The man was a brilliant scholar who took a double first; I didn't dare to accuse him of innocence and naivety. And I was probably right. He is now an international financier.'

6. Here, and elsewhere in both instalments from my meetings and correspondence

with Thomas Higham, I have supplemented what was said at the time from what he and Lady Ogilvie had compiled and sent, on 3 September 1966, to Malcolm Foster, in answer to Foster's questionnaire. I undertook not to use the material until after Foster's book was published, but have no doubt that Mr Higham would have wished it to be made available to other scholars.

7. Some of the photographs were shown in the Exhibition mentioned in item 11, n. 2.

15

The Colonial Serviceman

H.W. Cowper

This letter was written on 11 January 1961, to Professor M.M. Mahood.[1]

I first met Mr Joyce Cary when he was first appointed to the Administrative Service of Nigeria after demobilisation from the Nigerian Regiment at the conclusion of the First World War.

He was appointed to Kontagora Province of the Northern Provinces as assistant district officer. This province was administered by the Resident Major Hamilton Brown at that time. I was the district officer of Yelwa and Borgu Divisions. These two extensive areas are on the East and West side of the Niger River, Borgu division being on the West side of which the principal town was Boussa – near the rapids where Mungo Park lost his life. I am afraid that Borgu division was rather neglected as it was impossible for one man alone to cover such an extensive territory. On Mr Cary's arrival at Kontagora he was sent to me at Yelwa, as my assistant, to be instructed in his administrative duties. This I did to the best of my ability. When this was accomplished, Mr Cary was instructed to proceed by canoe with his staff to Boussa and then on into its interior as far as Kaiama which was to be his headquarters. He had first to have quarters built for himself, office and staff. When this had been accomplished, he was to make a thorough assessment report of the division. I had shown him a report as an example, giving population figures, a map, showing villages. The report also required historical and ethnological information; also of agriculture, details of various crops and of any industries. When he handed in his report at the end of his tour, he was complimented by the Lieutenant Governor, Mr Goldsmith, as one of the best reports he had seen. I should mention perhaps that in those days Nigeria was, as you probably know, divided into Northern and Southern Province by Sir Frederick Lugard (Lord Lugard) and the Governors were known as Lieutenant Governors.

One evening when talking to Mr Cary on his return to Yelwa, he told me that he had sent three stories of the Quartier Latin in Paris where he had studied before the War. These stories he had handed to a friend at Oxford who was a literary agent. These three stories were ultimately accepted, I believe, by an editor in New York. Mr Cary received a cheque for £240 with a request by the editor to know more about Mr Cary as he was very impressed by the style of his writing. Mr Cary said that if he could make £240 for three weeks work he would do better for himself in literature than with an assistant district officer's pay of £500 a year. He then proceeded on leave and that was the last I saw of him. I should mention that while he was out in Nigeria he suffered greatly from asthma. Probably this also made him decide to leave the Nigerian Service.

Cary was not an easy person to get on with. He took strong dislikes. Fortunately he liked me and we cooperated well together. He came from the Irish junior branch of the ancient family of the Cary's of Cockington Court Torquay. This probably you know far better than I do.

NOTES

1. Professor Mahood kindly gave me this letter in 1964, after completing *Joyce Cary's Africa* (see item 65), of which p. 33 ff. deals with the period described by Cowper. As she noted on the letter, the period was in fact 1917; and an Assistant District Officer's pay was then little more than £300 a year.

Cowper's letter of 27 February 1962 to Colonel Moody is in the Bodleian (MS. Cary Adds 4, fols. 44-47), and contains the additional comment that Cary 'got on well with the natives.' It ends: 'Cary was very straight in all his dealings, highly intelligent and very critical of men and things.'

'21 Blue Waters Drive, Paignton' was Mr Cowper's address in 1961; but I learned on 29 September 1987 from the present occupant that he had died before 1975 and that no one in the neighbourhood knew where his son and daughter now live. I trust that they will have no objection to the publication of this letter.

Part II

Family Man
and
Professional Writer

16

From Inishowen to Oxford

Lionel Stevenson

This interview took place in Professor Stevenson's home in Durham, North Carolina, on 7 July 1967.

[*If I could now have a further interview with Professor Stevenson, I would preface it thus:*] *You are the person who can best bring together the Irish, English, and also American aspects of Joyce Cary's life, because you shared family connexions and also literary aspirations. I have read the letters he wrote to you, and recognize that he wrote as the much older cousin, ready to be admired, expanding with good advice and also with admissions of his hopes and ideas, notably regarding his political theory, which he was clearly anxious to have discussed. Above all, the letters to your mother give insights into* Castle Corner. *I already have your permission to quote from them, and this I propose to do. But first I shall give my record of our interview, which began with the question, When did you meet?*

It is quite possible that I met Joyce before I left Inishowen, in 1907. But I was only five years old, and have no memory of it. I remember first hearing about him in 1908, as author of a book of verse, who was to be famous some day. I wrote to him in 1925 about the chance of going to Oxford University, and his letters to me date from then. But we did not meet until 1929, when my mother and I stayed at 12 Parks Road for a week or two.

He was then still going each day to the room he rented as a study.[1] He no longer wore a monocle, as I'd expected. But he still wore his magnificent evening cloak; he never gave up wearing that. His sight was in fact very bad in one eye, and he was always screwing up his face, to see better. My mother – his Aunt Mab – had very bad eyesight, and found writing almost impossible.

These portraits were all done around that time,[2] but the one of Joyce is too wan, and fails to convey his vital personality; the one of his father, with his gun, is typical; and Trudy's soft, dreamy look is well conveyed in the portrait of her. She had a vague, English manner, and

61

seemed a clinging vine, in the way she would say, 'Joyce, what shall we do now?' She probably had brains, as her brothers were brilliant, though she didn't have much sense of humour, and didn't get on with the Irish cousins, really. But she was totally loyal to Joyce, who was of course pleased to respond to the clinging vine manner. And she did manage everything for the family later, when Joyce had got a novel published, and was working very hard to keep it up.

In 1929 they had just bought a car, which she was learning to drive. She then most often drove. Joyce's eyesight might have made him – or her – feel unsafe, when he drove.

In 1933 I went to Oxford to do a B.Litt., and lived in Norham Road, from 1933 until 1935. My mother lived with me, and she played bridge with Gertie (as she, like most people except Joyce, called her). I remember one evening, when she and I called there after dinner, Joyce was in a dinner jacket, but alone. At that time they apparently always dressed for dinner, and Joyce expressed surprise at our apologies. We'd assumed he must have guests.

I think their friends of the 'thirties were probably Gertie's, including Dorothy Muir, who was at school with Gertie, and was tutoring in history. I think Joyce's closest friends were Duncan MacGregor of Balliol, and his wife Dorothy.

James Osborn was working for a B.Litt. between 1934 and 1936, and I remember mentioning Joyce to him. But I can't remember whether I introduced them.[3]

From around 1933, Joyce Cary made notes on your family lineage, which led directly into the writing of Castle Corner. *It seems likely that he was inspired by talking to your mother.*

He was always wanting to know more about Cary lineage, and wanted my mother to write about it. He felt identification with his Irish background; he felt strongly that it was his. Hence his desire to buy Castlecary, of which you've read in my family history. Our grandfather was ill when the remission of rents came, and in debt to Foster in Londonderry, whose daughter married Colonel MacNiece. When the Carys were evicted, Foster first let Castlecary to other tenants, and then to MacNiece. Colonel MacNiece's son became an Air-Vice-Marshal and lives in Oxford. His youngest son Donny stayed on at Castlecary, and the place had been let go when Donny offered it to Joyce. He was very tempted! My mother probably intensified his sense of familiarity with life in Castlecary, by talking about it, and he

was certainly proud of his aristocratic lineage. He had to set the novel
Castle Corner back to the time when his family had lived at Castlecary.

*His father must also have been able to recreate the life at Castlecary for
him. Or was your mother better at it?*

His father was very downright and practical, and though Joyce had
affection for him, they argued a lot – by the Cary method: 'Well of
course you're totally wrong.'

Did you see much of the Cary sons when you were in Oxford?

Tristram and George were only infants in 1929 – much younger than
the other two. I used to feel very sorry for Peter. I thought them hard
on him.[4] He was very shy; I remember him as gentle, shy, and
withdrawn in 1929. I met him later, with his young wife, when they
were living in Wimpole Street (in the house made famous by Tenny-
son's *In Memoriam*). You will find an affectionate letter to me from
Peter in my Joyce Cary file, in which he says that he hopes my edition
of Meredith will encourage people to read him. When it came to the
sons choosing which of their father's books they would like to take
away for themselves, the first editions of Meredith were left solidly
where they were, he said.

*They are in the Bodleian Collection, and no doubt valuable.
Would you say a word about Cary's American lecture tours?*

The young men used to lionize him.
   I remember how warm he was in 1953.[5]

[*The following extracts are from the letters mentioned above; where no
address or salutation is shown, it can be assumed that these are '12 Parks
Rd' and 'Dear Leo' or 'Dear Lionel' (the latter post-dating 1929, when
Cary evidently learned that his cousin preferred 'Lionel' to 'Leo'); the first
letter covers six foolscap pages, and begins:*]

Jan 15th '25

   I had always hoped that you would get a scholarship enabling you to
come here, but without that, or without at least a hundred a year by
which you could live as a non-collegiate student (an excellent course
for older men, and hard workers) I dare not suggest so desperate an

adventure. It would be cruel and wicked to advise you to abandon your present career, now well begun and promising a certain future, to bring you to this country, overcrowded with experts in all the learned professions and especially your own. [...]

[...] To understand and enjoy good writing and fine wit is a sensible ambition, and to me, of course, life would mean nothing without it; but books have the advantage of portability, and they carry their charms with them. I grant that the critical powers necessary to enjoy are not so easily borne to the middle of Africa or the suburbs of a provincial town such as Bristol or Burslem, but they can be acquired, given some natural bent, by reading good critics, among whom I don't hesitate to place Johnson, in his lives of the poets, and Hazlitt, and Masefield (in a little book on Shakespeare's plays) and of course Causeries du Lundi, but I need not write a list. [...]

Jan. 23 '27

[...] A critic to be any good must be very much more than a critic; but that is true I suppose of any artist. Chaplin I hope will give us his masterpiece after he had been tried and condemned on the evidence of public opinion by the press. He has given us several variations on the theme that there is no justice in a world where God himself makes one man big and happy and another little and sad; now he can give us his New Kid; Kid having another meaning.

I like your style, tho I am no judge of styles. I haven't any. I try only to put as much of my meaning as I can ascertain in words into the fewest possible, and in doing so no doubt I escape from the well-made phrase and the too appropriate adjective. Style in painting I do know something of; and I can see that in a great painter like Van Gogh (or Van Eyck if you like) it is of the least importance except as a medium of expression; but in a small painter like Hals or Orpen it is of great interest because no other nobler part of the work is interesting. We forgive Carlyle his abominable style on account of his matter, we put up with George Moore's stupid matter on account of his style; but I'm damned if anyone can stand Emerson.

[...] I'm ashamed to say I don't know anything about poetry and cannot criticize it. [...] when I open a book of poetry, it is usually the Golden Treasury or a Shelley. [...]

I wonder did you ever see a book of verse I wrote at eighteen. If so, I hope you burnt it.[6] It was worse even than the notorious first work of Shelley's, because it had not even high spirits. In Shelley's work one sees at least energy, in mine there was nothing but metre. My fault was in having nothing to say; the usual one at my age then. I had grasped nothing with force, felt nothing deeply; or what I had felt deeply had seemed to me too commonplace for expression. When one has nothing to write about the thing to do is to write extremely well and acquire the art of expression which will be useful when one has had a few unpleasant misfortunes or some of those disillusionments which must strike into every man to the advantage of his inward lighting; to write well one must study good models of good writing like Flecker. How I wish someone had made me translate from the French when I was a boy; then I might not have written such feeble stuff as I did at eighteen. Flecker's youthful work has nothing in it; but it is worth reading for style. I don't know a better model for the young – give him to your poetry class. [...]

June 2nd [1927?]

I congratulate you on a good opportunity. I take it there is a large opening at Berkeley [...] I wish you could have come here, but there was no possible opening, and what you could have done here can be done anywhere, or at least at Berkeley, where there must be plenty of enthusiasts ready to talk about books.

The English school here is new and not particularly good. None is good anywhere. There is world wide room for the pioneer. [...] the pioneer will be earlier than most of his kind in seeing the results of his enterprise. In spite of every discouragement, the revival has begun. We can see it in every newspaper we open, in cheap novels, in the theatre, in architecture, in clothes. Compare the modern woman's dress with that of 1905 or 10. You see the return of form, line, construction, in short the classical renaissance. [...]

Nov. 8. 32

Your plan sounds a good one and I don't think you'll regret it. [...] the Colleges recommended for an English student are Merton and Exeter, Merton for Nicholl Smith and Exeter for Nevill Coghill. [...]

Feb. 18 33

[...] Our own plans and future are uncertain because of our financial position which is extremely bad. We shall probably shut up the house for the present and goodness knows what we'll be doing in September. It depends on what America does in March among other things and also upon the future of my new book and its date of publication. [...] [...] We want to keep the house together for the boys, and I've no doubt that we shall succeed in time – the great crisis is in this year and next while our income has almost disappeared and my work is not yet producing anything. [...]

Oct. 27 '36

I was glad to hear that you enjoyed the Witch. the Americans are certainly treating me kindly; and my American publisher is particularly charming to me. [...] I hope Morrows[7] get some return for all this expenditure. [...]

Nov. 22 '36

Dear Aunt Mab,
I was glad to hear from Lionel that you liked my book. I think my new one is a better book but I don't know if it will be so popular.[8] Some of the scenes are in Ireland. I wish you were here to give me particulars about the pre-war Inishowen. I remember more than I thought; but not nearly enough. Trudy and I visited it this summer and were welcomed by many of the old ones whom you would know. George Orr spent a week on the Moville road to catch us each time we passed and Jimmy Ellis gave us tea. Both wished to be remembered to you. Of course I am not writing about places and people by name; and I am disguising all my descriptions. But the contrast between dying imperialism in Ireland and rising Imperialism in Africa is an interesting theme. I only wish I could take another year at it. [...]

Feb. 15 '38

Dear Aunt Mab,
This is the book. [...] the reviewers up to now have been very kind. The book was recommended by the Book Society[9] [...].
I do hope you are better, dear Aunt Mab. You want to rest a heart. Dad need never have died like that if he had not gone out to golf in a freezing wind without his zip jacket.
Morrows are not publishing the book in USA. They wanted something more like the last – but this is a better book than the last. As you see it's not about Castle Cary[10] but about a compound of C.C. and Whitecastle, and even Clare. [...]

Nov. 2 '38

Dear Aunt Mab,
I went to a Hallowe'en party with an Irish gathering – Boyles and Morleys from near Limavady [...] and it made me think of you.

Especially the way one of the Morley girls said 'Is that man expecting more tea?' meaning me.

The Germans have just published my book the A. Witch, calling it Ein Schwartzer Prinz.[11] They have done it well and Michael says that the German version is superior to my own – it is almost literature. But my new novel is stuck while I finish my damned political work [*Power in Men*].

Nov. 27 '38

Dear Aunt Mab,

[...] I am cheerful because, having just fired off the political book, I can begin to do some real work on stories. [...]

The agents are always [?bothering] me for short stories so I wrote some and now I like doing them so much I shall do some more. But I doubt if editors will like them. [...]

My love to you both – has Aunt Mabs yet written her memoirs – or even tidbits of them? [...]

Feb 12. 39.

[...] I have spent too much time last year on my political book. [...] But specialists up here are much interested in my idea, which is as far as I can discover the first and only coherent theory of the democratic state in existence. This may not be so surprising as it seems. I came to it from the side of modern dynamic or space-time philosophy which, even in Oxford, has not displaced the old idealism. But that idealism from Plato to Bosanquet was the father of autocratic theory and in fact, it made impossible any rational systematic treatment of liberty. Mill contradicted himself; Rousseau played with [?paradigms]. [...] I'll send you two or three copies, so that you can let the university library have one. I want the theory debated; however much it may disagree with the old anarchist and the old autarch, which are, of course, the same people. [...]

April 28. 39

I send you two copies of this book, one for your university library if it wants it.

Specialists down here tell me that its theory is original and that it solves some obstinate problems of political science. I hope it does for it is quite time they were solved. As you see, I approached the problem from a new and modern angle tho' I can still scarcely believe that I have done so much as they say. [...]

7.4.44

Dear Aunt Mab,

We went to see Peter yesterday in hospital [...]. He is lucky to be alive as the mortar bomb went off only a yard away. [...] Indians (Gurkhas) brought him down from the mountain. They are fine troops, soldiers by tradition; but the men who bear the brunt of this war are the P.B.I. the poor bloody infantry; and especially the English county regiments – their casualties, by percentage, are far the highest and they take on all the dirty jobs.[12]

We are all fit and well, and I am full of work. I have a new book being printed [*The Horse's Mouth*]. All the others are out of print but there is to be a collected edition after the war – I dread the necessary corrections. My first editions are now being held fairly tightly – I can't get copies myself. It made me laugh to see a paper advise the world generally to hold on to 'Cary firsts'. I can't take myself seriously as a collected author.

My film is being shot in Africa under serious difficulties. When I say mine, I wrote it, but god knows how much of my story will come through the mincing machine. [...]

Nov. 5. 44

Dear Aunt Mab,

[...] Peter's wounds are cured and he will be called up again in the next few days. I hope they don't send him off at once as the fighting in France is heavy, with a high proportion of officer casualties. Michael is still at the Admiralty. Tristram is finishing his training and expects to be sent East. I'm afraid this country, England, will suffer in this war, as in the last, much the highest proportion of casualties. A bigger proportion of Englishmen is in the front line than any imperial unit, or any ally, including Russia, and the wastage of the best lives, especially in the air Force, has been fearfully high. A very large proportion of Eton scholars of Michael's time were killed in the first years. [...]

Sept.15.45

Dear Aunt Mabs,

Thank you very much for your poems which bring me back my childhood in dear Inishowen. I enjoyed them greatly and shall keep them at hand. I don't know which I like best but the legend of the Giant's Causeway is a first class ballad and I heard it first when I was very small indeed, perhaps from yourself. Tho my recollection of it is mixed with a vision of the old stone bowl that used to stand at the door of Whitecastle and which, I think, must have been pointed out to me as the giant's porringer. [...]

March 25 47

[...] The American publishers up to now usually say I am too English for their public – this has not been an objection in Sweden, France, Germany, Italy etc. I shall send a copy of the Horse's Mouth which is all I can lay hold of just now. [...]

I look forward to your Thackeray. the new edition of his letters is valuable as giving new light on his character. Strange that neither he nor Dickens put themselves into their books, but only their aspirations. The bad husband drew virtue, the good one vice. The sentimentalist wrote like a cynic and the egotist wrote sentiment. [...]

April 11. 47

[...] I apologize for the Horse's Mouth copy. It was done for a readers union in large numbers and so I have some copies. It was to my surprise popular here; but Harpers thought it 'too exuberant for the USA.' You seem to be a cautious and prudent people in matters of art. [...]

Aug 8 47

[...] I am fearfully busy as we go away to Ireland in September and I must before then establish my book. A book is a mood and does not travel well. Also I am very behind with my patient and anxious publisher. I spent last year in India and in films and on writing a long poem – which is coming out this year and also on a book which I am now putting aside till next year. I am a wasteful writer and Trudy despairs of my tons of unfinished and unpublished MSS. I shall not finish 1/10 of my work in my lifetime. [...]

Jan. 2. 49

[...] An American batch of reviews on the Moonlight (over 8) has just come in. We both notice that American reviewers are for the most part much more intelligent than British ones. They are in quite a different class, and take more trouble. This is odd because circulations are much lower. My books sell 4 times the number (20,000 or so) on this side and there is still a demand. [...]

New Orleans
11.11.53

My Dear Lionel,

I am having a very good but *very* full time here – classes all the
morning and people all day. I am very comfortable except as you see it
is hard to find envelopes stamps [?d=in?] New Orleans. I don't know
where New Orleans is and tho I hear the ships blow on Miss – ippi as
they call it, I haven't seen the old crocodile myself and I want to see
her again. I have a passion for rivers. Thank you 1000 times for my
very good time you gave me in L.A. and my love to Lillian and
Marietta and Mrs. [?Sprogue],

            ever your affectionate cousin
                        Joyce.

Some haste – in 5 minutes I am to be whisked away to some negro
college.[13]

NOTES

(Continued from item 1:) Lionel Stevenson had been Professor of English at Duke
University since 1955. He retired from Duke in 1972, and was distinguished visiting
Professor at his Alma Mater, British Columbia, when he died suddenly on 21 December
1973.

His major critical studies are on Thackeray and Meredith, and he produced vol. XI of
E.A. Baker's *History of the English Novel*, subtitled 'Yesterday and After'(New York:
Barnes & Noble, 1967), in which the section on Joyce Cary occupies 15 pages; see also
'Joyce Cary and the Anglo-Irish Tradition', *Modern Fiction Studies*, IX (Autumn 1963),
210-16.

1. On the third (top) floor of a house in Rawlinson Road, owned by a Fellow of
Hertford College named Campbell; he had taken it in 1926, when Tristram was a baby,
and concentrated work at home was difficult.

2. They were on the wall above us, and done, I believe, by Toni Thompson (item
23).

3. He did not; see item 66.

4. I gained the same impression from others, including Michael Cary with respect to
his father. The situation is so important to our judgement of Cary as man and writer,
that I here venture the following comment. Letters exchanged between Cary and his
wife during the months just after Peter was born (on 9 Dec. 1918) show their deep
unhappiness about their own future (e.g. Cary's of 30 May 1919, quoted by me in *The
Writer and His Theme*, p. 88); in Cary this became desperation, as shown most
powerfully by the letter of 22 November 1921 (quoted by me in *The House as a Symbol*,
p.70). None of this was due to the child, whose only fault, perhaps, lay in not being the
girl they had both hoped for. Any baby would have suffered in this atmosphere, as
Cary's own theory of the telepathic powers of children would endorse (see *Art and
Reality*, p. 14); but it happened before he had studied such things, and the parents, too
aware of their own unhappiness, could have ignored the way it affected their baby's
character, at least until it was too late. Michael would have been armed already with a
self-confidence that could meet the situation, because for three years he had lived with

his mother and her parents at the Glade, Harrow, where the servants also, no doubt, gave him constant love and attention. Any such child would expect the attention he had known to continue, and his mother probably gave it to Michael, if only from habit. His father was a rival for her attention whom he had to accept, and doubtless wanted to accept, in many ways; but a baby brother as a rival was not only harder to accept but easier to fight; Michael himself admitted that he had been 'awful' to Peter. Since Cary was engrossed in self-analysis during the 1920s (as his notebooks show), he must surely have thought to compare his own relationship with a younger brother with that of Michael and Peter. Perhaps he expected Peter to stand up to Michael as Jack had stood up to him. But the future naval Commander had been a very different character from his artistically-gifted second son – as indeed Michael was different from Joyce Cary himself.

The relationship between brothers, which he knew from direct experience, seems to me a vital clue to an understanding of Cary's work. He made it obvious in *A House of Children*, and also the second trilogy. But it runs right through his fiction, even when he changes the relationship to one between sisters.

5. This final comment was made by Mrs Stevenson who, now Mrs Pollock, read and approved this record of the interview in February 1988.

6. Stevenson's copy, presumably first his mother's, was acquired by Texas University.

7. See N.3.

8. Cary refers back to *The African Witch* and forward to *Castle Corner*.

9. *Castle Corner* (N.4.).

10. Consistently spelt thus by Cary, but Stevenson uses 'Castlecary', as the name survives in the district.

11. The book is Cary A.21 in the Bodleian: 'Aus dem Englishen ubertragen von Willy Kramp, Copyright 1938 Munchen'.

12. During 1944, Cary wrote the bulk of his long poem, *Marching Soldier* (P.15), which is dedicated to the infantry; he had begun it in 1939; Peter was in the infantry, and he just escaped death in April 1944.

13. This last letter links with the reference to New Orleans in Tristram's account, which ends Part II, and Mrs Stevenson's comment, above.

17

Of Oxford and Ireland

Cary Clark

This interview at the Bungalow, Ireland, continues from item 6.

I was a schoolboy at Radley, near Oxford, from 1920 until 1924, and I used to see Joyce quite often. I loved talking to him. He was a brilliant conversationalist, and he made philosophy exciting to me, at sixteen or seventeen. When I used to visit them as a boy I was certainly a pretty uncouth individual, and over here in Ireland we must all have seemed a pretty 'through-other' family to anyone living in such a civilized place as Oxford.

I don't want to give the impression though that either Joyce or Trudy was critical of us in any unpleasant way. It was more, I think, that Joyce was amused and Trudy perhaps a little astonished at some of our Irish ways. She was rather critical of people. And she used to send Joyce on errands. If he stayed with us on his own he was one of the family. But when she came they became a separate group. They drove me nearly mad with making plans and changing them etc.

How did the children behave?

Very well. Michael and Peter were slapped and sternly brought up. With the second two they were more relaxed.

Judging from the number of letters in the Bodleian sent by Cary to his wife from the Bungalow, it seems that he stayed here quite a lot on his own, and felt more at ease writing his books here than in Oxford. But I'd like to hear more about Oxford, as you remember it.

I remember when Joyce and A.P. Herbert took me for a pub crawl. I should add, by the way, in case I've given a slightly distorted impression, that Joyce had a terrific sense of fun. I don't think I remember anyone laughing more heartily than when I fell into the Cherwell or Isis from the ferry and came to the surface with a startled

72

expression and my school bowler clamped firmly down on my ears. Of course to appreciate it fully I suppose you would have to realize how funny I look in a bowler at the best of times.

Another anecdote which I remember Joyce telling with great glee was when he was showing my mother round the medieval kitchen of one of the Oxford colleges – I forget which, but no doubt you will know as it is quite a show piece. At any rate Joyce had been expounding at some length to my mother, who appeared to be deeply interested, when suddenly she turned to him and said: 'You know, Joyce, I'm not at all sure that Mary Josephine is strictly honest.' Mary Josephine was a woman who came in once a week at the Bungalow to help with the washing.

I'm telling you these stories only to show that, much as I appreciated Joyce's more serious conversation, he was equally at home in family fun and gossip.

Although I don't think he liked whisky, I think he always came up to my mother's room and joined us in a night-cap when he was staying with us. And I also remember him joining me in one when I was staying with him at Oxford.

I didn't see him after 1949. Netta died in January 1949. She had been ill with osteomylitis since 1936.

Did she like his books?

She loved his stories – his pot-boilers. I remember him saying, 'It's easy enough to make money.'

But he wanted something more? What then impressed you most about him?

He looked objectively at – for example, impending disasters.

NOTE

See item 6.

18

As a Writer in Oxford

Thomas Higham

The interviews of 1967 and '68 are here continued from item 14.

Do you think Joyce Cary a worthy subject for study?

Yes, I think so. Americans made much more of Joyce than we did. They always do.

Where then does his greatness lie?

I think he had a poet's eye. (I made some claim to being a poet myself, incidentally.) Joyce had great power of expression in language. I recall the description of a lime tree in one book.[1] And he was always a perfectionist. He would never pot-boil. When we went on holidays and walking tours together (after he married and settled in Oxford), I came to realize that Joyce had a high standard. After being 'demolished' by Prichard, for example, he set himself to get at the truth.[2] Form in a novel was something we discussed a lot. I am perhaps old-fashioned – I like a beginning, middle, and end. But a slab of life was formless thought, Joyce said. However, Trudy agreed with me that *Mister Johnson* was better because it had more form.

Did you read his first novels when they came out?

Yes. I was poor when Joyce's early novels came out, and so was Elinor Wreford-Brown (now Mrs King). So we decided to take turns in buying copies. Joyce gave me *Power in Men*, *Process of Real Freedom*, and *The Case for African Freedom* – which is inscribed 'from his old affectionate friend the author'.

Clearly he wanted to interest you in his political writing. He was similarly poor during those depression years, I've gathered.

74

Yes. They divided their Oxford house, 12 Parks Road, sometime during the twenties; Joyce and his family lived on the first and second floors, and they let the ground floor and the garden. At a later date J.B. Priestley and his wife lived in the let-out portion.[3] There certainly was an acute financial crisis in the Cary household. Mrs Cary's father came to the rescue.

Mrs Cary appears to have been a marvellous housekeeper.

[...] Probably she owed her sense of wifely duties to her German mother, a sometimes formidable figure at family gatherings held at her own and her husband's expense in a Hotel at Blair Atholl. Suitors for her daughters' hands and would-be brides of her sons did not always win her approval. They had to show in some way that they deserved it. Gertie inherited from her the Germanic emphasis on Christmas celebrations – the giving of numerous presents (none of those received by the family to be opened until after tea), the singing of traditional songs and annual revival of traditional customs. Birthdays and other anniversaries had similar importance and rituals of their own. Gertie and I were always the best of friends. I think she liked me partly because I helped to prevent Joyce from overworking by taking him out for walks in Oxford and sometimes for a walking tour. I felt honoured when she asked to see me not long before her end. She had been having most painful treatment for cancer, but did not let her visitors suspect it and greeted them cheerfully. As you probably know, she did all Joyce's typewriting – and with good humour, a labour of love.

Would you say something about your holidays and walking tours with Cary?

The most memorable was our trip to Hungary, in 1922. During 1921, some undergraduates had lit a bonfire in King Edward Street, to mark the rejection of King Charles as ruler of Hungary. As a result they were invited to go to Hungary, and the visit was such a success that they were told to invite others, including some dons, to go there after them.[4] I was invited, and I said I'd go if Joyce went too. Julian Huxley and two Fellows of All Souls were of the party, and we spent about ten days in Hungary, and a night or two in Vienna on the way. There were strong Jewish persecutions, and quelling of radical disorders at this time in Hungary, and one of our number, who was invited to speak, was himself a Jew. In return for their hospitality, some Hungarians were entertained in Oxford at All Souls College, and I got the impression that these were Royalists. It was in fact an ordinary meal at All Souls, but it was reported in the papers, and annoyed the Hungarian ambassador. One of the All Souls Fellows on the trip with us was Dermot Morrah, who was Irish, and had some claim to descent from ancient kings. I recall spending one evening in Budapest writing limericks, and we couldn't finish Morrah's, until I suggested 'A putative kingly begorra', for which Morrah never forgave me. He took his royal descent very seriously.

Joyce and I had a walking tour in the Cotswolds for about a week, probably in the Easter Vac., in 1921 or '22.

The other walking tour we had was from 15 or 16 April 1930, when we spent a week touring Normandy and Brittany, on foot mostly, though we used buses too. I have postcards which I sent home from Hotel de France, Caen, 16 April; from Hotel de Normandie, Falaise, 17 April; from Mont S. Michel 20 April; and an undated one from Bayeux. We also visited Coutances and Mortain.

Did Cary have other close friends in Oxford at this time?

Yes. There were Duncan MacGregor and his wife Dolly. She was large and cheerful and vigorous – could bicycle 90 miles in a day – but she died comparatively young after serveral operations for cancer, and must have had sometimes difficulty with Duncan, whose health was impaired by war-service. He died a good while after Dolly; a Memorial Service was held in Balliol on 15 March 1939.

There was also John Macmurray, with whom Joyce used to take walks in the Parks and discuss philosophical subjects. He is still alive, and you should get in touch with him, if possible.
[*See item 25.*]

NOTES

See item 14, for biography.
1. See *To Be a Pilgrim*, ch. 98.
2. See item 14, nn. 3, 4.
3. Peter Cary gave me to understand that this was during the war.
4. From my copy of a letter lent me by Mr Higham, it seems that the invitation was issued to F.W. Ogilvie, Trinity College. Dated 29th May 1922, it reads: 'In expressing, on behalf of the Hungarian National Union, our grateful thanks to each individual member of the Oxford League for Hungarian Self-Determination, for their valuable work in the interests of Hungary, we desire to give concrete testimony of our appreciation of their efforts, by inviting you in the month of July next for a ten days' sojourn in our country. [...] the same hospitable spirit still exists as in pre-war days, restricted only by the limitation of our resources imposed upon us by the "Peace".'

19

In Oxford Circles

Helena Brett-Smith

This interview took place in Oxford on 3 October 1967.

I met the Carys when they came to Oxford in the twenties, at the home of Duncan MacGregor, whose first wife was my friend. Thomas Higham and his wife formed a group with us.

Joyce wore a monocle in those days, but I don't think it was an affectation – I don't think of him as an affected person. He didn't wear it for long; it probably didn't help much. We usually dressed for dinner in the evening, the women wearing long frocks. Wine at table was usual in Oxford in those days.

Joyce danced very well, and he was always a very good talker; he could talk about anything. He always called his wife Trudy, though others called her Gertie. Her sister Elsie (who became Mrs Carlisle) was at Somerville with me. Trudy was very fair, with fair hair, a nice complexion and blue eyes; that is, though not strictly very pretty she had pretty colouring. She was very English-looking, though in fact she was Scottish and German. She was very charming, and gifted musically, and when she took up painting – she went to evening classes – she became rather good. She played bridge with College dons' wives; we played in each other's houses. At her house, Joyce would come in for the tea break, but he never played.

Everyone went out a lot in those days, and I think they would have had a full social life and many friends. Looking back, I see it as a time of incessant parties; there was probably too much entertaining. The Carys were interesting, vital people.

What did you know about Cary's work?

People used to tease him, and speculate on what he was writing. They would suggest all sorts of mad ideas. People used to ask 'What does Joyce Cary *do*?' He took a room in Rawlinson Road, and he used to work there for definite hours, but no one knew at what. Then the

77

African novels came out. Lots of friends were interested in *Aissa Saved*, but the critics were slow to accept him. In America it took much longer.

Would his friends have been encouraging?

They probably discussed his books in senior common rooms, but dons are always diffident to talk, and it was an atmosphere where everyone was writing. Joyce didn't talk about his work. Oxford in those days was so packed with things to do and people coming and going, and it was much more closely woven with London life than it is now. It was a very alive sort of time, and the Carys never gave the impression of being out of things. Trudy was always very charming and enjoyed going about, and Joyce was so vivid, with such a wide range of interests. He wasn't at all donnish.

Trudy struck me as very practical and capable. They had servants and never struck one as short of money. But no one talked of money. Everyone rode bicycles, and would even go to dances on bicycles.

My husband and I played tennis with the Carys, at the University Tennis Club in the Parks – another indication that they did join into Oxford University life. They had connexions everywhere – Fred Ogilvie at Trinity, for example.

I can believe that Joyce might have been disappointed in not being made a Fellow of Trinity, but his fourth-class pass would certainly have been against that. I don't see why they didn't give him an honorary degree later. But he was a very well-mannered, generous-minded man, and I don't think he would have borne a grudge.

His letters to his wife, during their rare partings, give the impression that he was under a great strain, from lack of money, and fear of failure. Her family, too, evidently thought that he should get a paid job.

What you say makes me realize that there could have been a strain over their position, but such things weren't apparent. I knew them well, and saw them all the term, but not in circumstances where such facts would appear.

I knew them well until Trudy's illness, but at that time my own husband became ill and died; so I wasn't much in touch. Trudy's cancer seemed to come so suddenly, and she was desolated. She wanted to live so badly. She went to her brother-in-law, George Carlisle, who was then doing advanced treatment for cancer, and after treatment under him she did come back looking quite well. Then she got more and more ill, and from then depended entirely on Joyce. It must have been very distressing, and she couldn't bear the thought of dying; she wasn't very old.

I don't recall why I know about Trudy's thoughts about dying, except that she had a way of casting off a remark. I wouldn't know whether she was brave about dying or came to terms with it, but I think Joyce would have been an enormous support.

He told Edith Haggard that he'd always had to build Trudy up, even before she was ill.[1]

I can see what she meant, and that it might have been so. When Trudy was doing something quite well she would behave as though she was doing it badly. Even a good hand of bridge she'd describe as a bad one. In her manner she was perhaps not so talkative as some people, and I can see that she did rely on Joyce's support.

Did you know their sons?

I remember seeing them at school functions, and I remember Peter playing at friends' houses when he was an undergraduate. He was more musical than Michael, but wasn't so obviously brilliant, and lacked Michael's good looks. I think there must have been the expectation of success in the household; so they were very proud of Michael, and Peter was overshadowed by him.

Do you recall Lionel Stevenson, and his mother, Cary's Aunt Mab?

Yes. Trudy treated them very hospitably when they stayed in Oxford, and Mrs Stevenson played bridge with us. She had a caustic wit, and took the view that she had done a lot for Lionel, and now he could do it for her.

Joyce in conversation was always throwing things out, and watching one's reactions. He always had theories about everything, and he wasn't boring on them. He was amused at himself.

Did you ever hear him talk about Buchmanism?[2]

I wouldn't have thought he took it seriously, but I recall the son of a friend who was from Eton and brilliant, who became involved and vanished from academic circles. I remember a meeting at Lady Margaret Hall, where I went with a woman friend, and Joyce might

have been there, though I don't recall seeing him. The Buchmanites
took Oxford by surprise and some amusement. It was odd to see those
young men get up and confess to really most trivial things. A woman
don got interested, but I wouldn't have thought Joyce took it seriously.

*He was very distressed about its effect on a brilliant scholar (probably the
one you have mentioned),*[3] *and plots concerning 'The Buchmanites' appear
from that date in his notebooks – when he was also writing* An American
Visitor. *Buchman, as an American visitor to Oxford, influenced the theme
of that novel, I believe.*

I wouldn't have thought he'd have had anything so involved to say, as
what you suggest about the ambiguity of that title.

I think all his titles are ambiguous. Which of his novels do you like best?

I think *The Horse's Mouth* is wonderful.

*Well, Cary called it a very heavy piece of metaphysical writing; the French
recognized that fact, he said, but could not find a title in French to convey
his meaning.*[4] *He is involved, I think.*

I am reminded of Yeats, when he was in Oxford. He had a certain
following among the undergraduates, and they used to meet at a café
opposite Balliol. But Oxford was slow to recognize or bother with
anyone like that – it was rather bad in that way. Life seemed so full,
and one tended to treat everything rather casually. Joyce would have
been interested in Yeats, I think.

   Looking back, I do realize that the Carys could have felt a little out
of things, though they never showed it, and I was never aware of it at
the time. But you did tend to associate people with the Colleges, and
women who had been up at Oxford themselves had a feeling about the
place, which someone like Trudy could not have.

NOTES

Helena Brett-Smith (née Yates), was educated at St. Leonard's School, St. Andrews,
and Somerville College, Oxford. Her husband, H.F.B. Brett-Smith, was Goldsmith's
Reader of English Literature at Oxford University. She died aged 88, in May 1977.
   This interview was kindly arranged by her son John, who was then president of the
Oxford University Press Inc. New York.
   1. See item 47.

2. An evangelical movement founded by Frank Buchman (1878-1961); he was born of German antecedents in Pennsylvania, but his movement took root in Oxford, where adherents won it the name 'Oxford Group' (from 1929); 'Moral Re-Armament' (MRA) was adopted from a slogan coined in May 1938, but 'Buchmanism' and 'Buchmanites' were terms used by people outside the movement.

3. See item 20 (end, and n. 4).

4. 'An Interview with Joyce Cary', *Paris Review* (see Q.7).

20

Memories of My Father

Michael Cary

This item combines extracts from an exchange of letters in 1964, and an interview on 29 May 1967 (see notes).

For the past three years I have been working on your father's manuscripts in the Bodleian Library, and [...] so often I have wanted to ask you in particular for explanations, because as the eldest son you would be more likely than your brothers to remember the early years. Do you for instance remember a house in Saundersfoot called, at least by Joyce Cary, 'The Turkish House'? It had 'jutting balconies', and stood darkly against the hillside behind trees and creepers. It seems to have been occupied, in your father's imagination at least, by a slightly sinister elderly woman with a younger companion.[1]

I vaguely remember the Turkish House; up the hill, very umbrageous, slightly sinister, but I didn't know about the inmates.[2]

Do you think a complete list of the contents of your father's library could be compiled? What is in the Bodleian is invaluable for research, but knowing also what he left for his family would give a truer picture.

He started collecting first editions while still at Trinity. I have *The Correspondence of Horace Walpole*, *The Woman in White*, *Silas Marner*, editions of Peacock which Joyce gave my mother, some James and, amongst others, a small copy of *Ulysses*, printed in Paris and smuggled into England in 1930, which I gave him.

Who has his Ellis and Yeats edition of William Blake?

I've no recollection about that. As far as I remember, I instructed Win Davin to take out all the books containing notes, to be put in the Collection, and the family took the rest.

Do you recall anything about books of names? Lists of names suitable for characters appear repeatedly in notebooks, the names being evidently intended as clues to characterization.

The Oxford Dictionary of [English Christian] Names was given to my mother, but for the purpose of naming grandchildren, I think. I don't recall any other books of names, or discussion of names, except for family purposes. I suggest you ask Peter about the books.

How did you and your brothers get on with each other, and with your parents?

Peter in early life was very sensitive, and he and I quarrelled a lot. Joyce could have protected Peter from me, and could have been more sympathetic towards him, I think.

It's surprising that your father was unsympathetic.

He was fairly hard on all of us. He was very wrapped up in his work, and rather grudged the time away from it. We were conscious of money worries, which made him feel the need to work. He did play tennis, and liked games on the beach. But he would never play card games with us, or anything like that. He grudged the time, but always had time for long walks in the park, talking about Plato in particular, or Bergson. I remember Plato from the time I was seven, eight and nine years old. I used to dread, rather, the walks in the park.

What sense did you have of your father as an intellectual?

I think he had a very powerful intellectual equipment. He was good on political science, and a good humanist – ethical questions. I read philosophy, but I wasn't particularly interested in it; so we reached an understanding about what to discuss.

Was irony a strong characteristic?

I don't think of him as displaying irony characteristically, but rather sarcasm. I don't think of him as a wit, as such. He was a very good conversationalist – never rude. But he was pretty sarcastic about people at times.

Would you talk about his relationship with your mother?

They were devoted to each other. They recognized that there were areas on which one couldn't enter fully into the other's appreciation – for example her world of music. But Joyce enormously appreciated her views of his work.

And their relationship with her family? Your mother seems to have had a very close bond with her brother Fred.

Trudy found Heneage more amusing than Fred, but probably preferred Fred. Joyce didn't get on with Fred, and used to have frightful rows with him, especially about money. I know nothing about the tale you heard, that Fred was there on their honeymoon. But it possibly related to the difficulty of travelling at all during the war.

After your mother and her brother Fred died, your father seems to have formed a close friendship with Fred's widow.

Joyce was very fond of Mary Ogilvie, and he talked to me of his thoughts about marrying her, in about 1954 to 1955 (when he was getting ill). But she had her own life and interests. I don't think he was hurt by her staying away when he was ill and dying. He understood her reasons.

Do you recall visiting Ireland with your parents?

I remember a visit after the war. We went to Whitecastle, looked at Redcastle, visited that strange character Donny MacNeice at Castlecary, and stayed at Greencastle.

Did your father ever talk to you about the Montgomeries, with whom he evidently played as a child when on holiday in Moville?[3]

I don't recall that he ever did.

Does one rightly sense that he had strong feelings against the idea of 'experts'?

Yes, I agree that he was always against experts.

Regarding John Middleton Murry, your father wrote of him (in letters of 1917 and 1919 to your mother) as 'a scamp' and 'a rascal', who moreover owed him money. Did Murry ever pay his debts to him, and did your father remain bitter?

Murry never did pay his debts to him, and it did anger Joyce.

Murry's book, Between Two Worlds, seems likely to have angered him. Did he ever talk to you about his life in Paris?

He loved to talk of it. But Trudy did not like him to, and he respected her feelings.

Buchmanism was something against which he felt strongly, to judge from his notebooks. Was there a particular reason?

He shared his ideas against Frank Buchman with Alan Herbert. And he was particularly distressed about a brilliant friend of ours who became a Buchmanite shortly after entering the University.[4]

NOTES

Arthur Lucius Michael Cary (1917-1976), Joyce Cary's eldest son, was educated at Eton and Oxford, where he took a first in Mods and Greats. He entered the Air Ministry in 1939 as private secretary to the Secretary of State, but left to serve with the Royal Naval Volunteer Reserve from 1940 until after the war, when he returned to the Air Ministry. Between 1956 and 1958 he was counsellor to the British delegation to Nato at Paris. He was deputy secretary of the Cabinet (1961-4), then appointed Secretary to the Admiralty (the thirty-first and last holder of the post which Samuel Pepys had been the fourth to hold). In 1968 he became Permanent Secretary at the Ministry of Public Buildings and Works, and in 1971 returned to the Ministry of Defence, where he became Permanent Under-Secretary in March 1974 until his sudden death on 7 March 1976. He was made a CB in 1964, KCB in 1965, and GCB in 1976. Lady Cary has kindly contributed an account of their family life (item 35).

  1. From a letter dated 28 May 1964 from B. Fisher.

  2. From a letter of 30 May 1964, from Michael Cary to B. Fisher; the interview of 1967 follows.

  3. See item 5, and the preface to *Charley Is My Darling* (N.6).

  4. See item 19, n. 2.

21

His Second Son and His Wife Remember

Peter Cary   Elizabeth Cary

This interview took place in Cambridge on 14 October 1987, and was then developed by correspondence.

Would you say something, Peter, about the painting by your father, in which your mother is playing the cello and you are accompanying her on the piano? The reproduction in Time,[1] *though little more than two inches square, still conveys a wonderfully sympathetic quality, and you and your mother look remarkably alike. The date given in* Time *is 1934, when you would have been sixteen.*

[**Peter**:] Lady Cary has the pastel. Elizabeth and I are very fond of this work, which, as an example of art, is a delight.

For the concerts that you and your family arranged, did you ever have an audience?

[**Peter**:] We never played in public, although we sometimes played to friends. My mother was an excellent cellist; she was taught by Percy Such.

I have learned from both Michael and Tristram about their fast walks, as children, in the park with your father, who combined his need for exercise with his desire to share, and instruct in, his current philosophical interests. Which philosopher was he most interested in when your turn came? And did you, too, rather dread those walks?

[**Peter**:] Yes, I did rather dread the walks. His favourite philosopher was Hegel, I thought. He got a general introduction to philosophy from Joad.[2]

86

Which of your brothers did you feel closest to?

[**Peter**:] I was particularly fond of my youngest brother George. We shared the same interest in books and scholarship, especially the classics, which I also read for my first degree. We were always in touch, and I stayed with him in Trinity College, Cambridge, after the war.

George's death must have been particularly tragic for you.
*   Would you tell me, Elizabeth, how you and Peter met, and how you felt about becoming a member of his family?*

[**Elizabeth**:] We met in my mother's house through mutual friends. Of course I was immensely impressed by the Cary family, of which I was quickly made to feel a secure part.

Joyce Cary told Walter Allen that he didn't belong to a club, because he was a 'domestic man'.[3] Does that fit your idea of him?

[**Elizabeth**:] Yes, Joyce was very concerned with being a traditional 'family man', but he did belong to the Commonwealth Club in London.

I imagine you got on well with your father-in-law. His diary[4] records the gift of stockings to be bought for your birthday each year, and also how frequently you and Peter stayed for two or three days at a time. Have you any particular memories?

[**Elizabeth**:] I was rather young and immature at the time, concerned mainly with my relation with Peter and our future together. I don't think anything I can say would be of any interest to the general reader.
    I always enjoyed staying at Parks Road and even enjoyed walking in the Parks with Joyce!

When did you last see him?

[**Elizabeth**:] We both saw Joyce on the day before he died, Peter visiting his side at midnight on the day of his death.

Have you any books from his library that you particularly treasure, Peter?

[**Peter:**] I am particularly glad to have a fine edition of Chaucer which belonged to Joyce, as well as a good copy of Bunyan.

Can you add anything to Michael's answers, when I asked him about books of names?

No. But I recommend your looking at a book called 300 Years in Inishowen,[5] as it contains a lot of information about the Cary family there and other families in that area.

My question relates to his use of names for characters in books.
Would you be interested in talking about your Irish connexions, and your holidays in Ireland? What memories do you have of them?

[**Peter:**] My general memory is of the carefree, kind, utterly relaxed atmosphere I found with my Irish relations. With my parents, I remember travelling by boat from Liverpool, at night, and arriving at Belfast early the next morning. Those trips were usually preceded by a stay with my mother's sister Elsie, in Birkenhead. I liked her husband, George, very much, and he was a very good doctor. He cured some ear trouble my father had, which his Oxford doctor couldn't.

In 1941 I went to Ireland with my regiment, for a course of troop training. On that trip I travelled from Stranraer to Larne.

In Ireland, we stayed as a family at the Bungalow, Castledawson, with my father's Aunt Netta, of whom I was very fond. She married Jackson Clark (always called Peter), who wrote a book called *Knockinscreen Days* (the name of a village).[6] One memorable anecdote in it concerned the local train, which Peter used to catch each day; when one day he failed to appear, the whole train waited while the train driver telephoned to see what had happened to him.

Your Aunt Netta's daughter Toni kept a diary for many years, and her son Courtenay has kindly allowed me to have it copied. She records that you and Michael stayed at the Bungalow with your parents in 1933, between April 7th and 27th, during which time they visited Aunt Pearl at Gravesend, where tennis was played. Can you identify her, and her home?

[**Peter:**] She was formerly Miss Wishart, who married Leo Cary – my great uncle. They lived 500 yards from the Bungalow.

Toni also records that Muriel Munro invited you all to Flowerfield. Can you recall that house and family?

It was a beautiful house, overlooking the sea. Muriel was Saki's sister-in-law, and I remember her daughter, Juniper, who used to stay with us in Oxford, when she was at school at Wychwood.

Have you any memory of your Joyce relatives?

[**Peter:**] I remember that Bunny Ritter was the dead image of Joyce.

She was James Joyce's grand-daughter, and your father's first cousin.[7] That means that your father looked more like the Joyces than the Carys, even though he had the famous Cary nose, in profile.
Have you met any of Peter's Irish relatives, Elizabeth?

[**Elizabeth:**] Only Joe and Toni Thompson. I met them when they stayed in London during the 1950s, at the Grosvenor House Hotel. I celebrated my birthday there with them. I haven't yet been to Ireland with Peter, but his happy memories of it make me hope that we can visit it, together.

NOTES

Peter Joyce Cary (9 Dec. 1918-), Joyce Cary's second son, was educated at Rugby, to which he won a scholarship, and Oxford, where he read classics for his first degree, before joining the army at the beginning of the Second World War, serving in Africa, Italy and later Germany, where he was involved in the reconstruction of Cologne. He then returned, in peacetime, to read English at Oxford, where his tutor was one of his father's close friends, Lord David Cecil, of whom he has especially fond memories.

In 1950 he married Elizabeth, daughter of the late Dr George Simon, the radiologist, and Charlotte MacCarthy, a painter (sister of the painter Albert Houthuesen). They lived first in London, and then Cambridge, where Peter was able to continue developing his love of music, both as teacher and performer, as well as his love of rare books and scholarship. Elizabeth went to University College London to read Latin and Girton College, Cambridge, where she gained an M.Litt. in Philosophy. She has taught at Girton and now works in the Computer Laboratory in Cambridge.

They have two daughters, Rachel and Annabel, both of whom are studying English and painting.

On 24 January 1988 they kindly agreed to the publication of this interview.

1. (October 20, 1952), p. 48; see items 48, 49.
2. In the Bodleian, books by C. E. M. Joad from Cary's library are *Common-sense Theology*, 1922 (inscribed 'J.C. 1932'); *Guide to Philosophy*, 1936; *Guide to the Philosophy of Morals and Politics*, 1938.
3. See item 28.
4. N.155 in the Bodleian Collection.
5. By Amy Isabel Young, The Linenhall Press, MCMXXIX.
6. London: Methuen, 1913; reviewed in the *Belfast Evening Telegraph*, 15 October, 1913.
7. See item 6, n. 1.

22

His Third Son Recalls
Early Years

Tristram Cary

This item, with 38, is transcribed from tape recordings made by Mr Cary in Adelaide in November 1987. He is answering written questions, which relate to an interview in 1962, and to letters.

I'd like to develop our interview of 1962, by asking first whether you have any memories of people and places in Ireland. Your father recorded a visit with you in 1932.

That is the only visit I remember. There must have been others when I was younger that I don't remember, but I have a very vivid recollection of that. It was the only time I ever visited Castledawson, and so my recollections of Castledawson are those of a very small boy, never those of an older person. I remember Aunt Netta, who smoked enormous numbers of cigarettes, and Uncle Peter and Cary Clark and a whole sea of other faces. There was a sort of chauffeur-handyman called Willie Campbell. He was actually a very nice man, but he frightened me like anything. He threatened me with black eyes all the time, whenever I was naughty. And I was naughty a fair amount, and adventurous.

One of the things I remember, even as a small boy, was the hours they kept: very late breakfast, very late lunch, and I've always been – still am – a very early riser. I'm very bright in the morning, and so I used to roam around more or less unsupervised. I remember lighting a fire, of newspaper. I knew it was perfectly safe. It was just a nice big blaze for a few seconds, in the middle of the kitchen floor, which was stone. And I knew at that age that stone floors were perfectly all right to light fires on. But I got a reputation for being really awful.

And I had a confederate, a young Irish girl who was presumably one of the servants. She would have been about fourteen I suppose, and I was seven. And one very clear recollection I have is of the garden,

90

which seemed to me enormous. It may not have been so huge, but it was a few acres anyway, and there was some woodland. And Bridget and I decided we would have some hard-boiled eggs. So we got a saucepan and some eggs, and we lit a fire – tried to light a fire; I think it must have been wet, out at the back. We put the saucepan and eggs on the fire before it really got going. Well, Bridget probably suggested it to me, and she shouldn't have done, because I was much too young to handle paraffin. But she said, 'The way to make the fire go is to put some paraffin on it.' So, from the garage I suppose, I got some paraffin, poured it on the fire – which blazed up. It was in a bottle and the neck of the bottle was broken off by this sudden blaze and fell down and cut my leg. (I was always cutting myself to pieces.) It cut my leg open quite badly (I've still got the scar); so Bridget then got alarmed at what I'd done, and she'd done, and we ran into the house to have the wound dressed. We forgot all about the eggs, and it must have been an hour later, we said: 'Oh, what about the eggs?' We went back into the woods and there were the eggs. The water had almost boiled dry, but the fire was still going. And as the eggs had been boiled for an hour they were very hard indeed. I remember a game we had, throwing the eggs at trees to see if we could break them. And Willie Campbell said: 'I'm going to give you two black eyes.' I wasn't sure what 'two black eyes' was, but I knew it wasn't a very good idea. And I was terrified of getting these two black eyes right up to the very last minute.

I remember him driving us to what must have been the docks in Belfast to catch the boat back to Liverpool, and I was thinking, 'When am I going to get these? When is this punishment going to occur?' And I was really frightened of that. I remember the huge sense of relief, when I got on the boat and I'd never got those two black eyes. In fact of course he was a delightful man. It was just a joke. That's the kind of recollection I have of Castledawson. I've got a memory of driving about by a lochside or possibly the seaside somewhere, but nothing of that is particularly clear – just seven-year-old recollections.

I've been meaning to get back to Ireland for years and years, but never seem to actually do it. I've been to Dublin several times, but not to Belfast; so the Northern Irish part, Inishowen and all that, is still something I'm hoping to do.

There's one more recollection of Ireland that I have, and this is a very powerful one. I've just remembered, when we were all at lunch, at this huge table, and there seemed to be lots and lots of people. They were all sitting around and they gave me something to drink – just for a joke you know, and I suppose it was the first alcohol I ever tasted.

They were a joky lot; they were always having practical jokes on people. I didn't like the taste and I made a grimace at which they all laughed. Well, nobody likes being laughed at and so I sank down under the table. And I can remember crawling about under there with this sea of legs under the table contrasted with a sea of faces above the table. I didn't know what to do quite, because I wanted to stay there. And I did stay there until I was dragged out. I can remember them going on laughing about the antics of little Tristram and hating them all. So that's another recollection I have of Ireland.

In 1962, you first showed me an album, in which the early photographs were of your father in Africa. Does any discussion with him of his African experience live in your memory, and would you comment on his first three novels?

Joyce was always talking about Africa and his experiences there, in dinner table conversation and so forth. He had a lot of splendid stories about his time in Africa, and of course one recognized in the books the bits of biography that are there. As far as the first three novels go, I read them later of course. And I remember the family discussion and the jubilation about the Book Society Choice for *The African Witch* (in 1935), which didn't make him much money, but did put him on the map. It was a great feather in his cap to be chosen, and he was really pleased about that. But it wasn't the first three, it was *Mister Johnson* that I knew better, and of course that's full of autobiographical details. I was older too, when it came out. You see, I was only ten in 1935, and with *Aissa Saved* – well, it was just something that Daddy did. I didn't understand about writing books, and all the struggles they were going through in the early thirties; I discovered that later – the terrible financial time they were having after the depression, and the fact that he felt he was being rushed into publishing too soon, when he wasn't really ready, but felt he had to try to add to the diminishing family resources. So all I can say about discussion of his experience is that there was plenty of it.

Can you recall any incident in, say, Mister Johnson, *that you enjoyed hearing your father recount in conversation as autobiographical?*

There's a lot of Joyce in Rudbeck in *Mister Johnson*, and the building of the great road, because Joyce himself built some of the earliest roads – I think *the* very first road in his part of Africa. He had various stories about road-building and bridge building. For example, they did build about a hundred yards of quite good road, he said, for a car that was expected. It was probably the first car in that part of Nigeria which, when it did turn up, blew up after a few yards. It was a one-cylinder car (I don't know what make it was), but they built a special road for this car and it was never used of course, because the car blew up and never went again.

Joyce was very keen on the practicalities of things, and so was I. He wanted to know what makes things tick and how they worked. And he described how, on one occasion, intending to build a road between one village and the next, he said to the people in the first village, 'Where do you think the other village is?' And they all pointed across the hills. And he said, 'No it isn't. It's in this direction.' And he pointed at a direction about a right angle from the one they had pointed at, and they wouldn't believe him. Then he tried to show them how a map worked; how you'd survey things and how you divided the countryside into triangles etc. And then he said: 'All right now. What I want you to do is to place a line of sticks in the direction I'm showing you. You'll find, if you go on with this line of sticks, you'll turn up at this village.' Well, they put two sticks in the ground. And the first wrong thing they did was to stand in front of the first stick, looking at the second one, and he said: 'No, no, what you've got to do is to stand behind the first stick, line it up with the second stick and then put a third one behind that one. When you've done that, move down to the second one and put a fourth one behind the third one. This way you'll get a row of sticks sticking out of the ground all in line.' Once he'd explained this, he said, they got the idea very quickly. Then they were absolutely unstoppable, in the sense that he said: 'If you hit a river or some very difficult bit of country, you can, if you like, move a little aside, and move back to the line later.' But they didn't do this. They forged ahead through rivers, through bush, everything and, blow me, they turned up at the village. They thought that some sort of miraculous witch had predicted that this line of sticks would arrive at the village. Then with a straight line of sticks he said: 'All right now, we do have to make some diversions, because we cannot possibly cross the river at this point. So what we'll do is to make bridges where it's more convenient and then come back to the line of sticks later on.' I remember him describing all this and we did experiments on the beach. I was fascinated by the way you could make a straight line from one place to another.

What else? Bridge building! He used to tell of an engineer, a black man, completely illiterate, who had a marvellous sense of engineering. He explained to this man about triangulation – how a triangle was entirely rigid – by first of all going into a stream, into a fast-flowing stream, and saying, 'If you put your legs apart, so that you've got a strong triangle, it's only strong if you put that structure up and down the stream, and not across the stream. You can be pushed down easily across the stream, but not up and down the stream. And then by sketching it on a piece of paper he drew sets of triangles and explained that if you made groups of triangles you had something which was very rigid. As soon as this guy understood what he had to do, apparently almost overnight he became an expert bridge builder. He suddenly got the idea, and without any drawings and without any previous knowledge and without any education he was able to build strong bridges, and Joyce much admired this. [...]

There were a lot of stories to do with horses. It was very much part of what he believed to be a good education to sit on a horse properly. So there was a lot of horse lore which we had at the table in conversation very early on. We were taught to ride very early too. He used to talk about his polo games and the individual horses that he liked and disliked.[1]

Joyce was always talking about magic, too, and the effect of magic. He brought to life a sort of primitive Africa that one felt had probably disappeared or was disappearing. Then the question of juju and magic came back later on, when he was making the film *Men of Two Worlds*, in 1943. He said that it was amazing how the traditional magic of people they were playing affected the actors themselves. They were educated, sophisticated people. But they were nervous about dabbling (because the script wanted them to) in these things, because of the possible effect it might have. So he felt that these things were very powerful.

Hardly a day went by that he didn't mention Africa, either over a meal or on walks in the Park, which we very early joined him in. He used to walk tremendously fast; so when we were little we didn't get invited to go on walks with him, because we couldn't keep up. But as we got older the walks in the park were very much a part of the day. I used to find it boring sometimes. I didn't want to go, because I was doing something else. But one always felt if he said, 'Will you come for a walk?' that one should go, and in the end there were very often fascinating conversations on these walks. He did sometimes repeat stories many times, and sometimes there were small variations in these stories. But he certainly conjured up a world that was just as good as the sort of R.M. Ballantyne novels that I was tending to read when I was about eleven or twelve.

One thing he used to talk about a lot was the importance, if you're living in really wild conditions in the bush, of having enough luxuries – real luxuries; things that are not necessary at all, but lovely to have, like some good wine. And this went with another of his dicta: when you're broke, when you have a financial crisis, and really seem to have no money at all, the way to cheer yourself up is to buy something you don't need and can't afford, because it gives you such a lift. I find it a very good piece of advice myself, because I too have had many financial crises. And when you feel that you can't afford a meal, the thing to do is somehow to scrape the money and go and buy a picture – something you don't need at all, but it gives you great pleasure. It somehow lifts the spirits tremendously, and for him and for me a lot of the things I have in my house were bought in that sort of way – when you really felt that you shouldn't be buying things at all.

He never was a great drinker. He used to like his half a bottle of wine with his meal, and the only case I remember him telling me about, of being drunk for days, was in the bush when he had an appallingly bad tooth (although his teeth were extremely good; he kept all his own teeth, except for one that was knocked out when he was playing football). If he had not been in the bush on that occasion, a dentist could have fixed his tooth quickly; instead he kept a mouthful of whisky in his mouth, and that was the only occasion when he was the worse for wear.

I think he was probably a very straight man, surrounded by the usual collection of drunks and the kind of people you would find in the bush in those days. I think that, amongst them, Joyce was probably regarded as too straight – a very clean-living and straightforward person. I've always thought so, anyway - although I've often wondered what went on in Paris and Edinburgh and that part of his life, which I found he was never very explicit about; his youth before he met my mother. There might be all sorts of things that maybe his biographers know about, but we were never told, anyway.

We come now to the period with your mother, and the photographs you showed me (in 1962) of family holidays, many of them at Heswall. Would you say something about the Carlisle family there?

The Carlisles were great friends. Elsie was definitely my favourite aunt. I found George Carlisle rather a remote person, but my father had great admiration for him, as a successful, caring GP. Compared with us, they were much better off. There was a slight envy of their slightly better life style, because, being a doctor, he was able to afford good cars and all sorts of little luxuries. We never had a new car during my whole childhood; they were always second or third-hand cars. The ordinary middle-class aspirations we didn't have – we didn't have a refrigerator until after the war, and so forth. So we regarded the Carlisles as to some extent an affluent family. I got on well with Ian, who was my contemporary, and Griselda, and Mary. Antonia was the eldest, and married Ruari McLean, who published the Rainbird edition of *The Horse's Mouth*. Ruari was a great school-time friend of Michael's.

I have very fond memories of the Heswall holidays. We quite regularly went up there, and Heswall was then almost country. I remember running down green fields to the Dee, and trips into Liverpool – not many; we generally just had a nice time there.

My notes on your holiday photographs include:

Bournemouth May 1923; Barton August 1924; Anglesey 1925, August 1926, August 1927, June 1928 ; Borth-y-Gest August 1928; Bigbury-on-Sea Devonshire 1929; Cornwall April 1930; Spencer Wedding, 1930; Saundersfoot Pembrokeshire August 1931, 1932, 1933, 1934; Belstone N. Devon 1934; Borth-y-Gest August 1935; Sherford S. Devon August 1936, Summer 1937.

At which point do these names bring back memories – personal, or of things you've heard about these holidays?

The first thing I remember was when I was at Borth-y-Gest, when I was three. There was one of those traumatic things: I was knocked down by a dog – a friendly dog, that knocked me flat on the beach, and I was very alarmed. My father was very annoyed with these people for laughing at me. I can still remember this beach scene with me and the barking dog.

Your father recorded the scene in a notebook. You 'wept with fury', he said; but he gave your age as two,[2] whereas you were three – and three months in August 1928. Next comes Bigbury. Have you memories of that?

Yes, Bigbury, when I was four, I still remember. I've got a water-colour in fact, of all of us tiny children – one of my father's water-colours – at Bigbury, with Burgh Island in the background. I remember there was great controversy at the time about the hotel they were building on Burgh Island. My parents were environmentalists, and they didn't like building, they didn't like changes, they didn't like tourists and trippers – though we of course were ourselves tourists and trippers. On the whole they liked things to remain the same, and for summer holidays, when they found a good place, they tended to go back several years running.

I can't remember Cornwall, in 1930. But I remember the Spencer wedding. I was a page, and I wore a nasty green satin suit with pearl buttons which I hated. I thought it was girlish and horrible, and my portrait was painted in it, to add to the humiliation. It's a good portrait, painted by Richard Murry, but I can still remember not enjoying being dressed up in the nasty little suit and being a page. And I spoilt the main wedding photo by turning my head and making a grimace; so I was a fairly horrible child. But Ursula and Gilbert Spencer remained very good friends.

A notebook of 1930 records some of your sayings, which are almost identical with Ankatel's in A House of Children.[3] *Do you recognize yourself as Ankatel?*

No. Of course, I read the book when I was a teenager, and I was five in 1930. But I was famous in the family for what they used to regard as comic sayings.

Did your father work regular hours at his writing while on holiday, as well as at home?

Well, yes. He'd usually work in the mornings. He was on holiday, and so he didn't work such long hours. But he would usually work after breakfast, as far as I remember, until, if it was a really fine day, we might get a lunch – a picnic lunch – and go out say at eleven o'clock, down to the beach for the day. If it was a wet day, he'd work for longer. (I hope I'm right on this; I was about my own business, you know.) But even on wet days we would always have a swim. We'd go down and swim in the pouring rain, or take a wet walk. He was a great walker, of course, both in the country and at home. So, yes, he worked. He usually tried to arrange that there wasn't a deadline – a pressing deadline. He valued those holidays tremendously. He couldn't really afford it. They were very expensive for him, but he thought it was important both for him and for us.

My mother of course worked just as hard on holiday. She was charging around making picnics and seeing to things, just as much as when she was at home.

Did your father spend time sketching or painting while on holiday?

Not very often. As I said, I've got the water-colour he made at
Bigbury, which is very amusing – a caricature of us all sitting in a row.
My mother was the great outdoor, sketching-without- drawing, or
rather painting-without- drawing person. Joyce taught her how to do
that, and she took his instruction. But he, with his pastels and so
forth, was more of an easel painter, and he liked sittings, and time,
and giving time to it. He always carried a notebook, but that was for
putting words down, rather than drawing pictures. He did do one or
two. I've got one, for example, in my autograph book, when I was
about ten; he did a very amusing little sketch and a rhyme to go with
it. But he wasn't the sort of person who, you'd suddenly find, had
been sketching you: 'Here it is!' He didn't do that.
   He'd go off into brown studies very easily, Joyce. He would detach
himself from any conversation, from the noise of the kids and
everything, and go into a complete trance almost, obviously thinking
about what he was going to do in his writing.

We now come to Saundersfoot, from 1931 to 1934.

I almost grew up in a way there – I was six till nine. In Pembrokeshire,
we visited castles; we had many happy holidays in Saundersfoot. I can
remember the boarding house we stayed at – certainly the rocks we
swam off.

When I asked you, in a letter [of 1980], *whether you remembered 'The
Turkish House in Saundersfoot', which haunted your father's imagination
(to judge from his notebooks), you replied:* 'I've had a good look at the
relevant pages in the photo album, but none show any house that
could possibly be this. [...] I think the Carlisle children came down
once or twice – maybe Tony McLean or Mary Hall could help.'[4]

I wrote to both, and Antonia McLean replied: 'We stayed in a boarding
house, part of a terrace overlooking the beach and facing due east
since I once watched the sun rise out of the sea.'[5] *I also wrote to Mary
Hall, who remembered, she said:* 'a very be-creepered house, though
that was not where we stayed. A fierce and character-ful colonel and
his family were there – one summer anyway, and we used to sail model
boats with them.'[6] *Do either of these memories revive any of yours?*

I'm afraid they don't. The truth is, I think the Cary children were regarded as rather stand-offish by the others, and I was never a great gang person; so when there was a boat-sailing party I used to shoot off on my own very often. We were all slightly loners. There were all sorts of what I'd call 'hearty' activities which I didn't take part in very much, and I'd go off on my own.

Did you enjoy Belstone, North Devon, also in 1934?

Belstone, as far as I remember, was rather disastrous. Certainly the car broke down; the secondhand Armstrong Sidley couldn't cope with those Devonshire hills very well, and I remember Belstone being wet and unmemorable. [...]

You mentioned that your mother did most of the driving; did your father drive?

My father did drive, but he was a rotten driver. He had very poor eyesight, but he was also curiously nervous. Put him on a horse and he was never nervous, and was generally an un-nervous man. He could face up to danger, face up to thugs, and I've seen him lose his temper and be a very fierce person, at times. He was perhaps not good at machinery; I don't know. But he wouldn't allow anybody to talk in the car when he was driving, and you always felt unsafe. I never felt happy with Joyce driving, and he was never happy himself. He was always laying down rules about how to drive, which is always a bit suspicious. He was not an instinctive driver.

My mother on the other hand was. My mother knew nothing about machinery; she'd open the bonnet, and she hadn't the faintest idea what everything was. But she was a marvellous instinctive driver, just as she was an instinctive pianist. She could do the most difficult things on the piano without really knowing the musical theory behind what she was doing. And she drove beautifully; so she did most of it.

Once in Devon, when we had the Armstrong-Sidley, an early pre-selected gears model, the whole gear-box went completely wrong. Eventually it broke down so much that only reverse and neutral would work. But without turning a hair, my mother drove backwards for about five or six miles. We were out in the country somewhere; she knew she had to get home, and without hesitation and, as far as I can remember, without much nervousness, she just reversed the car, for mile after mile. My father would never have done that. She was indomitable in that sort of situation, my mother. So, yes, she did most of the driving.

You seem to have looked to her to manage everyday things, rather than your father.

I did see more of her and talk more to her when young – and there were times when I was furious with both of them. You have to remember the big gap between me and Peter. In my childhood the 'boys' were remotely old compared with the 'babies', and those labels for the pairs still stuck when we were all grown up. George and I had tremendous quarrels, but they were nothing to the Michael and Peter battles, which would reverberate through the house while George and I trembled in the nursery.

Joyce had enormous regard for Trudy's brain, and was always praising her intelligence and her astute comments on the manuscript when she was typing it. She always put herself down and would be the despair of a modern feminist. 'Men always do things so much better,' she'd say. She was greatly alarmed by anything she regarded as 'deep conversation', and never ventured opinions even when Joyce knew she had them and said so. She used to try to persuade him to tone down the naughty bits in the books, and he would explain that graphic descriptions of 'that sort of thing' were sometimes necessary. When it came to things like sex, in fact, Joyce did all the explaining.[7]

Your account of your mother is fascinating. In our survey of family holidays, we have reached 1935, when you returned to Borth -y-Gest.

That is not quite so clear in my mind as the early holiday. [...]
I was eleven, twelve in Sherford, the South Devon holidays, which I remember very well indeed. It was the end of an era as far as agriculture went. The old horse-drawn reaper and binder was still there. The threshing machine was carried around from farm to farm. And Joyce as usual was terribly interested in the technical side of everything. He asked lots of questions, and these later went into books, about the way machinery worked and so forth.[8]

I did a lot of riding, and I used to run errands for the farmer. We were within reach of a number of beaches. I enjoyed Sherford more because I was more independent. We didn't have millions of cousins staying with us. The parents used to think this was a lovely idea for everybody to get together. But I don't think they really enjoyed it very much either. There was probably a good deal of friction amongst the grown-ups as well. But at Sherford it was a complete change. I've always had a taste for what you might call the labouring man; I'm what you might call a public bar person. I enjoyed very much making friends with those farm boys, and the labourers, and I spent a lot of time in the farmyard, mucking around with them. It was something so different from our rather cosseted middle-class existence in Oxford. To spend time on a real farm was very exciting.

Did you go boating on the Kingsbridge Estuary, which your father calls the Longwater in his novels? And do you remember a passenger ferry called the Queen running to Kingsbridge, which he calls Queensport (as shown on a map in a notebook)?

I don't think we went boating at Kingsbridge. Kingsbridge was a place to go shopping, and I remember the ferry. But I don't think I ever went on it. We motored everywhere.

Tolbrook Manor in To Be a Pilgrim *is supposedly four miles west of the Longwater. But in some respects the house suggests Ugbrooke, near Chudleigh. Do you remember visiting Ugbrooke, or have any reason to suppose that your father created Tolbrook with Ugbrooke in mind?*[9]

I can't remember about Ugbrooke either. We might have done. But there again, if it happened, I might have been frightfully bored, and I might have forgotten about it.

My last date for your album of photographs is 1937; but your father's manuscripts suggest that you were there also in 1938 and 1939.

Yes, we were there. Certainly we were there in '39. I can remember hearing about the war. We were filling up with petrol. We were on our way to the beach. We'd stopped for petrol, and the man filling us up said, 'The war has broken out.' I can still remember the guy saying, 'The war has broken out.' And my father was completely calm and resigned. He said, 'Right. I'm not at all surprised. I'm very sorry, but the holiday is now at an end. We are going to drive back to Oxford today. We're going to see to the blackout and all the various things we've been told to do.' I remember that very clearly. The outbreak of war there.

Have you any memories of your father's activites during the war, in connexion with defence?

He was Post Warden, and went on bomb courses, and tried to get as involved as possible. Thank goodness, the Germans didn't drop bombs on Oxford, because he would have been heavily involved. My mother was permanently alarmed at him getting too active, and getting himself killed.

He often remarked what a strange thing it was that these middle-aged and elderly men – the whole group – were in charge of the defence of some of the most valuable property in the entire country. All those laboratories in South Parks Road and Parks Road, the new Clarendon, where atomic research was going on (we didn't know of course), were being looked after by just a group of people in Rhodes House. If there had been bombs, millions and millions of pounds worth of property could hardly have been defended. But he really enjoyed that diversion, during the war. He made new friends, and enjoyed the bomb courses he went on. And, as usual, he took a tremendous interest in the technology in everything.

Later on, of course, I was in the war myself, from 1943, when I was in the navy; so I wasn't at home as often. But it gradually became clear that the war was not going to be lost; and so the urgency of the defence side of it wasn't quite so great at the end of the war as it was at the beginning.

In 1968, in a telephone conversation, I asked your opinion about 'It's a Gift', which appeared as a theme in your father's notebooks around the very time that the film of that title, starring W.C. Fields, was showing at the Scala Cinema in Oxford (March 1938). You said: 'Trudy and Joyce went frequently to the Scala, on Monday nights, and Trudy got printed notices of films each week; so Joyce would have seen the title on notices lying around the house, even if he didn't see the film. I never remember his discussing Fields, but I know he admired Sid Field – his golfing sketch – and I think Sid Field probably took his art from W.C. Fields. He adored Chaplin, but thought his films unimportant after Modern Times.'

Have you any further thoughts on that question?

I think I was probably exaggerating the amount they did go to the films. They went much more often to the theatre. They were very keen supporters of the Playhouse. And I think Monday was a cheap night there too, and so they went to the Playhouse more regularly than to films. Joyce's taste in comics and so forth was fairly old-fashioned. He used to go back to things he used to laugh at in his childhood.

That explains a lot about his visits to films during his American tours [see item 43; Mr Cary's account continues in item 38].

NOTES

Tristram Cary was born in 1925, and lived in England, working there and in Europe, till 1974, when he moved to Australia. He was trained in radar during his war service, and used his technical knowledge to become a pioneer of electronic music, building his first studio in 1948. During the '50s and '60s he wrote numerous scores for film, theatre, radio and TV, gaining an Italian Prize and several other awards. In 1967 he founded the electronic music studio at the Royal College of Music, London, and was involved in the first ever concerts of electronic music in London in the late '60s.

In 1973 he went over for a lecture tour of Australia, and was Visiting Composer at Adelaide University in 1974, later accepting a permanent post. He has received numerous commissions over the last ten years, and his music has been widely performed and broadcast in the South Pacific area. In 1986 he left the University to resume self-employment, and at the moment is writing a major book on musical technology for a London publisher, and establishing a personal composing studio.

1. See item 47, Cary's letter of 30. Dec. 1952.

2. MS. Cary 254/N.30.

3. MS. Cary 257/N.37, fol. 11, dated 1930, records Tristram's remark: ' "It's Brownade – and when it's full it's a skemeton" '; which is almost identical with Ankatel's words in *A House of Children*, ch. 13.

4. Letter of 2 Jan. 1981; the Carlisle family shared summer holidays with the Carys until 1932.

5. Letter of 4 Oct. 1981, quoted in *The House as a Symbol*, p. 126, n. 41, and acknowledged here with thanks.

6. Letter of 10 Jan. 1982; having been appropriately quoted here, Mrs Hall's contribution is not shown as a separate item, but it is gratefully acknowledged.

7. These two paragraphs are from a letter of 23 Nov. 1987, which I have Mr Cary's permission to quote.

8. The most obvious use of this background is in *The Moonlight*, which exists in an early draft marked by Joyce Cary, 'book written at Sherford'.

9. This suggestion has been made by Mr J.R. Pim, who kindly assisted me with research in Devon in 1966. The name, description, and history of the house, including an Adams room used for storing farm equipment, may well have contributed, even if Cary did not visit Ugbrooke, though it seems quite likely that he did – e.g. in 1934, while staying at Belstone, which is comparatively close. But cf. his letters of 22 Nov. '36 and 15 Feb. '38 (item 16), which show that he deliberately disguised descriptions and combined sources of inspiration.

In 1966, Mr Pim drove me to the farm at Sherford here described: Homefield, where the daughter of Mrs Ellen Cuming (owner during the years of the Carys' stay there) remembered the family, and the fact that Mrs Cary organized everything while her husband wrote.

23

My Cousin in Ireland

Toni Thompson

This interview took place in September 1963, at Mrs Thompson's home, 'Charleville', Castlereagh, on the outskirts of Belfast.

I remember Joyce at the Bungalow (Castledawson) in 1913, and his stories about Montenegro. In one the King of Montenegro had offered him his daughter for a wife.

How old were you then?

I would have been five.

He must certainly have made a great impression on you. How did you get on with him when he visited you with his wife and children? Did you find them easy guests?

I found them very critical. Joyce and Trudy would smile secretly, to one's embarrassment.

Do you identify any of the characters in his books with people you know?

I think he scrambled his characters. But one of the people, in his painting of them on the boat in *A House of Children*, looks like Netta – my mother.

[*Knowing, from this meeting, that Mrs Thompson had kept a diary during the 1930s, I asked her son Courtenay's permission, in January 1988, to have relevant extracts copied.*[1] *They mainly concern Joyce Cary's visits to the Bungalow (usually with members of his family, on holiday), and the first links directly with Tristram's account, opening item 22.*]

April 1932 / 9 Saturday

After breakfast I practised the banjo and waited for the arrival of Joyce, Gertie and party; they were much later than expected. After tea unpacking went ahead. I showed Tristram the toys and Michael the musical instruments. I played billiards with Michael till lunch time. After lunch we managed to persuade Tristram to go for a walk with Bridget. [...]

April 1932 / 10 Sunday

Was just thinking of getting up when young Tristram came in and made a very good effort to wreck my room. When I got down Gertie and Daddy were both on the sick list; Gertie was still troubled with earache. After tea I went up and chatted to Gertie and played her the banjo. I helped Og[2] to put Tristram to bed before supper. After supper Joe[3] came in, and he and Joyce had a long discussion on yachts and Joyce told us stories of the war in Nigeria.

April 1932 / 11 Monday

After breakfast Tristram, Joyce and I went over to the works to post a letter and on to the Hillhead. When we got back I thought it would be a good idea to paint Joyce.

April 1932 / 12 Tuesday

After breakfast I prepared for Michael's portrait. Joyce seemed to think an outdoor background would be suitable and made me sketches of his idea. Daddy was still in bed but Gertie got up and she and I chatted about dresses till lunch time.

After lunch I went on with Michael's portrait, then we made up a four for tennis. Michael and I took on Joyce and the Og. We had some good stories about Africa from Joyce at supper.

April 1932 / 13 Wednesday

Joyce and I set about arranging the background for Michael's picture. The picture of Joyce was too sticky to go [on] with today. After tea [*morning*] I went out with Tristram and saw that he did not kill himself roller skating. After lunch I went on with the background of Michael's picture and Joyce did a very good enlargement of grandfather from a small picture by Aunt Hessie. We all went to tea with Aunt Pearl [*her Uncle Leo Cary's wife*]. I helped put Tristram to bed.

April 1932 / 14 Thursday

The Og, Joyce, Michael and Tristram were going to Derry and on to Limavady, so Gertie and I watched them depart. I had tried to get Joyce to give me tips about the background for Gertie's picture, but I couldn't get him to really interest himself.

At tea time we discussed a suitable dress for me to wear if I go to Oxford for the 4th June celebrations at Eton. In the afternoon Gertie and I played tennis and the others returned in time for supper.

April 1932 / 15 Friday

Gertie, Michael, Tristram, Og and I went up to Belfast, leaving Joyce to do some work and potter about alone.

April 1932 / 16 Saturday

After breakfast I got hold of Joyce to paint but found everything very difficult. We had to cease fire early as we were going to Lisnalinchy races [*point to point between Glengormley and Ballyclare*]. Gertie and Joyce, Michael and myself went.

Michael was the only one to win anything, and we didn't stay for the last race.

April 1932 / 17 Sunday

Got up fairly early as I wanted to do some painting before going to Portstewart. Joyce's picture was in a half dry stage so I did a sketch of Michael.

Couldn't get the car started and arrived very late for lunch but Cousin Muriel was very nice about it. Og, Joyce, Gertie Michael, Tristram and myself went to the beach; Michael practised driving on the sand. Came home after tea leaving Joyce and Gertie to spend the night. I put Tristram to bed and Cary [*her brother*] told school stories.

April 1932 / 18 Monday

Rested until tea time. Tristram was out with Bridget. At lunch Tristram was very full of some adventures he had had with Bridget. They had found some old pots, made a fire and boiled eggs over it.[4]

After tea Michael and I took on the Og and Cary and were beaten in two sets. Joyce and Gertie returned from Portstewart just as I was finishing the cider I felt I had earned after the tennis. Joyce and I went down to the river to seek a suitable background for Gertie's portrait. I got Joyce to put it in for me as I didn't feel like painting and he made quite a success of it.

April 1932 / 19 Tuesday

I painted Gertie for a bit this morning, chiefly the clothes. Joyce seemed pleased with it, but Michael seemed to think I had made Gertie too young looking. Gertie herself wasn't pleased with the colour of her hair.

April 1932 / 21 Thursday

Got Joyce to sit for me and got on very well. I am afraid that Gertie wasn't very pleased with it and seemed to think that if she had met someone who looked like my portrait she would not have chosen him for a husband!

Gertie gave me a cheque for £6-6-0 for the portraits which was very pleasant.

April 1932 / 22 Friday

Great stir and bustle as Gertie was packing for everyone. I didn't take part as I would only have increased the confusion.

At lunch poor wee Tristram was very upset because we laughed at him when he tried some cider and announced with a horrible grimace 'I like it'. He had previously been scolded for squirting ink on the table while trying to hit Willie Campbell. I expect his nerves were upset.

They all left about six and the house seemed very empty without them.

May 1932 / 10 Tuesday

A letter from Joyce asking me over in June.

June 1932 / 3 Friday   [in Oxford]

[...] Gertie very thoughtfully met me, [...]

June 1932 / 4 Saturday

Was down in time for breakfast which was rather wonderful. We got ready for the Eton celebrations. We met Michael very beautifully dressed with a yellow buttonhole and did some of the school buildings; had lunch with him in the school. We had tea in Michael's study and were joined by Joc Lynam[5] who had been roped in to give me supper.

June 1932 / 5 Sunday

I was only a fraction late for breakfast. then it was church time, Gertie, Tristram and I went in the car to Lynams, after the service I chatted for a few minutes to Joc Lynam. [...]

June 1932 / 20 Monday

[...] Gertie and I went to an art class in the afternoon. After supper Joc Lynam turned up for a sing song.

June 1931 / 22 Wednesday

We got [up] fairly early this morning. Poor Joyce wasn't feeling a bit like going to Wimbledon as he wanted to go on with his book. We filled the car with food and called for Eleanor. Joyce was driving and vented his bad temper on the car to such an extent that Eleanor had to ask him to go slower. We had a very good day and stopped for supper on a very pretty common. We gorged ourselves on strawberries and cream.

June 1931 / 23 Thursday

Felt pretty tired but was down in time for breakfast. I did some strenuous packing. After lunch I looked at some caricatures with Joyce and then said good bye to him as I didn't want him to trail to the station to see me off. I ate a rather late supper on the boat, and rather disturbed by a man who wanted to pick me up.

[*Recording Joyce Cary's visit in December 1932, concerned with selling property inherited through his mother:*]

December 1932 / 15 Friday

I was actually down fairly early as I wanted to make a start on a portrait of Aunt Mabs. I worked fairly hard for about an hour. *Joyce* arrived just as I had got my board about covered, there was so much excitement that I stopped painting. After lunch Joyce and I retired to the schoolroom and had a look and criticism of my pictures. I was delighted as Joyce seemed to think I had progressed. After that we went for a walk round the Brough.[6]

December 1932 / 16 Saturday

Got up very late indeed. Joyce was having a hideous time trying to make business calls to Derry.

December 1932 / 19 Tuesday

[...] after tea Joyce had to do his packing as he was crossing tonight. We had supper a little early and then he departed, having left some lovely chocolates for me.

[*Record of Joyce Cary's visit to Castledawson in 1933, with Michael, Peter, and their mother:*[7]]

April 1933 / 7 Friday

Got up fairly early to do the flowers, had just done one vase when I found that Joyce, Gertie and the boys had arrived very silently, long before we expected them. We chatted for a bit, had some tea, Gertie did some unpacking and I wandered about helping her and showing other members of the party around.

Joyce and the boys and Og and I went for a stroll round the Brough – it was a glorious day. We played tennis most of the afternoon [...]

April 1933 / 8 Saturday

Got down in time for breakfast much to Michael's surprise. After breakfast the boys played the violin, piano, and gramophone alternately, Joyce wrote, Gertie knitted and I cut out a frock. [...] After supper Gertie, Michael, Joe and Peter played bridge with myself auxiliary to help Peter.

April 1933 / 16 Sunday

Easter Day Today was a glorious opportunity to stay in bed all morning so I made full use of it. When I got down [...] Joyce, Gertie and the boys had gone to church. [...]

April 1933 / 20 Thursday

Got up late and prepared for the visit to Portstewart. Gertie and Peter were heartily sick on the way over. Cousin Muriel had a large lunch for us, to which everyone did full justice. Afterwards Gertie and I felt throroughly lazy but Joyce and the boys went for a stroll along the beach. We ate a huge tea when the others came in. Poor Peter was again sick on the way back.

April 1933 / 22 Saturday

Again this feeling of tiredness so got up fairly late. We were going to the Antrim races *[point-to-point]*. Michael was the most lucky backing horses, Peter won once. Gertie and I lost all the time. Had tea in the Air Force tent and home.

April 1933 / 24 Monday

[...] Joyce had a large quantity of proofs to correct which were boring him considerably. Soon after tea Michael went off. He is crossing by himself as he wants to attend an Old Boys' dinner in Oxford. He went by bus, Cary and Joyce saw him off. [...]

April 1933 / 26 Wednesday

[...] Uncle Leo came in for tea. He and Joyce had a discussion on the causes for bankruptcy in shops in London. It came on to rain but Joyce and Gertie were brave enough to go for a walk in spite of it.

April 1933 / 27 Thursday

Got up with the intention of sketching Gertie but found she was busy packing. Later I changed into tennis things for Dorothy's party.[8] After lunch Joyce and I set off. [...] We left fairly early and Gertie and Peter went off to the boat. Joyce went with them.

April 1933 / 28 Friday

I stayed in bed with my throat [...]

April 1933 / 30 Sunday

Stayed in bed, Joyce came up and talked to me about his book which was very interesting.[...]

May 1933 / 2 Tuesday

I was still in bed. Joyce came up to visit me and we talked about marriages and how few were successful – nice and cynical!

May 1933 / 3 Wednesday

[...] Uncle Leo came in for tea and he and Joyce had a great chat about ancient members of the family. [...]

May 1933 / 4 Thursday

I felt fairly well – Joyce came up to see me and we discussed a name for the heroine of his book. [...]

May 1933 / 8 Monday

[...] In the evening Cary *[her brother]* and Joyce had an interesting talk on books about Victoria's time; also on the politics of the world.

May 1933 / 10 Wednesday

[...] At about twelve we set off for Flowerfield for lunch; it was a glorious day. Joyce and Og in the back of the car were discussing very ancient family history. We arrived there in good time for lunch. After lunch we had coffee and walked down to Portstewart before tea to enjoy the sunshine. We took Joyce *[home]* by way of Portrush as he had never been there. We also chose the Kilrea road and saw a 'hiring' fair there.

May 1933 / 25 Thursday

Got up fairly early. Joyce gave me a splendid talk on picture composition.

After lunch I got everyone into their coats and collected the picnic Minnie had made for our expedition to the Giant's Causeway. We went to Portrush and to 'Dunloose' Castle and we wandered round the ruins with a guide book. We had our picnic and went on to the Causeway. We stopped at Bushmills to telephone that we would be late home. Og and I had been there before so we sent the others off to see the long walk while we sat in the sun. We stopped at Garvagh for bacon and egg supper where we ate with tremendous appetite.

May 1933 / Wednesday 31

[...] We all listened with great excitement to the broadcast of the Derby and were delighted to find that Joyce had won third place in the sweepstake draw with 'Statesman'.

June 1933 / Thursday 6

[...] Dr Thompson came in about *[morning]* tea time. He and Joyce had a chat about curious characters. Poor Joyce had a boil inside his nose so Dr Thompson prescribed for him. [...]

June 1933 / Saturday 10

Francis[9] came along and performed a lancing operation on Joyce's nose which must have been very painful as he stayed in bed until lunch time.

June 1933 / Sunday 11

[...] Tony and I v. Joyce and Shiela[10] had two sets of tennis before lunch and got beaten.

June 1933 / Tuesday 20

Got up early and dressed for the party at Limavady.[11] Mud gave us a good lunch. We saw over Tommy's chicken farm, beehives and pigs. Bunny came along and we set off for the tennis tournament. We had tea at the Club House. Joyce did a beautiful sketch of the return of the dance party to the Bungalow.

June 1933 / Friday 23

[...] After supper Joyce and Tony, Shiela and I danced to the gramophone till bedtime.

June 1933 / Tuesday 27

Joyce was going to Derry – Shiela, Tony and I decided to accompany him. On the way Joyce and I were interested in imaginary picture building. When we got to Derry Joyce shot off on his business and Tony, Shiela and I did the Cathedral. The Cary Tomb we found after much difficulty – a verger with a 'preaching' voice showed us round. We met at a café for lunch which Joyce stood us. We went to Portstewart afterwards as Joyce's business was finished. Ethel Munro was there to greet us. Cousin Muriel came in to tea. We played tennis and back after supper.

June 1933 / 30 Friday

[...] Left for Belfast. When we returned Joyce had painted a lovely picture from a sketch that I had made at Ballintoy and tried to paint.

July 1933 / 3 Monday

Staggered down late and decided it was just the day to go on a bathing picnic to Toome and a wonderful opportunity for me to sketch. We got home in time for a latish lunch after Joyce had sketched me in the 'bones' of a picture of the eel farm. There was rather a depression in the air afterwards as Joyce and Shiela were packing. We did get in a set of tennis before tea, then more packing before we set off for the boat to see them off at the boat. We met [?Mustand] on the boat and all had supper. Sad farewell and then home.

July 1933 / 4 Tuesday

Another lovely day so a picnic to Toome seemed entirely indicated. I cleaned my paints and set off in great heart, but I became very tangled. I missed Joyce and felt inclined to shriek for him.

June 1934 / 29 Friday

Shiela and I went bathing in the morning and got back late for lunch. we found *Joyce* had arrived unexpectedly and was lunching with Daddy. He and Shiela went over my pictures after lunch and he cheered me a lot about them. [...]

June 1934 / 30 Saturday

I decided over breakfast that it was a good day for bathing and painting. I drove Joyce, Lionel[12] and Shiela over to Toome. I got Joyce to choose me a sight to paint.

He knocked it in in charcoal and then I began the serious business of painting. After lunch we went off to the tennis party at Bellagby. In the evening we went for a stroll to the river and discussed art with Joyce.

July 1934 / 1 Sunday

After breakfast Joyce and I got enthusiastic over paint. He wanted to try painting yesterday's sketch in a more dramatic style and I wanted to get exactly what he meant. I got him to do the painting while I watched.

July 1934 / 2 Monday

After tea Joyce started me on a new sketch, this time copying a picture he had done a long time ago. We carried on from lunch till tea time, when Joyce pronounced it more or less finished. Then Shiela and I were seeing Joyce off at the boat.

NOTES

Mary Antoinette Clark, usually called Toni (1909-1974), only daughter of Joyce Cary's Aunt Netta, married Joseph M. Thompson of 'Charleville', Castlereagh, chairman of the Thompson-Reid Motor Company of Belfast, on 13 June 1936, their children being Antoinette (1937-), Peter (1938-), and Courtenay (1943-) who was Joyce Cary's godchild.

1. He kindly agreed that this could be done by Mrs Jean Gallagher, to whom I am greatly indebted. Each entry occupies a page, headed as shown; but it is written in pencil, now blurred and faded, and location of what is relevant to our purpose was extremely difficult.

2. 'Og' refers to her mother, Netta; is the nickname formed from the initial letters of 'Old Girl', perhaps?

3. Her future husband, Joe Thompson.

4. It will be noticed that Tristram's parents were away at Flowerfield when this adventure occurred.

5. Here wrongly spelt 'Jock Lineham'; he was then on the staff of Oxford's Dragon School, and became its Headmaster from 1942-1965, succeeding his father, A. E. Lynam, known as Hum, who was Headmaster throughout the years that Cary's sons attended the School; see also item 4, n.3.

6. The Brough is the name of the townland just south of Castledawson.

7. It seems likely that the reunion between Joyce Cary and Dorothy Lake's mother occurred during this visit, as she tells us that both Michael and Peter were present (see item 5); but no record of it was found in Mrs Thompson's diary.

8. This *Dorothy* appears frequently in the diaries, but was not Dorothy Lake, who was always called 'Do'een'.

9. Presumably Dr Thompson; these ailments suggest that Cary had not yet recovered from the exhausted state in which he had arrived in Ireland, following the completion of *An American Visitor*; it was for this reason that he had stayed on there for much longer than usual; it seems to have been from this date that his wife changed from the 'clinging vine' whom Lionel Stevenson first encountered to the capable manager recalled below by Vivien Greene.

10. Cary's half-brother and sister had apparently just arrived.

11. Next described is a visit to the family of 'Bay' Beasley (see item 5); 'Mud' is Maude; for Bunny, see item 6. n. 1.

12. Presumably Lionel Stevenson; see item 16.

24

At Tennis and Tea-parties

A.N. Bryan-Brown

This interview took place on 5 August 1968.

Sometime after 1928, over a period of two to three years, my wife and I played tennis with Cary and his wife, mainly on our court or the Williamsons' court, which was also in Headington – where they too lived. Cary was quite good at tennis in a rather portly way, though I got the impression that he was not particularly keen but felt it was good for him (perhaps socially as well as physically). They dropped out long before the war, and were in fact much older than my wife and I, though our son Christopher was at the Dragon with Tristram.

I met Cary at tea-parties too, occasionally, and did get the impression that his other life was obscure; he may well have felt diffident about it. He never attempted to discuss anything significant with me, but I can believe that he might have with John Macmurray, a very strong-minded man, whom I knew in the Student Christian Movement; it was intended to encourage Christians to support whatever denomination they belonged to, and was going strong during and after the first World War.

NOTE

Armitage Noel Bryan-Brown (1900-1968) was educated at Marlborough, and Balliol College, Oxford; he became a Fellow of Worcester College, Lecturer in Classics (1922-1967), and followed Thomas Higham as Public Orator (1958-67). His wife Teresa was the daughter of Professor Herbert Wildon Carr, whose philosophical theories and writings profoundly influenced Cary, to judge from notes he made in August 1942 in MS. Cary 271/N.82, from Carr's *The General Theory of Relativity*, 1920, and *A Theory of Monads*, 1922; possibly he had read these works earlier, and was now relating them to his own beliefs.

25

The Shaping of his Ideas

John Macmurray

The letter quoted below is dated 10 November 1967.[1]

[...] My wife and I knew Joyce Cary well during the last year or two that I was a Fellow of Balliol. He fell into the habit of coming to see us for tea on most Sunday afternoons when we were in residence; and he and I used to go for afternoon walks upon occasions beforehand. In those days we were both great talkers; and I think our discussions were most often on aesthetic subjects, though we often strayed into more general philosophic fields. I am sure that I shared with him the ideas of which my mind was then full. Those were the years in which the guiding principles of my philosophical views, as they were later published, were taking shape. It is quite likely that they had an influence upon Joyce, though he never said so to me, and I should hesitate to claim it. We were fond of one another and very open to one another on topics of general interest. But he did not talk much or in any detail about his own writing. We were aware that he was working hard, and having great difficulty with and finding little acceptance for his writing. Our share in it amounted to little more than comfort and encouragement.

After we left Oxford for London and then for Edinburgh we did not meet Joyce, and correspondence was very limited. I enclose a copy of the last letter we had from him. This was a reply to a letter of sympathy when we heard of his illness. [...] If there are any points in his writing where you might suspect my influence, or wished to seek my confirmation I should be happy to do my best, though in many cases I suspect that your guess will be as good as mine.

[*The letter enclosed is dated 13th October 1956, and reads:*]

My Dear Betty,
How nice of you to write. Yes, those old days were grand, when I used to come to see you so often. I still remember those long walks with

116

John along the Cher discussing Corbusier and functionalism, and it was a great pleasure to see you again in 1953.[2]

I don't really deserve so much sympathy. I have, on the whole, very little pain, and I still do plenty of work. If you and John ever come to Oxford do come and see me.

Love to him and to you
Ever yours
Joyce

NOTES

This obituary in the *University of Edinburgh Journal* reveals why Macmurray would have inspired Joyce Cary:

'John Macmurray, MC, MA, LL.D: in Edinburgh, 21st June 1976, aged 84. Professor Macmurray was educated in Aberdeen, at Glasgow University and Balliol College, Oxford. After service in the first world war when he was awarded the MC he became successively Lecturer in Philosophy at Manchester, Professor at Johannesburg, Fellow of Balliol and Grote Professor of the Philosophy of Mind and Logic at London. From 1944 to 1958 he was Professor of Moral Philosophy at Edinburgh. Professor Macmurray was that rare combination, a philosopher who both speaks to the layman and also makes an important contribution to his subject. In his earlier days in London he was a successful broadcaster and his books of broadcast talks and popular lectures such as *Reasoned Emotion* are still much read after forty years. In his lectures at Edinburgh, which sometimes seemed more like the sermon of a prophet than a discursive argument, he aroused in his large audiences enthusiasm for philosophy, affection for himself and a concern for humanity. As a philosopher he was not part of the modern analytic tradition; he was a man of independence and originality rather than a follower of fashion. His Gifford Lectures in 1953 and 1954 and later published as *The Self as Agent* and *Persons in Relation* form a major work of philosophy.'

I should like to hear from any surviving relatives regarding the publication of this item.

1. It is addressed to B. Fisher, and its significance is evident, if, for example, Macmurray's *Creative Society* (1935), in which Christianity and communism are compared, is read in conjunction with Cary's *The African Witch* (1936); for a more detailed comparison, see *The Writer and His Theme*, pp. 117-19.

2. On the occasion of receiving his Hon. LL.D.

26

Recollections

Vivien Greene

This interview took place at Mrs Greene's home, Grove House, Oxford, on 29 May 1968.

I first met Joyce Cary in 1933. I had just had my first baby, and had no help, and could not go out in the evening. But I remember walking to their house with the baby. Joyce had written to Graham about a recently published book.[1] Graham admired Joyce immensely.

Soon after that we went to London, and our home was on Clapham Common – a Queen Anne House, built in 1712. But early in the war the house was destroyed by an incendiary bomb, and I became an evacuee. I went first to the south coast, but returned to Oxford at the end of 1940. By then I had two children, and I was billeted with the President of Trinity, John R.H. Weaver.

Mrs Cary was so sweet. She had a most charming personality and created a wonderfully warm, cosy atmosphere. Her sons seemed devoted to her, and seemed to look to her rather than to Joyce, as a pillar of strength. (This sort of situation was more obvious in wartime, when basic needs depended largely on a woman's capable handling of rations etc.) Life was dreary and hard for children, and Mrs Cary gave lovely, scrumptious-looking teas and parties, out of nothing, for other people's children much younger than her own. She was so good with children; she never talked down to them. I was an evacuee and paying guest, who had to give up my rations and therefore could not return the hospitality. But she understood, and I found it such a break for my children. I don't remember our conversations, as they were usually held when I called to thank her for the teas – which she had given for eight to ten of other people's small children.

I thought her infinitely attractive, physically and in every way. One son had made her a virginal for her birthday, and I remember her look when showing it to me. She was obviously very musical, and I remember that they were keen on madrigals. But she seemed very retiring in that regard, and I never heard her play. I was rather

118

uncomprehending about music at that time, and I was very much overworked. I had also begun collecting Victoriana, with the idea of furnishing and decorating a dolls' house. I began partly to compensate for the loss of my home, and I became absorbed with that as a hobby. But I remember thinking how hard it must have been for Mrs Cary, acting as her husband's typist as well as doing everything else she did. I think he would have been rather formidable.

According to both Michael and Tristram Cary, his father greatly valued his mother's ideas regarding his work.

I have occasionally given suggestions to Graham. But I think that in a novelist there is a certain hard core of knowing. A writer has to please himself. Graham always used to say that what a writer is goes into his work and what you meet is what's left over. I don't in fact read novels much; I prefer biographies and memoirs. I decided that Joyce Cary is more a man's writer, and I don't like novels about foreign countries. But Graham admired him very much, as a writer, and as a friend.

How else did Cary strike you, as a person?

To me he always seemed so stupendously distinguished, with his fine profile, and the way he held his head – very poised – struck one. It therefore seemed all the more sad that the end came as it did. However, he was so natural about his illness, and about being irritable. The mood was, 'I am helpless, and it is a nuisance.' You felt he wasn't being too heroic, as for example about having his arm in the crane. I didn't have a feeling of sainthood.

It was almost like a salon at his home on Sundays, from about four to six o'clock. I think it was Lady Ogilvie who suggested that I should go along. I hadn't seen Joyce since the war, until 1956, when he was already ill. All sorts of distinguished people were there – I remember Maurice Bowra. But it was all very casual, which Joyce liked. He liked to be brought news and gossip. The Davins were always there, and Enid Starkie, who would make him laugh.

You must have seen Mrs Cary after the war, if you saw the virginal of which you spoke.[2] And you have made your war-time hobby into a life's work. You must be a world authority on dolls' houses, and your museum is world-famous.

I have written a book on eighteenth-century dolls' houses, of which I have seen two thousand, and own fifty. England has more, and better, dolls' houses than any other country, because the type of society suited them.

I'm sure that Joyce Cary, who claimed to write as a social historian, would have had interesting thoughts on that fact, too.

NOTES

Vivien Greene (née Dayrell-Browning) married Graham Greene in 1927, and they had one son and one daughter. The Dolls' House Museum is in the grounds of Grove House.

On 27 October 1987, Mrs Greene kindly agreed to the publication of this interview.

1. Prior to 1933, Graham Greene had published *The Man Within*, *The Name of Action*, *Rumour at Nightfall*, and *Stamboul Train*.

2. See item 35.

27

About Each Other's Writings

Graham Greene

These written answers to the questions were kindly sent on 4 December 1987.

Can you recall how you met Joyce Cary, who was sixteen years older, married, with two children, when you entered Balliol as an undergraduate in 1922?

I don't remember when I met Joyce Cary first. It was in any case a long time after Oxford.

Letters from Cary to you, now in the Bodleian, are a guide to your common interests. The first, dated 'Feb. 3. 36', concerns men 'complete as Nigeria made them', whom he could immortalize in a character sketch, and also his admiration for England Made Me, *as 'the most brilliant piece of work I'd seen for years.' In the second, of 'July 25 36', he wishes he had been 'with you in Liberia',* Journey Without Maps *having recalled his own treks in Nigeria and the Cameroons. The last, of '28.1.54', begins: 'I'm delighted you should like my book'. Would that have been* Except the Lord, *which was published in November 1953?*

The book I liked so much cannot have been *Except the Lord*, which I have never read. I know I wrote a fan letter to him on the subject of one of his earlier books *An American Visitor*, which remained with *Mr Johnson* my favourites. My admiration for those books continues to this day.

That letter of 1954 continues: 'It's an odd thing we haven't had a proper good talk for 20 years. And yet we both have the same fundamental feeling about the world – we both wonder that people can do without a god – more still how they can make any sense of their own lives and reactions.'

Looking back to a date around 1934, can you recall any 'proper good talk' of the sort that Cary had so obviously valued?

Or do you remember an unexpected encounter in Sierra Leone in 1943, when Cary was script writer to Thorold Dickinson's film unit, and delays allowed time for long discussions?

I certainly remember our unexpected encounter in Sierra Leone in 1943. It was a very pleasant occasion for me as I was getting more and more bored with my duties there for M16 and to have Cary to talk to was a great pleasure. It was not so comfortable for him as he was lodged briefly between planes in a rather miserable Nissen hut. I can't remember now what we talked about. It would not have been about my work. I imagine we spoke mainly about each other's writings.

In Journey Without Maps, *you write of Freetown:* 'I had never found myself in a place which was more protective to women; it might have been inhabited by rowing Blues with Buchman consciences and secret troubles.' *By that reference, you imply that Buchman's activities in Oxford might have concerned you as greatly as they did Cary, whose notes about 'Buchmanites' date from the 1920s. Can you recall discussing Buchman with him?*

I only knew Buchmanites by repute and certainly had a prejudice against them. I didn't take them seriously enough to discuss them with Cary.

Do you think that the theme of Cary's novel An American Visitor *might be associated with Buchman – as an American visitor to Oxford? And is your novel,* The Quiet American, *possibly inspired by a similar reaction to such characters as Buchman and his followers?*

I certainly didn't have Buchman in mind when I wrote *The Quiet American*. The character Pyle was a picture of a certain type of naive thinking on the part of Americans in Viet Nam. It put a great belief in a Third Force which would be neither Vietnamese of the south or Vietmihn to something in between.

Would you give your opinion of Cary's books as a body of work, to indicate how far you think they deserve to be remembered?

I certainly feel that Cary's books should be brought out in a Collected Edition if possible by Penguin. They are memorable and should be remembered.

NOTE

Graham Greene was born in 1904 and educated at Berkhamsted School, where his father was the headmaster. On leaving Oxford he worked for four years as a sub-editor on *The Times*, and on his return from Liberia (mentioned above) became film critic for the *Spectator*. He was made a Companion of Honour in 1966, and his vast and varied output of writing includes more than thirty novels. He was busy 'trying to get a book right for publication' when this contribution was sent. That is surely a measure of his esteem for Joyce Cary.

His agreement to the publication of the above was gratefully received on 16 January 1988.

28

Novelist of the Creative Imagination

Walter Allen

This item is compiled in response to a letter of 30 November 1987, in which Professor Allen kindly answered the questions below.

[...] everything I have to say is already in the British Council pamphlet and *As I Walked Down New Grub Street*.

With your permission then,[1] I shall first quote from your British Council pamphlet (from which my own interest in Cary originated). You begin by contrasting the objective and subjective imagination, the extravert and introvert artist, using Coleridge's famous distinction between Shakespeare and Milton by identifying Cary with the former as:

'the one Proteus' of the English novel to-day. [...] all the characters that seem typical of Cary are in the grip of what can only be called the creative imagination. [...]
   The creative imagination: Cary is its novelist and its celebrant.[2]

As I Walked Down New Grub Street *records your first meeting with Cary in 1948, at an Oxford University Summer School, as*

the most rewarding experience that this Oxford venture gave me. [...] We were not unknown to each other, for it fell to me, as Michael Joseph's literary adviser, to be the first reader of his manuscripts, and I gathered he always wanted to know what I had said of them. I had known his novels since the early thirties, for John Hampson had introduced them to me. Cary was little known then. The only thing John and I knew about him was that he was completely unlike any of his contemporaries. In many ways, his work seemed to contradict most of the qualities that for us made a novel modern. He seemed an odd-man-out, but his power was unmistakable, and we admired him greatly. He did not achieve anything like adequate recognition until the war-years, though by 1947 his reputation was higher in America than it was at home. In that year, I remember going with Robert Lusty, Joseph's partner, to visit the man who was to be my American publisher in his London hotel. He had just read the typescript of my new novel and was flattering about it, but he had reservations. 'I certainly hope we can do it,' he said. 'The trouble is, it's too British.' [...]

Bob Lusty was anything but sympathetic towards Thayer Hobson's reaction to my novel. 'Yes,' he said, 'and look what happened to the last novel you turned down as "too British".' It had been Cary's *The Horse's Mouth* which, published by another house, had been the choice of the Literary Guild and a best seller for many weeks.

[...] It was from his transvaluation of values, following the life of a man of action largely removed from literary occupations, that his fiction sprang. [...] It was a ten years' struggle [...]. By 1948, things were different; he had warm friends and admirers in people like Lord David Cecil, Enid Starkie and Helen Gardner. He invited me round for drinks one evening. He was, I think, the handsomest man I have ever met. With his lofty brow and Roman nose, Cary looked proconsular: it was not difficult to imagine him ruling alone over thousands of natives in a country the size of England. He looked a ruler and a wise one at that. Meeting him, it was impossible, I think, not to be convinced of the beauty and loftiness of his mind.

I was struck, too, by the impression he gave me of certainty. Here, it seemed to me, was a man who never had to question himself, who *knew* as by direct intuition. Alert and wise, he sat there in surroundings which were his own and in which he was at home. [...] He spoke rather jerkily in a lightish voice, a jaunty voice, which in retrospect reminds me of Lord Montgomery as we used to hear it in the war. Whether this similarity, if indeed it was a fact, was due to their common Anglo-Irish origins I do not know, nor do I know whether Cary thought of himself as Irish. I am inclined to think that similarity of voice may have arisen from their being both men of action used to command. That he was a writer would not, I think, have been your guess on meeting him for the first time.

[...] He explained to me his way of writing. 'I do not,' he wrote somewhere, 'write one novel at a time. The process is more like collecting [...].' When he had an idea for a novel he would set aside a special folder for it. The idea might be implicit in a report that had caught his attention in a newspaper or be enshrined in a scrap of dialogue. He would put it in its folder and add to it in the course of time any notes he might acquire towards it, sketches of characters, impressions of scenes and so on, until the material accumulated to the point where it needed only to be edited into a whole, as it were.

He made writing novels sound easy, much easier than he can actually have found it, but the method was one that he had developed for himself out of his own experience, for his early years as a writer were strewn with more or less abortive novels. The method also throws light, I feel, on the nature of his novels, which strike one as somewhat improvisatory or at least very fluid. They are, so to speak, in no way set; one feels that scenes could be transposed from one to another without much difficulty, and though this contributes to the strong sense of life they have, their apparent provisional nature was not something a writer who had tried to bring himself up in the manner of Flaubert could easily adapt himself to.

I cannot pretend I knew Cary well. My meetings with him were more or less casual, at the cocktail parties Michael Joseph gave, I think at two-yearly intervals, and at the Society of Authors. At the cocktail parties, he was usually accompanied by one or other of his sons and their wives, which throws light on a comment on himself he once made to me. He did not belong to a club, he said, because he was a 'domestic man'. In memory, his house in Oxford as I saw it in 1948, struck me as being very much lived in [...]. One felt a web of family activity, with Cary very much at its centre. [...]

Both as novelist and thinker, he was, as I have said, a self-made man, what Eliot, writing of Blake, called a 'resourceful Robinson Crusoe'. But he was also, of all our contemporaries, the novelist and celebrant of the creative imagination. That for him was the central factor in human life, since it made every man the creator of his own life and destiny and, as he shows in such novels as *Mister Johnson*, *A House of Children*, and *To Be a Pilgrim*, the protagonist in tragedy and comedy alike. Tragedy and comedy are, indeed, reverse sides of the one coin. My memory of him is of nobility.[3]

Does any one of Cary's novels stand out as for you his best; or any as unsuccessful; or do you possibly see them as all necessary parts of one whole work – as he himself did?

I've always liked *To Be a Pilgrim* and think it the most successful. The least good seems to me *Castle Corner*, though it is fascinating. It is so formless as almost to be the *reductio ad absurdum* of his way of writing novels.

Might his view, that his novels form a whole, accord with what you say of them in your Memoirs: *'one feels that scenes could be transposed from one to another without much difficulty'?*

I suspect my comment on the fluidity of his novels would chime with his view of the novels taken as a whole.

Would you relate this very fluid quality, as you call it, to your description of Cary as ' "the one Proteus" of the English novel today'? Is it related to his capacity to assume such a wide range of characters so easily?

This fluidity is certainly related to his Protean quality and his apparent ability to assume a wide range of characters, though I ought to say I now have serious doubts about the validity of that passage in the pamphlet. He didn't dissent from it himself, but I was seeking to make a distinction between him and contemporaries that I no longer think exists.

The creative imagination has always been what you have stressed regarding him. Do you think the creative imagination was for him the mind of God, through which each of us is joined in the eternal recreation of the world? Does that fit the man who impressed you in the way I have quoted?

Your idea that his notion of the creative imagination as being his idea of the mind of God is one that's not struck me. I can only say that at this moment it strikes me as very probable, but I couldn't generalise further about it or relate it to what was first and foremost a visual impression. The beauty and loftiness of his countenance is what impressed me, and I read it as expressing the quality of his mind in a temporary attack of Platonism.

Do you think that his novels would be appreciated more, if the ideas behind them were understood?

I'm not sure of this. Novels are only incidentally (and accidentally, I think) the expression of philosophy.

Do you think a new generation of readers may be more ready to accept his ideas than his contemporaries were?

I wouldn't know about this. I'd have thought there was a constant interest in Cary over the years. It's difficult to think of any other novelist of his generation who has generated so many critical studies on him.

NOTES

Professor Walter Allen was born in Birmingham in 1911, and is a graduate of the University of Birmingham; he became a reader and critic, author of several critical works on the novel, and a distinguished novelist himself, the most highly praised of his six novels being *All in a Lifetime*. He was appointed to the Chair of English at the New University of Ulster in 1967, at which point *As I Walked Down New Grub Street* ends. He hopes to finish another novel by June or July, 1988, and the time he spared from it to deal with these letters and questions is therefore to be doubly appreciated.

1. From a letter of 9 Dec. 1987 to B. Fisher: 'I need hardly say you have my full permission to quote me.'

2. *Joyce Cary*: Writers and their Work: no. 41, for the British Council and National Book League (London: Longmans, Green and Co. Ltd, 1953; revised edition, 1963), pp. 5, 9.

3. *As I Walked Down New Grub Street: Memoirs of a Writing Life* (London: Heinemann, 1981), pp. 182-86.

29

From Michael Joseph's First Associate

Robert Lusty

This item was compiled from conversations and letters exchanged between November 1987 and January 1988.

With your kind permission I am quoting the following from your autobiography, Bound to Be Read.[1]

Victor Gollancz had published a novel or so by an author with whom he said he could make no headway and whose books were unsuccessful. He was about to reject him from his list but just wondered if we might be interested. He had the manuscript of his new novel and its title was *Charley Is My Darling*. The author was Joyce Cary. Thus we recruited to our young list a novelist destined to be recognized as one of the most brilliant and significant of our time. No author could have presented fewer problems of temperament. He was an unforgettable character; a man who lived and wrote with great intensity and power and compassion for his characters. He was not, in current terms, anything like a best-seller, and only after his death was recognition and success accorded him in America. He wrote his novels in quick sequences which he numbered and then fitted together to bring order and unity. He was a delightful man, too, with his rather puzzled look and alert, quick glance. He spoke rather as he wrote, his thoughts moving faster than he could either talk or write. Only his wife could decipher his rapid scrawl, and her death a few years before his own was a sad deprivation.

I visited Joyce Cary in Oxford very shortly before his death, which he awaited with the greatest composure. He had never given the impression of being other than mildly careless about his appearance. He seemed to ignore such irrelevancies. But on this occasion he was immaculate, with almost the look of a dandy. He lay on his couch in the neatest of jumpers, and carefully pressed linen trousers rather deeper in colour; his socks were gay and his shoes neat and highly polished. A monocle dangled from a chain; his face, a little pale, achieved nobility and his eyes had lost nothing of their brilliance. He seemed more relaxed than I had ever seen him. He gave the impression of having done with the worries of the world. We talked of this and that for a while and I made my departure. Within a very little time he died (pp. 81-82).

Every once in a while, if a successful author has the wisdom (and the confidence) to remain with one publisher, a uniform edition becomes a possibility and few operations give more satisfaction to an author. [...] It has been my good fortune to contrive five of these uniform editions, of which three contain the Michael Joseph imprint, and two the Hutchinson. I like to think there is a certain aptness in their names. C.S. Forester has his Greenwich Edition, Joyce Cary his Carfax Edition, and H.E. Bates his Evensford Edition. [...] it is likely that these editions will carry them into the future more certainly than might otherwise be possible (pp. 143-44).

As you had kindly given me permission to quote from your correspondence with or concerning Cary, I wrote to Ms Dereham of Michael Joseph Limited and received the following answer:

Since Sir Robert Lusty's day, we have moved offices three times and on each occasion have cleared our files. All we have in our Cary files now is correspondence relating to low reprint royalties.[2]

How do you feel about that situation, Sir Robert?

Publishers should not destroy their files before photo-copying them and what treasures disappeared in the Joseph moves is alarming to contemplate – the Readers' Reports, the correspondence with authors etc etc.[3]

NOTES

Sir Robert Frith Lusty (1909-) was educated at the Society of Friends' School, Sidcot; became a local journalist, and then entered publishing, first with Walter Hutchinson, then Michael Joseph, in December 1935; nominally he began as Editorial and Production Manager, but he became a director when they broke away from Gollancz; in 1956 he resigned as Deputy Chairman, to become Managing Director of Hutchinson's, until his retirement in 1973; from 1960-1968 he was a Governor of the BBC.

1. (London: Jonathan Cape, 1975).

2. Letter of 7 Dec. 1987.

3. From a letter dated 7 January 1988, from Sir Robert to B. Fisher, in which he also explains that he made the decisions, such as the name and colour used, for these editions, 'all these, of course, with the approval of the various authors.' He also gives his own approval of what is here published.

It is appropriate to add that the Harper files (discussed in items 40 and 45) contain material related to what Michael Joseph has lost. In the letter of Sept. 1949 (quoted in item 40), Fischer says that Sir Robert expected *A Fearful Joy* to be more popular than Cary's previous books; it is his only novel that no contributor to this book mentioned!

30

From his Literary Agent

Spencer Curtis Brown

This interview took place at Mr Curtis Brown's London office on 7 June 1968.

I was very fond of Joyce Cary. But there is nothing, it seems to me, which I could tell you, which you could not learn better either from his sons or from his many friends in Oxford.

Perhaps you know more about him as a writer.

People are not 'writers', but just men.

What sort of man was he to deal with, in business?

I believe the business side did not interest him at all. He was a man of great moral integrity, though not an orthodox Christian. I believe he did have a sense of mission, and he was fascinated by historical problems.

I think *The Horse's Mouth* is his worst book.

How did your relationship begin?

I don't know how he came to me – there was no acquaintance before our business relationship. The first thing we sold for him was to Gollancz. I always dealt with him personally, directly with the books. I don't recall anyone else in the firm dealing with him.

I think of Joyce Cary as a man of great vitality, and full of curiosity, about everything. He talked a great deal, about everything. He was a man of great impatience, and for this reason, a careless writer.

Can you recall any particular conversation?

No. I can't remember anything about our conversations particularly. He threw off ideas like sparks. But he was not a logical thinker, though he thought he was. He talked frivolously.

Did you visit him at his home?

I used to go down to see him when he was ill, but not before. I didn't see the sons until the end, if then. But I think he was closest to Tristram.

Do you think that he was setting an example, to them in particular, by the way he faced death?

I would not think of his death as exemplary. I think it was not exceptional.

His doctor, Ritchie Russell, said that some people do feel their death must be an example.

Joyce Cary was a modest man – but not in every way. I think David Cecil was his closest friend, and the best source of information.

Do you have any correspondence with him?

There would be no letters of any value, because we could discuss matters verbally, and a letter would be of the kind, 'Herewith the MS.'

What value do you place on his manuscripts in the Bodleian?

I think the manuscripts are the best source of information. And the unpublished work is important. He died comparatively young, and there might be work that he would have published had he lived longer.

'The Split Mind of the West' and 'My Religious History' are long essays that have been submitted and rejected, I believe; but I think they deserve publication. And his last treatise, 'Real Freedom', would not suffer, as a novel would, from being unfinished. What are your views about the notebooks?

I cannot judge the notebooks, because I haven't read them. I think Michael would be the one to decide whether they should be published.

Speaking generally, do you think the notebooks of writers of interest for publication?

On the whole I don't think much of notebooks of writers. But I don't think there would be much to write in a biography of Cary, and a study of the books would be more important – and possibly the notebooks.

NOTE

Spencer Curtis Brown (1906-1980) was educated at Harrow and Magdalene College, Cambridge (History Exhibitioner); became Personal Adviser to General Sikorski, Polish Prime Minister, 1941-43; then served in the Intelligence Corps, and in 1945 assisted in reorganizing the book trade in liberated countries; from 1945-1968 he was Chairman of Curtis Brown Limited, London, literary agents.

On 13 January 1988 a copy of this interview was sent to the Director of Curtis Brown now concerned with Cary's literary estate.

31

The Power of Love

Enid Starkie

This interview took place in Dr Starkie's Oxford home on 4 September 1967.

I got to know Joyce Cary in 1941, when my book, *A Lady's Child*, came out at the same time as *A House of Children*. Joyce wrote to congratulate me on my book, and I found only then that he lived just around the corner from me. He must have kept very much to himself for this to be possible, I decided. I had not read his earlier novels, but had read *Mister Johnson*, and thought it very good. I was interested in *A House of Children* because I knew that part of the Irish countryside.

When we met his personality struck me as very reserved and non-Irish. He was very much the English officer. I was even more surprised that we hadn't met previously when I found that his wife was Fred Ogilvie's sister, as I had known Fred and Mary Ogilvie for years. But Fred came back to Oxford as Principal of Jesus only in 1948. Then, within a few months, he discovered that he had cancer. When he saw the X-rays he just died; he never came out of the nursing-home. Freddie died before Trudy, but it was at the party for Freddie, when he became Principal, that Joyce told me Trudy had cancer. They only just knew.[1]

I had a severe operation myself early in September 1949, and Trudy cycled to the Acland hospital to see me. Then, at the end of September, she and Joyce went on holiday and took their bicycles. On December 7th I went to Joyce's birthday party, when I presumed he was fifty-one, as there were five candles round one in the middle. Trudy was dying in the next room, through the folding doors, and they must have known she was dying, but nothing was said. She had had all sorts of treatment, including (I think) poison gas. By this time she had cancer of the liver, and was very yellow. I went to Paris on December 8th, and was away when she died, five days later.[2]

She had been very much the wife, but was amused by Joyce's idea of women's role – as I said in my lecture.[3] I gave the lecture just three months after Joyce's death, and invited all the sons. Tristram didn't

135

like it; I think he wanted me to eulogize Joyce more, as the greatest living novelist, and so on. I would rank him high among English novelists, but I haven't read all his novels, and the English novel is not my field. I don't think either Michael or Peter came to the lecture.

I think Tristram was Joyce's favourite son, because he saw in him many qualities that he would have liked in himself. He thought (as I did) that George was the most brilliant of the four, but they used to have the most dreadful fights, and as an adolescent George was very rude to his father. Joyce didn't like it, but Joyce couldn't have been rude to anyone. George was more like the Ogilvies than the Carys. Joyce forgot all about those arguments as soon as George died.

Joyce also thought Peter's wife brilliant, and I think he was possibly right. I got on well with Peter, and when I was there, just after Joyce died, he gave me a picture of Gerald Wilde's. But I've never regarded it as my own, and I intend to give it back to Michael [as the executor]. I think Michael the best of them. It was sad that his post was in Paris during Joyce's last illness, so that he could not visit him much.

Joyce had a great admiration for the academic. He thought Mary Ogilvie wonderful, with a marvellous brain and so on. But I didn't think her wonderful at all. He dedicated *Art and Reality* to me as 'Dr Starkie', and I thought it odd that he didn't realize I would have preferred 'Enid Starkie'. I myself had no original leaning to the academic, and did it only because I had to make a good living (to support my family).

Do you recall discussions with him about Baudelaire? There was 'something Baudelairean' in his nature, he once noted, and he was annotating your 1942 edition of Les Fleurs du Mal *while writing* The Horse's Mouth.

He wrote to me in November 1942 about that book. But I don't think there was anything Baudelairean about him; for Baudelaire's chief quality was a sense of guilt, and Joyce had nothing of that. My book, *Baudelaire*, was published on 21 June 1957, and was dedicated to Joyce, 'In Memoriam'. I do say in my dedication that we discussed it a lot, but I'm afraid that I can't recall, now, anything particular of our conversations.

I think there was something very English in his character. He didn't for example pay compliments for the sake of it, as a Frenchman would. He was English in the way he faced his wife's death, with a 'stiff upper lip', which I found so hard to bear, as I said in my lecture. His heart was breaking with grief.

The most Irish thing about him, as I also said in my lecture, was his irony. The jewelled woman I referred to there was Rosamond Lehmann, incidentally. He used to talk about himself ironically when he was ill, and say things like 'Next year you'll see me in a bath chair.' I was the first to notice the onset of his illness. It was in October 1954. I had walked him all over Paris, and so it showed up. That is, he was weak in the right leg. He was in Paris to lecture at the British Institute.[4]

What I think most valuable in your lecture is your memory of him as 'utterly genuine and good', because the message of his books must be rooted in those qualities. You have shown this by ending with his thoughts about his dying wife, recorded in a notebook for no eyes but his own:

[...] I was made to feel, I suppose, for the first time, the *absolute need* of love to make life possible, and the continuous everlasting presence of love in the world. And so the fearful bitterness of this danger to T. and all our memories together, was mixed with the sense of something that can survive any loss, the power of love.

NOTES

Enid Starkie (19??-1970), born in Dublin, was educated at Alexandra College, Dublin and the Royal Irish Academy of Music. With a scholarship to Oxford, she took a first class honours degree in 1918, followed by a doctorate at the Sorbonne. From 1929 she was a lecturer in Modern Languages at Oxford, later a Reader in French Literature, and a Fellow and Tutor of Somerville from 1935. Her best-known works were on Baudelaire and Rimbaud, and her most famous honour that of Officier de la Legion d'Honneur, from the French Government. She was made a CBE in 1967.

1. They knew when they returned from London on 27 April 1948, when the doctor confirmed Trudy's fear regarding a lump on her breast, discovered on 25 April.
2. On 13 Dec. 1949; for Enid Starkie's recollections of Cary, including her account of his Christmas party in 1949, see 'Joyce Cary, A Portrait', Tredegar Memorial Lecture, read on 24 Oct. 1957; *Essays by Divers Hands*, being the transactions of the Royal Society of Literature, n.s. xxxii, ed. Joanna Richardson (London: Oxford University Press, 1963), 125-44.
3. 'A Portrait,' p. 136.
4. On 27 Oct. 1954.

32

The James Tait Black Prize

John Dover Wilson

This interview took place at Professor Dover Wilson's home, Three Beeches, Balerno, near Edinburgh, on 23 August 1968.

I had to award this prize regularly, and couldn't keep up with all the prize-winners.

But you did keep up with Joyce Cary. I have been reading your correspond-ence, which you gave to the National Library. What did you think of him as a person?

He was a grand fellow to know. He stayed with us when he came for the prize – and kept me up all night talking. My wife detested him. She 'couldn't away with him.'

Was that because he kept you up all night?

She thought him a very untidy Irishman, too.[1]

What did you think of his lecture?

The lecture didn't hang together. It was a very bad lecture. My impression was that he hadn't prepared it.

He had spent months preparing it; I know from his notes and drafts in the Bodleian. Perhaps he lacked sleep, and was over-excited. But I think that getting the prize, and actually meeting and talking to you, gave him the confidence he needed. Would you agree?

Yes. He told me as much. He did most of the talking, but perhaps he got something from me too. He told me that his father hadn't wanted him to come to the Art School, and that he had gone to the Balkan war because he thought, 'this is the last war of civilization.' I think he was

138

quite a good artist, judging by the water-colours he did for me.[2] I had a strong impression that he had several novels in his head at one time and, in his own words, he had to 'shove them away in a drawer' – which I took to be metaphorical. I think he was essentially an artist, poet, writer of imagination all compact. Talking to him that night, 'I felt I was as near to the act of creation as I was ever likely to be, with all my ideas about Shakespeare simmering at the time.'

Have I your permission to quote these as your exact words [repeating the words in quotation marks]?

Yes, you have. He was incalculable, I should think. I don't know how his wife got on.

Would you say something about his novels?

I hadn't known the African novels at that time, and I thought *A House of Children* untypical. But I read *The Horse's Mouth* at a time when I was myself suffering great distress, and this most vital book had been a tonic.

The remarkable thing is that his visit here largely inspired it, to judge from his letter to you, which I read in the Library last night.[3] What do you think of the trilogy as a whole?

I thought Sara the best character in the first trilogy, and *Herself Surprised* one of the finest books of the kind since the eighteenth century – reminiscent of *Moll Flanders*. I think it a very good book, though short, and would put it next after *The Horse's Mouth* as Cary's greatest. I don't think much of *To Be a Pilgrim*.

From what you have just said about Shakespeare, I am reminded that The Fortunes of Falstaff *was published soon after, and that Cary annotated his own copy; it was given to him by a friend who may well have discussed it with him.[4] Do you recall discussing Falstaff?*

I think we very likely did.

When talking about the great characters of literature (usually Tolstoy's), Cary said that such characters are not real people, but symbols, and that is why they are great. Is Falstaff similarly a great symbol?

Yes. I would agree with that.

What is your view of the symbolic use of words, and names in particular?

I would shock most Shakespeare critics by saying that I don't think it very important. But I must say that the two comic names Dogberry and Verges are delightful and absolutely right.

Since you found Gulley Jimson's book such a tonic, may I ask what you think is the real importance of laughter in literature?

I discuss laughter and the comic muse in my book on Shakespeare's Happy Comedies, published by Faber. I suggest you read that.

The way Falstaff makes a joke of honour is not unlike Gulley's humour, and we know from Not Honour More, *and what Cary said about Conrad's influence on him, that honour was central to his thought. Would you comment on that?*

I wonder whether Cary ever commented on *Troilus and Cressida*, where the idea of honour is strange – Shakespeare derides honour. It was written for an undergraduate audience at the Inns of Court – a bawdy undergraduate audience, and Shakespeare used that sort of humour to please them.

I have just remembered seeing [in the Library] the postcard he sent you of Shakespeare's bust [in Stratford-on-Avon]. He had written on it, 'Is this the man who wrote Troilus. It has given me a shock.' It seems likely that something you said made him send that. What interests me most in The Fortunes of Falstaff *is what you say about Shakespeare's 'conversion'.*

Then you should read my introduction to the Sonnets, where I quote Mahood as suggesting that the rejection of Falstaff is Shakespeare's treatment of his own rejection of the young lord. We don't know why Shakespeare left London, but I think it probable that he went back to Stratford every year and wrote his plays when the theatres closed. He said his farewell to London and the court in *The Tempest*. But you can't tell how imagination works – what set Shakespeare on fire. I think Shakespeare used his own feelings though.

So, when you said that your ideas about Shakespeare made you feel near to the act of creation when talking to Cary that night, it was because you felt that Cary's feelings had set his imagination on fire. That suggests a direct link between your discussion and the way Cary began creating Gulley on the train journey home.[5]

NOTES

John Dover Wilson (1881-1969), born in London, was educated at Lancing College and Gonville and Caius College, Cambridge, where his lifetime interest in Shakespeare was kindled by Alfred Ainger (as his preface to *The Fortunes of Falstaff* states). He was Regius Professor of rhetoric and English literature at the University of Edinburgh from 1935 to 1945, and from 1936 had lived at Three Beeches, because his wife Dorothy (née Baldwin) disliked the city. They had two daughters and one son, who died in active service in W.W.II.

I trust that publication of this interview will be approved by surviving members of his family, whom I regret having failed to trace.

1. I learned from his second wife that his first wife had been a very practical, house-proud person; as this description conflicts with others of him as a guest, I suggest that he was already assuming the character of Gulley Jimson (as shown below).

2. In copies of *A House of Children* and *To Be a Pilgrim*, now in the National Library of Scotland.

3. Dated '5.12.42, it begins: 'I was going to write to you when I had drawn in your book. But to be honest, I had some ideas about a new book, in the train coming south and since then I have been throwing off scenes, characters and dialogue at thousands of words a day. Most of it will be scrap but meanwhile, like Manet, as he painted his first drafts, I am learning the forms and necessary conjunctions of my matter, discovering its weaknesses before they are fatally included in some general plan, and getting to know my people by putting the question.

It will be a damn queer book but my agent told me to write what I damned well liked and to hell with the publisher; and then the publisher smiled upon me and told me that whatever I wrote would receive his highest consideration or words to that effect.' (See the views of his publisher and agent in items 28 and 30.)

4. Mary Ogilvie, in December 1944; see Cary B.188 in Bodley.

5. For my development of this idea, see *The Writer and His Theme* (1980), pp. 225-6.

33

Cary – and Raffalovich

Arthur Melville Clark

This interview took place in Edinburgh on 26 August 1968, and was followed by correspondence, as shown.

When Cary received the James Tait Black prize, I chaired his lecture. It was open to the general public as well as students, and held in one of the largest classrooms. The lecture was a bit higgledy-piggledy, but very agreeably delivered. His manner as a lecturer was good; it wasn't the manner of someone who was master of his audience, but more in the nature of a talk – and therefore he rambled.

We had a discussion afterwards and I liked the man very much. But he was an untidy writer, I think. He kept a number of novel ideas boiling, but didn't work with all-out concentration on one. It therefore seems that he was not a consecutive thinker – his thought comes in flashes. He tried to objectify the 'confusion' in his mind, I gathered; but it would have been better if he had concentrated longer and allowed an idea to shape itself before he wrote it down. I think he was defeating his object. He sent me a pamphlet after he got home, and a letter to explain what he had been saying. I'll look them out and send you a copy of the letter, if you like.

I'd appreciate that very much. Could I now ask you about André Raffalovich? He appears in Cary's notebooks as a key influence, and you knew him well, I've been told.

Yes indeed. I was a regular luncher and diner at his house. If there were people of interest in Edinburgh he found them; he ran lunch, tea, and dinner parties. We always called him Raffie, and his chatelaine was Florence Gribbell.

She was originally from Devon, but she'd had an unfortunate love affair, and to cheer her up she was sent to Paris, where she met Raffie's mother (some time between 1870-80). She became governess to Raffie, then a little boy, and she took to him. His mother ran a famous salon, and couldn't be bothered with him; so, when he was about eighteen, Florence Gribbell went with him to Oxford, where he got a house. He took responsions (I don't know at which College), but then he gave up and went to London, intending to start a salon there. It was Oscar Wilde who chiefly discouraged him, from all accounts; and when he found, after a summer visit, that he liked Edinburgh, he decided to settle here. He bought 9 Whitehouse Terrace, which is where I used to visit him, and where he lived to the end of his life [...], 1934.

He was very wealthy. His father was a Russian Jew, a banker (money lender) in Odessa, who went to Paris, and there married this very beautiful, intelligent Jewess, named Marie – Raffie's mother. Their eldest son was in the Russian Embassy, and their third child, Sophie, married an Irish nationalist, William O'Brien, through whom she became devoted to Ireland. She was converted to Catholicism (as Raffie was also), but the mother kept to the Jewish faith, I believe, even though she went to live with her daughter, in Dublin.

Raffie was the second child, and such an interesting person. He was so peculiar to look at, though. He had a kind of monstrous beauty. He always wore a high choker, which you thought would have been fashionable in the nineties. And he had a rather big mouth.

That reminds me at once of Nussbaum in Castle Corner, *who is obviously drawn from Raffalovich. You may remember that Nussbaum has a huge mouth which makes his smile ugly; so he always wears a gloomy expression to make it less evident.*[1] *I sense that Cary had formed that impression of Raffalovich, and might therefore have seen him quite often.*

You can see portraits of Raffalovich and his friend, Father John Gray, at the Dominican Priory in George Square. And you can read all about them in a book called *Two Friends*.[2]

[*This I did, and two weeks later received a letter from Dr Clark, dated 5 September '68. It begins with a discussion of how Cary might have met Raffalovich,*[3] *and continues with a copy of a letter that Cary wrote to him on 20 December 1942, regarding his lecture on 27 November – three weeks before. This copy of Cary's letter includes:*]

'I meant to write to you some time ago. but I have been too busy since I came back to reflect on our discussion.

'I told you I was afraid that my superficial remarks in a general address might mislead your class.[4] I said that meaning existed before

the symbol and that there could be therefore a direct reference from
the mind to a reality objective to that mind, and that the reality
consisted, in its most obvious form, of primitive characters of feeling.
This was of profound importance to the artist (I leave the other
implications, theological and philosophical, out of this account)
because it enabled him to compare his symbol or expression with what
it was meant to contain and convey. It cut out the root of the
expressionist theory which seemed to me a disaster in philosophy and
art. I had not time to add that the objective real was much more than
primitive characters (love, hate, fear, appetite, curiosity etc) and
consisted largely of what modern semantic writers call a universe of
discourse. Of vast importance to art and to history; and itself a
product of art in its widest sense. A created idea realised in living
memories, which are so far objective; not merely between one man
and another; but between one man's mind and his own memory, as
the psychologists have shown. But the point I wanted to make was
that the universe of discourse, without that root, that reference, in the
primitive feelings, and the total objective real, is an escaped balloon,
floating in the void, and too often, as I think, filled with very doubtful
gas. It is not healthy breathing for artist[s], at the least, and has
choked a good many of them. [...]'

[Dr Clark continues:]

[...] The pamphlet which Cary sent me (along with the letter) is
Process of Real Freedom [...].

I find, to my astonishment, that I was Cary's chairman at the lecture
in 1953. I had forgotten this. You date the lecture tentatively in
January. But I am pretty sure that it was considerably later [...] I may
as well give you my notes [...][5]

NOTES

Arthur Melville Clark, D.Litt. Edin., D.Phil. Oxon. (1895-) was on the staff in English
Literature at the University of Edinburgh from 1923 to 1960. His many publications
extend from *Realistic Revolt in Modern Poetry* (1922), to *Sir Walter Scott: The Formative
Years* (1969), and *Murder Under Trust* (1981).

1. See Carfax edn, pp. 275, 408.
2. *Two Friends:* John Gray & André Raffalovich, edited by Father Brocard Sewell,
St Albert's Press, 1963.
3. Through Charles Mackie, John Duncan, or Henry Lintott (see item 11).
4. Dr Clark adds in a footnote: 'It was an open lecture and many not students
attended it.' It was published as 'Tolstoy's Theory of Art' (E.6).
5. These notes clearly form the basis of the laureation address of 3 July 1953, in

which Professor Matthew Fisher asked the Vice Chancellor to confer upon Cary an Honorary LL.D (as shown by MS. Cary 335 in the Bodleian); it seems therefore that the address had been prepared by Dr Clark – a fact that he himself had forgotten, as he assumes in his letter that the occasion for these notes was his own introduction of Cary as lecturer; but the only lecture Cary gave in Edinburgh in 1953 was on 20 January.

34

With Film Makers

Thorold Dickinson   Joanna Dickinson

This interview took place in London on 5 December 1967.

[*Joanna*:] We came to know Joyce Cary when I found *The Case for African Freedom* in a bookshop, and bought it. I was amused to find my own relations' Liberal ideas reflected there. Then I found *Mister Johnson* and bought that, at about the same time – 1942.

[*Thorold*:] At this time I was in the army, and had built up a training film unit in the army. Then I was asked, with Carol Reed, Ustinov, and others, to go over to the National Film Unit. I was assigned to getting interest in bolstering up the British to get beyond the immediate war problems and consider the future of British rule – that is, to get past merely bolstering up the war. The war had drawn the talent of colonial development into the armed forces. The Ministry of Information wanted to have a film to entertain and instruct.

We had a sketch for a film about Africa written by E. Arnot Robertson, and Public Relations men in the Ministry were interested. It was to be a Two Cities Film.

[*Joanna*:] At my suggestion, about ten days before Christmas 1942, John Sutro, our producer, wrote to Joyce Cary to come in with us, to rescue Arnot Robertson's sketch. We wanted someone who understood the country. The letter came through the box, and was in a bright orange-yellow coloured envelope. Joyce stuffed it in his dressing-gown pocket and Trudy noticed, but said nothing then. Then on Christmas Eve she said, 'What on earth was that letter?' He said he didn't know what she was talking about; so she went and found it in his pocket. He wrote, and we all travelled down on Boxing Day to the Randolph. We sat in the lounge watching people come in through the swing doors, and we were all sure it was him when he came. He said he was interested, but would have to go home and ask Trudy. We phoned next day, and he said he would come.

[*Thorold*:] It was difficult to buy the right clothes etc. during wartime, but Trudy found his original tropical gear, with which he turned up. In those days red was supposed to be a protection against the sun – like a topee – and Joyce's underwear was a flaming colour. He made it all right, and we met at Glasgow Central. All was very hush hush; we went out into the Clyde in an open boat and were put on a Canadian Pacific Liner, *The Duchess of Richmond*, with 5,000 troops in it. The smell was appalling. Having been a major, I had a cabin with another army officer, and Joyce had a cabin with Desmond Dickinson, a camera man. The Art Director Tom Morahan and the Production Manager made up the party – five of us.

Quite soon Joyce said: 'Let's go up on deck and talk about the script', and I looked in my bag to find that the Arnot Robertson story was left behind. When we got up on deck, Joyce said he had left his copy behind too – by accident. I wondered whether there had been some subconscious prompting. Anyway, Joyce said, 'Thank God,' and we started again. We gave an acknowledgement on the film, 'From an idea by E. Arnot Robertson'. But she'd put in a lot of niggly things about boys' schools etc; we decided to develop the story out of the country.

The great stimulus to Joyce's writing at this time was the cockney Desmond Dickinson – a real dyed-in-the-wool cockney, with rhyming slang and all. Without being rude, he would bring Joyce down to earth in what he was talking about. We had a table in the officers' saloon, and where other tables were rather quiet and tense, ours was full of talk and jollity – as when Desmond told Joyce that his favourite film star was Greta Garbo, and Joyce asked, 'Who's she?' He'd never heard of her!

Shortly before disembarkation we were told that we were not going to Lagos. Instead, we were put ashore on an open beach at Freetown. The harbour was full of shipping. There we sat on our suitcases, until taken to a cricket pitch, to be told that there were 450 people who had been waiting for transport for weeks. We were then directed to walk up the hill to a hut to get lunch. We went into an ante-room with a bar and decrepit furniture, and the man behind the bar directed us through another room to a room beyond where we would get a meal. And there we found Graham Greene! [... *see item* 27.]

Faced with the possibility of being stuck for six weeks, we went to the Governor who, at dinner at Government House, told us that there would be seats on a plane at one airport, but we got there just as it was taking off. Three weeks later we got a plane to Monrovia, then flew to Accra; got another plane to Lagos, another to Khartoum, then a plane to Dar-es-Salaam, where we found we could work best.

Joyce was ill once – his stomach was apt to be upset. I was very ill at the end, as we ran into rains, and I got malaria.

For local conditions we studied witchcraft, and found a witch doctor, though everyone said we would not. An Englishman who was about to retire was allotted to us as doctor; then we found an intelligent chief's son who became Swahili interpreter and guide, and he became very friendly; he found us a witch doctor in full practice. Having got our story we flew home.

I was ill with malaria in Dar-es-Salaam, and we had still found no girl for the main lead. So we got into a plane and flew to Kampala, in Uganda, and I was put into a hotel bed and doctors were called. Joyce went off to find a girl. He met the African ministers of Uganda, a minister's wife gave a tea-party for educated girls, and Eseza Makumbi was there. Joyce came back and said, 'I've found a most wonderful girl. She's taking us to a tea-room where it will be acceptable to talk.' I was helped to dress and Joyce took my arm. We got to the steps of the hotel (a flight of about forty steps), and there were three buses at the foot, having brought about eighty people off the plane – district commissioners and officers. She drove up in a small car and got out, and Joyce called out, 'Yoo-hoo', and waved. When all these people saw who was waving to him, they froze. She was the daughter of a government official and was very intelligent. She is now [1967] the leading woman politician in Uganda.

The plane we left on was an old German crate from Cairo, and we flew to Stanleyville. It rained all the way from Dar-es-Salaam, until we left Africa. [...]

In October 1943 I was back in Africa and was there for ten months. Joyce did not come, but he took a great interest when we worked at the film studio. We started in Denham in '44 and finished the film in '45. For the negro composer we went to Dr Felix Brown, a psychiatrist, who took on the actor as a patient, and was paid to treat him, so that his behaviour was convincing. But he was affected by performing as a man of two worlds [see Cary's view, item 22]. The film was ten years before its time, and the fascist woman in it, especially, was not appreciated. Phyllis Calvert was under contract and had to be in it; but people *did* overdress out there (so she wasn't really wrong). Eric Portman was tiresome; too full of gin after 4 p.m.

Joyce was very civilized and professional. Many writers aren't. But other film people wondered how I got on with him. They expected him to be unrealistic etc. And he was a little. I remember in Lagos, we were told that on Sunday morning, after Church parade, the Governor's lady would be on the verandah and would like to meet us. Joyce and I went down early for exercise. But Joyce insisted on going for long walks in very brief underwear, and by the time he returned the Governor's lady was there to greet him. Joyce forgot about his underwear until I reminded him; then he rushed off to change. The Governor's lady was very proper, but all passed off without evident embarrassment.

Would you talk now about his trip with you to India, in 1946.

[*Thorold:*] The reason for the Indian film was that I had made *The Next of Kin* for the army, which was intended to show the importance of keeping their mouths shut. The Chief of Intelligence for Wavell [*the Viceroy*] had seen it, and said: 'The Security Officer is the most unpopular man, but the film made people sympathetic towards him.' So Wavell decided, 'If a film can do that for the Security Officer in the Indian Army, perhaps a film can make the British popular in India.' But it was too late.

[*Joanna:*] During the Indian trip Joyce was dogged with proofs of *The Moonlight*, and worried about Trudy – they'd had a hard winter in England. 'I can't think why I wrote the damn thing,' he said. We had lunch with the Wavells. Gielgud was there, and two people who were fascinated with Joyce named Casey – later Lord Casey, and his wife; she was particularly so – they were terrific fans.

[*Thorold:*] Joyce came in a consultative capacity, and the film was made in 1952. He gave us the title: *Secret People*.[1] While making *The Next of Kin* I had been indoctrinated regarding the CID, and was told a true story, on the topic of when the end justifies the means: in 1939 an Irish Republican put a bomb in a square in Liverpool – this was the germ of the film, which people found violent and improbable – though it was based on fact. The film *Secret People* nearly caused a riot in Leicester Square; it concerned a wife who gave her husband up to the police – and had to be changed surgically and given a new identity – this is not infrequent. Irene Worth was in it. This film, too, was ten years before its time.

[*Joanna:*] Thorold was ill when Wavell asked him to go to India, and he made what he thought were impossible conditions, including my being there. In fact, I could find out about women's problems as no man could. But Joyce resented my being there, even though I pointed out that he and Trudy had been together throughout the war, whereas Thorold and I had been separated. He missed Trudy, and worried about her. Thorold became very ill in India, and had to come back to England before he could have a certain operation. But he gave up the only available seat to Joyce, who was so put out at the thought of being delayed – so concerned that he of all people should not get left. He could be the most difficult man under the sun. No small boy stamping his foot in a rage could be more unreasonable.

Trudy did everything for him. I used to feel mad at the extent to which she pampered him. During the war when food was a problem there would still be an enormous spread for the ritual afternoon tea, at about four-thirty to five.

In India, I decided that Joyce had to take some responsibility, so he was put in charge of the petty cash, to pay all the carriers. He admitted that since he'd married he hadn't even bought a railway ticket for himself.

I think of him as not well integrated – underneath he was a snob; the voice in which he would say, 'Don't you know so-and-so in Oxford?' We didn't think he had really overcome prejudice against the Africans. He thought they were hundreds of years behind, and weren't really ready to make decisions.

We thought of Trudy as an optimist, and strong, though Joyce dominated the conversation. She used to think of herself as closest to George – they didn't even have to talk. We hadn't known of her death – hadn't realized that it would be so soon. We saw Joyce about three weeks after, and Trudy's name came up, and he just said, 'Didn't you know, she died?' There was an awkward silence, but we felt it difficult to see how he felt, and he made it difficult to express sympathy.

He could be very difficult, and he used to make me boil the way he took everything Trudy did for granted – running the house, and then going off with his manuscripts to type – no-one else could read his writing – every word he wrote.

At other times he could be so sympathetic and tactful I could have just hugged him.

NOTES

Thorold Dickinson (1903-1984) was educated at Clifton and Keble College, Oxford, where he read History, and also developed his interest in the cinema. He joined the film industry in 1928 as a film editor, and from 1936 onwards worked as a script writer and director, showing an exceptional sense of style and structure, to become one of the most important directors of the British cinema; besides *Men of Two Worlds*, *Secret People*, and *The Next of Kin* (discussed above), he created such classics as *Gaslight* (1940) and *The Queen of Spades* (1949). He was head of film production at the UN, New York (1956-60); then founded the Department of Film at the Slade School of Fine Art, University College, London (1960), where he became Professor of Film (1967-72). He also wrote books, and *A Discovery of Cinema* (1971) remains one of the best books on the cinema.

Irene Joanna Macfadyen (1903-1979), had a Quaker upbringing. She studied architecture at the Architectural Association (1925-29), and became an Associate of RIBA. Her work in the 1930s included kindergartens and schools; during the war years she assessed bomb damage and rebuilding programmes for the Ministry of Works. She became a strong critic of anti-social trends in post-war British architecture, and her skills and advice were used in the development-aid programmes of the UN.

Marriage to Thorold Dickinson in 1929 involved her increasingly in film work, and they were co-authors of *Hill 24 Doesn't Answer*, made in Israel (1953-5).

1. MS. Cary 278/N.127 contains Cary's plot and synopsis for the film; 278/N.129 has documentary evidence concerning it from Dickinson and Scotland Yard; versions by Cary and Dickinson are in MSS. Cary 222, 223.

35

Marriage into the Cary Family

Isabel Cary

This interview took place at Lady Cary's home, Huntswood House, Harpsden, on 14 December 1987.

My main memory of Joyce is that he was wrapped up in his children. So if people came to Parks Road, he didn't ever talk to anybody else. He just talked to his own family. And the very first time that I ever met them, when I was first engaged to Michael, I think he hadn't seen Michael for some time. And I was simply amazed: they were awfully nice to me, but they weren't a bit interested in me, they just wanted to talk to Michael. It was very characteristic of that house. Joyce was so admiring of his children, and wrapped up in them, and loved it when they came; so if there were his own sons in the house, there was always very good talk at meals, and nobody else's conversation signified. Nobody else could break into it very much. It was just between Joyce and his sons. He loved having arguments with them; loved having them there, and was so proud of everything they did. I remember how terribly pleased and touched he was, when Michael made a pair of virginals to give to his mother.

Michael only started doing woodwork in 1946, after we were married, and he made his first clavichord in 1947. He bought a clavichord from Henry Lamb in 1944 because a flat I had before we married was too small for a piano. Henry Lamb advised him to get advice about tuning from Thomas Goff, and Thomas Goff thought Michael could make a better one himself; so he made the first of many in 1947, the year Lucius was born. The next instrument he made was the virginals, with a double manual. The virginals were used for a year in a London hotel, which laid on an Elizabethan evening with appropriate food and music.

You certainly had an extraordinarily talented husband – as his friend Stephen McWatters stressed.[1] Had Michael prepared you for the relationship you have described between father and sons?

152

Not at all. Michael hadn't read his father's books when I met him first, and that's extraordinary. They just knew he wrote, and they didn't read his books. Michael started round about then because he sometimes read me Joyce's books aloud. We read *The Moonlight* on our honeymoon.

If Joyce Cary thought so highly of his sons' opinions, I imagine he was hurt that they didn't read his books – though too proud to show it.

No. I don't think this. And they did read them as they grew up.

I do have the feeling of Joyce having very changeable moods often. He could be wonderful company; he loved having people to come in to have drinks, and he loved being admired, which people of course do. He expanded. But he also had another side of him, which would be sometimes very gloomy and depressed and sad.

Do you think he had been very strict with his children?

Not really. I think he was probably stricter with his children than he ever was with the grandchildren. He was very, very nice to my children – to his grandchildren, and very interested in them. He did not like to be left alone with small children when he got ill, in case they fell and he could not rescue them.

We went to 12 Parks Road for all the Easters, and all the Christmases. Joyce was a great traditionalist. I am sure it was Trudy who started the customs, but once they were started they had to be kept up and mustn't be changed.

Where do you think Trudy got them from?

From her mother, who was German. Her maiden name was Wolff. I'm sure it was her mother who had her children acting plays and learning music, and Trudy did the same. When they were children they lived in Chile, where Trudy's father [*William Ogilvie*] was building railways. He was a Scot.

Joyce organized his life marvellously. He had the 'piggers' up at the top, and everybody knew he went up there after breakfast. He always had breakfast at the same time – at half-past eight I think it was. After breakfast he went up and wrote until about twelve, and then he came down and said, 'Will you come on my walk?' They didn't really want to, but one of them always did go and walk in the Parks with him. He'd have his lunch at about one, and then he'd work again in the afternooon. But he never worked in the evening. In the evening they used to play the piano – he'd only listen. He only had about one song, 'My old man's a dustman'; he used to sing that. But he loved having discussions at night, or hearing them play or listen to their concerts. He had dinner at about seven thirty.

Did he still dress for dinner when you knew him?

No. But everybody was always tidy for dinner, and it was always a rather formal dinner. After Trudy died it still was. He stopped having puddings then; they used to have puddings when the children were younger. But he did like it to be formal; he liked to have something, and then something, and then a savoury. And he'd have wine, and the table would be nicely laid with silver. Joyce liked the boys to be properly dressed, and used to despair of Michael's untidy clothes.

What I think is interesting is that, when they first lived in Oxford, and had very little money, Joyce luckily had his father-in-law who liked him, and supported them, and they did have a nurse, who took the children for walks. (I suppose nurses were very cheap then.) He lived a very organized, routine life. He slept very badly, but he never complained about it. He said, 'If I'm not sleeping, I rest; I don't work.' And of course, he was wonderful when he became ill.

The first time that we knew about it was in 1955, which was also the first time he saw Kate; she was born on 27 January '55, when he was lecturing in Greece. When he came back from Greece he came to stay with us, in Blackheath, and when he got up after dinner, he fell. He thought it was because his leg had gone to sleep, and what hurt him then was not so much that he fell but that he hit his head on something. Michael was very worried about him, and hired a car and drove him back to Oxford. That was the beginning of it all. It started with the big muscles of his leg. He tried all these awful things to try to cure it, like snake venom. He was frightfully brave about it; very uncomplaining.

He had been terribly knocked by Trudy's death, and then he went to America. He had been reluctantly persuaded to go for this lecture tour, and it absolutely set him on his feet. He hadn't realized how much people had read and enjoyed his books, and how good their questions about them would be. Some said that reading his books had changed their lives. He came back rather inspired by it all, and that's when he started to make all sorts of new friends. That's when he got to know Wendy Purdie, who later went to Africa to plant trees. And that was when he met Gerald Wilde, who amused him enormously. People used to think Gulley Jimson was modelled on Gerald, but Gulley came first.

Were you yourself really fond of him?

Yes, very. He was a very up and down person. He used to get very gloomy and depressed. I can see him sitting sometimes at breakfast, sunk in thought about something. I remember once saying something about his family, his ancestors, and he said, 'Oh, they're a very dull family, really.' That was not what he really thought, but he did at that minute. He could be very depressed and gloomy at times.

It seems important to stress that, as so much was made of his zest and exuberance, when he was at the height of his fame.
Did he ever talk to you about his work?

No. But he had all these themes and ideas, that he would repeat. One was 'The death of the symbol', and he'd tell about the artist who painted the girl on the swing, and suddenly nobody wanted to buy his paintings. He'd go on saying this, in various versions, over and over again.

That artist became the father of Gulley Jimson in The Horse's Mouth, *as you doubtless know. Did he ever discuss his novels with you?*

No, never. And I don't think he did with his sons. He often talked of the importance of imagination. In all the books it is the person with imagination who is at the centre of the action.

So he wanted you to understand his themes and ideas, which would prepare you to appreciate the novels. But he wanted your reading of the novels to be your own experience. That is what I would have expected.

NOTES

Isabel Cary (née Leslie) was born in 1913 in Johannesburg, and when she was five her family moved to a farm near the village of Zwartruggens. Her father was killed soon after in a railway accident, but her mother stayed on, and she was brought up in this very isolated place. She went to school in Johannesburg, and at seventeen came to England. From 1933-36 she read Modern Greats at Somerville College, Oxford and, after doing the Mental Health Certificate at the School of Economics, she became a Psychiatric Social Worker. She then went to America, but returned to England when the war started, and was working in the psychiatric clinic in the Middlesex Hospital when, in 1943, she met Michael Cary. They married in 1946, and their children are Lucius (born in 1947), Tristram (1949), Anthony (1953), Kate (1955), and Richard (who was adopted, 1957).

Lady Cary kindly agreed, on 6 January 1988, that this record of our interview, and also Sir Michael's (item 20), might be published.

   1. In item 8.

36

Memories of a
Daughter-in-Law

Margaret Robertson

This item developed by correspondence from an interview in Cambridge on 14 October 1987.

Joyce Cary's youngest son, George, was born on 12th August 1927. He went up to Trinity College, Cambridge, in 1945 as a scholar from Eton, where he had been admitted as a scholar. He then went on to gain a 1st class in Part 1 of the Classical Tripos in 1947, followed by a 1st class the following year in Part 2 of the Modern and Medieval Languages Tripos.

It was while George was up at Cambridge that I first met him and the Cary family, owing to the fact that my mother wanted somebody to coach my younger brothers in the holidays. George came both to my home in Wiltshire and on a ski-ing holiday to Gstaad in Switzerland. We were married on 23 July 1949.

Where were you married?

In the Spanish Catholic Church in Warwick Street (off Regent Street) in London. I made it difficult for everyone by choosing to be married there, since the reception was in Chelsea. My father was not a churchgoer, but during the 1930s, when he was British Minister in Vienna, my mother became a Roman Catholic, and I was brought up in her faith.

Did Joyce Cary ever discuss religious belief with you?

He said he was glad that I did go to church. He compared the support it gave me in confession with that of a psychiatrist, which seemed to me at the time a surprising remark.

I shall always remember the startled look on the face of my mother's solicitor in London, when Joyce came with us to discuss our Marriage Settlement and he said, 'Of course we never left our stock certificates with our solicitor; they would not have been safe!'

What was your own first impression of Joyce Cary?

As having Irish eyes – he was not typical of the English in Oxford. I first met him when invited to their home, and he began telling me stories about his Irish ancestors, making them sound rather wild (at which Trudy looked worried). But he had lovely ways of telling a story.

Did you feel that his wife rather restrained him?

I don't know, but she was certainly devoted. George felt that she was overworked. He was very close to his mother.

And his father – what did he think of his books?

I don't think he read them. But when he came to coach my brothers, and met my family, we started reading his father's books. I don't recognize Joyce's family in his novels – as one does with Evelyn Waugh, for example.

Do you think his other sons read his books?

I think Tristram did. But I always remember the story about Michael, who said of one of his novels, 'It reads well in German.'[1]

Did you ever discuss his books, or literature generally, with him?

I remember that he talked about Tolstoy, and his ideas about *Anna Karenina*. But I loved best the glimpses of life in Ireland that he gave me, in the many anecdotes about his family. There was a freshness and originality about the way he spoke – especially when he spoke about Ireland – that made him stand out as different from his Oxford surroundings.

It was clear that Ireland meant a great deal to Joyce and that his childhood there had been a happy one. In a letter to me dated 4th November 1956 he writes: 'The Cromwell House article has come out in the New Yorker for 3rd November. It is about Uncle Tristram and Aunt Doll at Cromwell House, where Jack and I used to spend so much of our time as children.[2] I hope you will read it because it gives a picture of a quite unusual world, which has now disappeared, and it links Christopher with his ancestry.'

Our son was born on 23rd April 1950 and we christened him Christopher Alexander George. George had first started to be interested in Alexander the Great while still at Eton; and in 1950 he was awarded a Research Fellowship at Trinity College, Cambridge, after submitting his dissertation on 'The Medieval Alexander', a study of the Medieval legends about Alexander the Great. After his death it was published as a book by the Cambridge University Press (in 1956). This gave Joyce great pleasure and he wrote to me on 20th January 1957: 'What very good news about George's book. I am simply delighted that the poor boy is to have something of the name he deserved, for certainly his name is now established and I feel a great deal is due to you and Donald for your efforts in getting the book published.'

Christopher was only two and a half when George died on 9th January 1953. I shall always remember the way Joyce tried to comfort me by saying that George had had a full and normal life although he only lived to twenty-five.

Professor Donald Robertson, your second husband, clearly wrote the tribute to George, signed 'D. S. R.', in The Cambridge Review *of 14 February 1953;[3] and it certainly stresses the fullness of his life and interests. It mentions your holiday in North Africa together, which I am sure greatly interested Joyce Cary.*

NOTES

Margaret Ann Robertson was the daughter of Sir Eric Phipps. She was born in Paris in 1925, and lived in Vienna from the age of three until 1933, when her father became British Ambassador in Berlin, until 1937, when he was transferred to Paris; she was at a French convent in England from 1935 to 1939. Before she became engaged to George Cary, in 1948, she was planning to go to the Courtauld Institute. But later she took a degree in Modern Languages (in 1973), as a 'mature student', at Newnham College Cambridge.

On 10 December 1987 she kindly agreed to the publication of this item.

1. It was *The African Witch*, as Joyce Cary revealed in a letter of 2 Nov. 1938 (item 16).

2. The article is republished in *Selected Essays*, pp. 43-65.

3. Professor D.S. Robertson was Regius Professor of Greek at Cambridge, Fellow of Trinity College.

37

'He'd asked for a history scholar'

Cecilia Dick

This interview took place in Oxford on 8 September 1967.

I met him in 1950, well before the end of the academic year – that is, nearer January than June. The occasion was that he'd asked Anne Whiteman for a history scholar to do some simple research. It concerned ensuring that Chester [*in the second trilogy*] could not be confused with Lloyd George, by checking that facts concerning Chester did not tally. They were such questions as: 'Was there a Ministry of Production?' If there was not, then Cary would have this. Or: 'What exactly did Lloyd George think about supporting French policy at a given time?' He was already talking about *Not Honour More* in 1950. I remember his telling me that he'd woken up in the night and worked out a particular scene for *Not Honour More*, which had altered all the previous conception. *Prisoner of Grace* was well planned by then – that is, by 1950.

I was amazed to learn that Mrs Cary had died only in December 1949. It confirmed what I had always thought: that it was impossible to rock him. He talked a lot about her, and of his extreme loneliness. but he fixed up his life – that is, he saw certain people at fixed times.

He went to America in January 1951. This was before I became engaged, and Joyce asked David Cecil to 'look after' me. That is, he felt very paternal (avuncular or what have you) about me. I was married in the summer of '51, and was in America until the summer of '52 or thereabouts. In February '53 I moved house, and then he asked if he could come to tea regularly once a week, on Tuesdays. He would stay until supper was on the table, and then left.

Would you say more about your view that it was impossible to rock him?

He insisted for example, that his mother's death had not wrecked his life at all. I don't think he had any special relationship with his father;

but I have a feeling that his father had been a gay dog, and that Joyce in some way approved. Somehow I think he adjusted early to being a 'rock'.

What sort of woman did he most admire, do you think?

He liked women intelligent, and he liked them with style – able to come into a room with a grand entrance; women like one of Hemingway's wives, whom he met. He recalled the prostitutes of his French student days with admiration and enthusiasm. He thought there should be prostitutes and they are good and kind. I think he was flattered by being taken up by these women. They were so good to the students, etc, he said. He talked of Marguritte.[1]

Would you say that Edith Haggard[2] had style, in his view?

I agree that she did, but not of the sort Joyce most admired. I did not have it either.

How did he treat other women whom he employed?

Edith Millen kept her place. She assumed a professional role, and did not mix with visitors. Joyce did have an idea of the place of the housekeeper etc. But certainly he was friendly from the start with me; very direct. He looked you straight in the eye.

Basic to the female nature, he thought, was that women are masochists and want to be beaten – not beaten in a physical sense, of course. He talked a lot about his wife, and this idea related to what he thought about her: she was always boiling up into a state, which led to the beating, which Joyce thought was what she wanted.

Have you any idea of his views on sexual relations outside marriage?

He talked a lot about the sex relations of his friends and others. He could see cases where he thought special relations were justified.

I thought him wholly amoral. Much of his conversation was amoral. For example, one of many stories that he repeated often concerned Dylan Thomas and his wife Caitlin, who would dance solo at parties and this infuriated Dylan. There was no moral attitude in Joyce's comments. He enjoyed it as a human situation.

Yet he did take moral attitudes. For example, you shouldn't allow your daughter to slap you, which I did allow, if my child felt annoyed with me. I remember too, when Michael's child Anthony was staying there, and at lunch, there was a scene, and he was smacked and put out of the room, where he cried. He was a very small child, but Joyce approved of the treatment. The child had to be taught. But I must say that he was very good with children. His manner was so easy and direct.

What do you think of his work?

I don't like much of his work. I think he treats people coldly, objectively. The best bits of his books are those where he has painted the scene, as a painter would. But his characters are rather nasty. I remember his telling me that *Not Honour More* was about the problem of good and evil, which I thought an incredible answer to my question.

He got his ideas into pigeon holes, and they were rather simple. I thought him naive. His religion was simply that goodness exists, and that is God. He was convinced that all women are masochists; that all women would like to be at home doing the flowers, and he thought it terrible that all these other pressures were put upon them to do other things. His views were rather nineteenth century.

Might it possibly be truer to say that he believed a high standard of civilization could best find expression in and through the home; and that he thought it tragic that women's power to create and develop this, and the importance of their role in doing so, were not recognized?

That seems quite possible.

NOTES

Mrs C.R. Dick, MA, was a student and subsequently Lecturer at Lady Margaret Hall, Oxford, and is a fellow of Wolfson College.

On 16 December 1987, Mrs Dick kindly agreed to the publication of this interview.

1. The girl described by Middleton Murry in *Between Two Worlds* (1935), and by Cary in MS. Cary 253/N.9.

2. See item 47.

38

The Years Following my
Mother's Death

Tristram Cary

This item was compiled in November 1987, from a tape recording and letters
(continuing item 22).

*Your earlier account reveals how traumatic your mother's illness and
death would have been for your father. For that reason alone, it is
significant, I think, that the first book published after she died has the
title* Prisoner of Grace. *Until three months before, perhaps the month
before only, it was called 'The Turkish House'.*[1] *I wonder whether*
Prisoner of Grace *has any particular significance for you as a title. I
wonder also about the significance of Machiavelli in this book. You have
told me that Machiavelli was the political writer in whom your father was
most interested. Do you think he was identifying with Nina, in chapter 77
of* Prisoner of Grace, *where she discusses Chester Nimmo's '"machiavel-
lian tactics"'? You may recall that the chapter ends with the general
observation that* 'People don't need to be hypocrites. They can so easily
"make" themselves believe anything they fancy.'

To answer your question adequately, I'd have to re-read *Prisoner of
Grace*, which I've not done for a long time, and consider it properly; so
I can't really give an adequate answer. Certainly, when I was reading
philosophy myself, in 1947-48, he used to talk about Machiavelli.[2]
    Joyce always had a soft spot for villains, and of course he regarded
Machiavelli as not really a villain himself, but a political theorist that
he admired for his ingenuity. I don't know whether Nina was
speaking for Joyce in that line, 'People don't need to be hypocrites.'
But certainly he felt that everybody had their place. Words like
'phoney' he didn't think about, because he thought that the charlatan
and the cheat, in a way, are just as genuine human beings, but they're
playing a different sort of game. That was one of his strong characteristics: that he had a very soft spot for villainy of one sort or another.

163

But he was absolutely straight himself. He could write very well about unscrupulous characters, but he was very far from unscrupulous himself. In his early life, of course, he had met a great many fairly unscrupulous people.

Your mother's musical gifts were clearly inherited by her sons. Do you think your father learned from them also – I mean in a theoretical way? Do you, for example, see special significance in these words, concerning uncomprehending critics: 'My wife says why don't you tell them what you're doing. But this is like asking a composer to put his music into words – a translation that falsifies the whole construction.'[3] *Could he have been trying, in a tremendously broad way, to give his novel series something of the form of a symphony? This idea seems to me strengthened by other remarks, in essays and interviews, as when he says of* To Be a Pilgrim: 'Lucy was only one character, one motive in the symphony.'[4]

I don't think he thought of it in that way. [...] Your symphonic idea may be the sort of romantic notion that he had, but the symphony itself of course is pretty vague. The heavier weight cyclic symphonies with a theme running through them tend to come in the romantic and late romantic time. Very often the finale of an eighteenth century symphony was simply a jolly piece of music to send people home with a tune in their ears. It's hard to know what Joyce's attitude to music was. But he certainly was not someone who could relish the idea of sitting through long symphonies. He was not a great concert goer; he left that to my mother. [...] But it's certainly a fascinating idea that the whole of his corpus of work could be regarded in a way as one piece. [...]

When I turned into some sort of a composer, he was always asking questions, and again, showed great interest in the techniques involved. On one or two occasions, he actually asked my advice, whether a person would say this; whether it was technically viable to say a certain thing, in referring to a piece of music. We used to have long conversations about the sort of parallelism between the arts; whether you could talk about music or writing in terms of other arts. I used to think that you could, and find more parallelism than was there. He always warned me of the dangers of this, and, although in general there is a creative parallel, he said that every art has its own rules. For example. when you are reading a book you can turn back; you can go back to page 100 and find out what happened. But when you're listening to a piece of music the thing goes by, and the whole thing takes place in the memory, and in the anticipation. It's a different sort of art form. The only sort of parallel tag that he mentioned was with *The Moonlight*, as a kind of answer to Tolstoy's *Kreutzer Sonata*. But I think that was not to be taken very deep.

Probably not in musical terms. But he does say in his prefatory essay to The Moonlight *that he began writing an answer to Tolstoy's novel immediately on reading it, and his notes concerning an 'anti-*Kreutzer Sonata*' date from 1931, which is the date inscribed in his copy of* The Kreutzer Sonata *novel, so that it influenced all his writing. I should have thought that the choice of title by each novelist must relate to his conception (however shallow or unacceptable to a musician) of the meaning and effect of these pieces of music.*

When I started writing music seriously, he did ask me quite a lot about it, and he was very interested in Mann's *Doctor Faustus*, and asked me whether I thought the character depicted there was particularly valid (Schoenberg of course being Mann's reference in that book). Joyce was very pleased that I was going in for some sort of artistic career, and he probably hung on my words much more than he should have, because I was only a student, just starting out really.

He was very pleased when I was adult and we could go out for walks in the Parks and talk, more or less straight talk between two artists about what they were doing. He was very pleased that things had developed to that stage, and it was very tragic of course that we couldn't go on talking; that he died before I'd really got going. Apart from a few small concert pieces, things like sonatas, played at the Wigmore Hall, most of the music of mine that he heard was in the service of something else: film music or radio music with literary texts. When he was very ill he went to see *The Ladykillers*, which was the first feature film that I did; he quite enjoyed that.

He was sometimes a hard conversationalist, because he would go off into a brown study; he would just go off and disappear from the conversation. You knew that there was something going on inside and there wasn't any point going on talking. He had a special way of saying, 'Yes, Yes,' which meant that he wasn't listening at all, but 'Keep talking'; and one got the habit of drifting off. Then you'd stop and he'd stop saying 'Yes', and it meant that for the moment there was going to be no communication. I would sometimes be rather impatient as a young man – young and enthusiastic. I would start on some explanation that he had actually asked for. He'd say: 'Tell me so and so.' And I'd get myself together and start on a long explanation; halfway through it he would obviously be somewhere else completely, and being young and impatient I would say, 'Well, hell, what's the point of going into this?' But then he would often come back to it later and really pay attention and want to know.

So I wish it had all gone on longer. It was a terrible time from '49 when my mother died until '57 when my father died, with George dying in the middle. And I was trying to get my career going as well. All those agonizing trips down to Oxford went on. And of course the conversations became less coherent and more urgently practical like how you could communicate at all on any level. So it's difficult to say when serious conversations with those lovely walks in the Park and all that really stops, because from the time that Mrs Lightburne was living in the house and the time that Edith Millen was working there, everything was different really. I was rushing down from London and one didn't have these conversations. So there's a kind of lack of coherence about the time when I was in my early to middle twenties, and becoming much more grown-up and much more mature in my attitudes, when conversations with Joyce would have been so tremendously valuable. And possibly conversations with me would have been valued by him in a musical context, when it all had to stop.

The fact that you cared so much makes his death all the more tragic. Would you end in whatever way you think best – perhaps regarding the way you think he deserves to be remembered?

What a hard question! When you are somebody's child, your whole attitude is coloured by the fact that you've known them on a different level. And very often when I meet people and they talk about Joyce, the impression one gets is different from one's own, in the sense that he made a different impression on outside people.

But one of the great things I think about Joyce is his tremendous originality. His style isn't particularly way-out. I don't mean it in that sense, but originality in the sense that he thought everything out for himself. When he made that joke about being self-educated at Clifton and Trinity he really meant it, in the sense that he took from literature, and history, and biography what he needed, and he thought everything out for himself. He leant very little. Apart from his great love of the nineteenth century novel and particular writers like Hardy, all his philosophy (and he read lots of philosophy of course) was his own. He really did come through completely with his own ideas.

So you've got someone who is a real original, living in that academic and knowledgeable, creative hothouse of Oxford. He didn't join any of the streams. He had a few academic friends but not many; he wasn't part of the academic society at all. He detested the literary mainstream; things like Foyle's literary luncheons. When he became famous he didn't want to join the London literary stream at all. And yet he made an instant appeal to everybody. His honesty absolutely shone through, so that when he had radio interviews, or in conversation, he made friends very easily, because he didn't force anything. He was a completely unforced sort of person.

He was very old-fashioned in many ways; he was an old-fashioned gentleman; he wanted to dress right and be right for his occasions. But I think of the American thing; his impression in America, both ways round. He was enchanted by the Americans and their love of life and the way they did things, and he was an instant success – when he got the freedom of the city of New Orleans, and was shown round the meat yards of Chicago by the boss of the meat yards personally. He was very touched by all these things, but of course they felt extremely honoured too. And so he was a very much loved man by all sorts of people who hardly really knew him. Nowadays, when you talk to people about Joyce, there's never any sort of sense that they're holding back the bad bits, which you do get with some people, trying to find nice things to say. People don't have to try to find nice things to say about Joyce, because it's very easy.

One of the strongest things of course was his lack of bitterness. I mean, he didn't succeed really till the end, when my mother had died and he was going to die shortly. He had many years of fighting against indifference – as most artists do; most of us aren't very successful when you come down to it. But he gave out a tremendous lesson in not being bitter about it. I remember he said to me very early: you mustn't expect the people of Liverpool to like your string quartets. It's not their fault for not liking them. Why should they? They prefer their dance music and so forth. In a way it's your fault for writing a string quartet. You have to persuade people to like your work, and you mustn't get embittered at failure or things going wrong.

That was the lesson of Gulley Jimson, of course. Most people read this book as a comic book. But it's not a comic book at all. It's about a man who is desperately fighting the tendency for artists to get bitter about not succeeding, and it turning in on them and ruining their work. So Gulley took it out on other things. But he didn't take it out on his work.

I don't really know how to sum it all up. He'll probably never be a hugely popular writer because he doesn't have that kind of thing in his writing. In a way he's a very quiet writer. That's why there haven't been splashy television serials and that kind of thing, though there may be. He might suddenly take off in a new age, and perhaps that will happen fairly soon. His fans are real fans. I mean, he's got a solid core of readers around the world who really adore his work, and probably adore it above a whole lot of others. I know from my share of the royalties coming in that, it's not an enormous sale, obviously, but it's a steady sale coming in around the world.

What else can I say? He was in a way an innocent. By that I mean that he could clear everything away at will and look at the world like a child – and he impressed on me that it was very important for an artist to be able to do this – look at a problem as if it were the first one in the world and think it through from the beginning. But he did absorb new information, right up to his final decline, with the innocence and enthusiasm of a schoolboy, and he never employed cunning or snide methods to get his way – I can't recall a single instance of being conned into something by the kind of trickery lots of parents use – all propositions were perfectly straight, and his orders and intentions were always crystal clear.

He approved of other people being outrageous in a way, but he didn't want to be himself. One example I can think of is S.B.P. Mace, who used to be a figure in Oxford, and always dressed in very colourful clothes, and Joyce said, 'I admire that. I think they're tremendous, those clothes, but I couldn't possibly wear such clothes myself.'

I am reminded of his early notes, that life is 'a battle with the code'; 'a battle by the rules which are simply legal'.[5] *Does his originality lie in the way he challenges us to examine our rules and codes; or in the faith by which he claimed to live and write; or essentially in both?*

NOTES

See item 22 for biographical note.

1. See notes in MS. Cary 284/P.108 headed 'Sept.4.49' concerning Nina 'In Turkish House'; cf. 'Prisoner of Grace Beginning *Nov* 1949' on drafts in MS. Cary 118-20, which could date the change of title; MS. Cary 287/N.145 is a maroon-coloured file on which 'The Turkish House' as a title has been cancelled and replaced by *Prisoner of Grace* (later changed to *Prisoners*); MS. Cary 253/N.3 is a file identical with N.145, labelled 'POETRY' and containing love poems to Trudy Cary. My suggestion is that, near her death, Cary and his wife read and sorted his poems and also their letters, in which he calls himself 'a Prisoner' (20 Aug. 1916) and her 'the Lady of Grace' (15 Oct. 1916).

2. Cary C. 918 in the Bodleian Collection, Cary's own copy of *The Prince*, is much annotated in his handwriting of those later years.

3. From a letter to Harper of 8 Nov. 1949, in the Bodleian.

4. *Selected Essays*, p. 8 (Q.7).

5. MS. Cary 256/S.4.K.

Part III

International
Fame

39

From the Editor of
Adam International Review

Miron Grindea

This contribution was gratefully received in January 1988.

Oddly enough, it was during one of my visits to Paris, shortly after the liberation of France, that I first heard of Joyce Cary's writing. René and Christine Lalou, both well-known literary critics and translators, asked me whether I could supply them with the more recent works of fiction and with Cary's novels in particular; (at that time it was difficult for them to buy foreign books). In *Les Nouvelles Littéraires*, René Lalou reviewed *Mister Johnson* as 'Le livre de la semaine';[1] it had been translated by Yvonne Davet, whose translation of *Herself Surprised* appeared in 1954 (as *Sara*). Like them, Yvonne Davet (who was for many years Gide's secretary), contributed greatly to making Cary's work appreciated in France. In a letter she expressed her 'vive admiration' for *Prisoner of Grace*, 'très riche d'observations psychologiques neuves et subtiles, admiration aussi pour l'art de ce roman, l'habileté de l'éclairage indirect.'

The special issue of *Adam* devoted entirely to Joyce Cary (no. 212-213 December 1950) gave him great joy. He spoke delightedly of Nicolas Bentley's drawing, which appeared on the front cover: 'Thank you very much for the original – I have thanked Bentley, who wrote me a letter, which is itself a work of art.' He never forgot during his lectures in the USA to speak of the journal. Writing from America on December 23rd 1953, he said: 'I am sorry to hear that *Adam* has been missing a beat. I have talked about your paper over here. I was very shocked to hear of Dylan's death and I shall write you a note if it is not too late. He was a very important poet and will grow bigger in the landscape of time.'

He spotted a serious mistake in one of the conversations with Lord David Cecil; there was a word 'scientist' instead of Aquinas, and he pointed out, 'it does not make much much sense', but very gently

171

took the blame. 'It's my fault,' he wrote, 'I ought to have corrected it
in the proof. I am a lazy devil about any past work. I am always
looking forward to the new. Your new numbers (on Christopher Fry
and Jean-Louis Barrault) are v. good. Have you done a number on Ivy
Compton Burnett? She is an interesting person. Or Graham Greene;
his first book is his best.' Once again he informed me that 'I
mentioned *Adam* often in the USA. It might be a good plan to send
copies of one or two good numbers to members of the English
departments at some of the American universities.' I intended to
publish some more work of his but at that time he was under extreme
pressure writing new prefaces to a number of his novels. On May 24th
1952 he wrote: 'Just now I am polishing some short stories. My
secretary, working on the 8th version of one, says, with a sigh, they
are as bad as verse.' The last letter I received from him at Christmas
1956, when his hands were suspended in the most complicated and
poignant system of wires one could imagine, but he was still heroically
determined to use one of his hands. He wrote, 'If you want anything
more, ask me. I have now finished six prefaces for the new edition next
year.'

The fact that his novels were becoming better known in Europe was
a source of increasing satisfaction. It was in Italy that his first trilogy
first appeared in one volume, under the title *Tre modi di peccare* (July
1953). Like *Les Nouvelles Littéraires*, *La Fiera letteraria* was drawing
attention to him in reviews and articles, notably by Giacomo Antonini, as 'Joyce Cary: un trittico puritano.'[2]

Answering *Adam*'s questionnaire on l'Entente Cordiale, Cary
alluded to a member of the House of Lords who, in a letter to *The
Times*, had deplored the increasing usage of the French language as a
major factor contributing to this country's downfall, and continued: 'I
agree that any serious decline in the use of the French language would
be an immense loss of civilisation, but I don't think that that is very
likely. French literature is too rich. As for getting the English and
French to understand each other, there are already plenty of under-
standers on both sides. That immense difference (which Monsieur
André Siegfried has so eloquently pointed out [in *Adam*]) between the
Latin education and the Anglo-Saxon makes it easy for wilful misun-
derstanding to create prejudice. True, their favourite cliché – Anglo-
Saxon want of form and logic, French insularity and lack of sense – are
getting rather threadbare, but it is wonderful how they are still made
to serve a columnist short of matter and time.' He was reticent,
though, when it came to writing on French literature: 'I should not
venture on a critique of the French novel. I have read many of the

masterpieces but I am in no position to judge them. I think you will find all you want in the prefaces. If you can't have them, I'll write you something to the point about the function of the novel.'

I last saw him in February 1957, two months before his tragic end. His face was still serene, his eyes expressing resignation and calm. I couldn't possibly tax his energy by asking questions about the formative years he had spent in Paris, something which I simply neglected to ask on my previous visits to 12 Parks Rd. I could never forgive myself though for having hesitated to ask him everything he might have told me about Marc-André Raffalovich, the extraordinary character who had known both Mallarmé and Huysmans. Raffalovich was so ugly that his own mother would not see him when he grew up. He took refuge in writing, and his book on *Uranisme et unisexualité* had a great impact on the decadent literature of the period. Cary's recollections of this self-hating Jew converted to catholicism would have been invaluable, but they may still come to light in a book on Joyce Cary and France.[3] The manuscripts zealously kept in the Bodleian Library at Oxford would be a rich source of information.

When I wrote my 'Envoi' in the Joyce Cary number of *Adam*, I hoped, in my naivety, that the High Priests of the Swedish Academy might soon have considered him as an important candidate for the Nobel Prize. Sadly, that did not happen, though Herbert Tingsten, editor of *Dagens Nyheter*, ensured that he was well known and appreciated in Sweden.

NOTES

Miron Grindea (1909-) was born in Rumania, and in 1941 launched the Anglo-French Literary Magazine *Adam*, to which many of the greatest writers of our time have contributed – Gide, Cocteau, Eliot, for example. He has lectured at many universities, in England, Asia, Canada, and the United States, and he was awarded an Honorary D.Litt. at the University of Canterbury in 1985. The French gave him the Legion d'Honneur in 1978 and he was made Commandeur de l'Ordre des Arts et Lettres in 1986; he then also received an OBE. He has lived in England since 1939.

1. Paris, 26 February, 1953, p. 3; for his review of *La Bouche du Cheval*, see the issue of 28 October 1954.

2. (Rome, 7 August 1955), p. 2; for other articles on Cary by Antonini see *La Fiera letteraria* (1 January 1953), p. 6; (14 February 1954), pp. 1-2; (19 July 1955), pp. 5-6.

3. For evidence that Raffalovich was the prototype for Nussbaum, see *Castle Corner*, p. 275.

40

Links with Harper

John Fischer

This interview took place in New York on 20 July 1967.

How did Cary's association with Harper actually begin?[1]

Elizabeth Lawrence suggested that Harper should publish *The Moon-light*.[2]

That is what I assumed from the Harper letters in the Bodleian. She certainly evoked a wonderful response in Cary, about his work, through those letters.

She is a very sweet, sensitive, and kindly person.

But the letter I remember most vividly is in fact your own; the one in which you describe your first meeting with Cary, in September 1949. For the first time in your life, you said, you felt that you had met a genuine 18-carat genius.

Did I say that? I hope it doesn't sound too extravagant.

I don't think so. Do you still have as high an opinion of Cary?

I believe I do. But I don't expect many people in Oxford would agree with me. Joyce Cary always thought he had been hardly done by in Oxford. He hoped that Trinity might have made him a fellow. Oxford didn't take Cary seriously.

Did you ever discuss Memoir of the Bobotes *with him?*

I did. But Cary thought it juvenile.

What about his painting?

He couldn't say what he had to say in the medium of painting. He thought he would never be more than a second-rate artist. I thought his paintings early post-impressionist, reflecting a juvenile form of cubism. Cary was also against painting as a limited medium. The Harper fragment[3] shows the parallel between writing and painting. But Cary approached writing as an artist. He talked about the methods of 'getting colours on the palette first'. That is, he talked in terms of getting patches of colour. His description of Gulley's painting was of patches of colour, and he thought of a novelist's technique in the same way. He wasn't thinking so much of the composition of the subject, with the central theme in a key scene round which the rest built; but of colour.

Presumably he thought of colour as the most direct way of conveying feeling. Did he ever talk with you about Tolstoy?

Yes. He talked often about Tolstoy's moral theory and of his admiration of Tolstoy as a novelist.

Did he discuss his religious ideas with you?

Yes, a lot, because our children were all at the age of needing religious ideas clarified. We had shortly before joined the Unitarian church, and Joyce talked at the Unitarian church at White Plains, at least once. White Plains, where we live, is about thirty-five miles out of the city. Joyce discussed religion with my wife and me, and also with the children, with whom he used to go for walks around White Plains, when he stayed with us there. You may know the magazine article where he talked about our daughter Sara.

'A Child's Religion', published in Vogue.[4] *Can you recall anything Cary said about his method of putting his ideas across in his novels?*

He talked a lot about *To Be a Pilgrim* in technical terms, and about cross-references. He thought of that novel as a major exposition of his religious ideas, which he wanted to set in juxtaposition to his aesthetic ideas. He thought all three books of that trilogy were varieties of religious expression.

No doubt he had William James's Varieties of Religious Experience *in mind when he said that. I always think that the way he refers to James's book in his preface to* The African Witch *is highly significant, almost as if he were begging readers to see how profoundly it had influenced him.*

Certainly his own annotated copy in the Bodleian leaves no doubt that it had. Did he ever discuss Judaism with you?

No. But he used to visit a Jewish neighbour, Bernard Lubar, who was a playwright. He used to talk to Bernie about dramatizing the novels, and possibly religion came into their conversation.

Cary had all the prejudices of his time and class; he would have denied that he had conscious intellectual prejudices against Jews, but they were there. He was always consciously judging his subconscious.

Do you think he studied the subconscious through children?

Yes. Walking with the children he would tell stories about the houses with eyes. He used visual ideas. He seemed to like talking to children, because he thought it stimulated his ideas. You should talk to my daughters about him. I'm sure we can arrange it.[5]

Now could you tell me more about his relationship with Harper's, and with you?

I don't think Cary had had much editorial help before. But publishers in England tend not to develop close relations – except in firms influenced from America, as with Eliot's. When I met him he was working on the second trilogy. He was at work when I arrived on the morning train. He immediately suggested a walk in the Parks, and talked hard.

He talked about *boredom* as a creative force in the world, and about his technique, including his use of the historical present, which he defended as an experiment, but rather agreed that it was not a good technique to use. I found him more articulate about his work than most writers. He could outline the second trilogy then; he knew at least that he had a trio as in the first trilogy, and wanted to get into politics. He wanted to portray two kinds of political minds, including the mind common in the civil service and the army. 'Why all this rottenness' was the phrase he used. He sympathized with the Welsh mind as the more realistic, and had in mind both Lloyd George and Nye Bevan.

He told me about meeting Bevan and his wife, Jenny Lee, in a first-class railway carriage (which Cary implied that he normally didn't use, but on this occasion the train was too full in the second class). He was in the same first-class carriage with Bevan and they asked him to move, as they had things to discuss. Cary refused (as *he* usually travelled second). There was a bit of a scene, and then they finally unpacked the hamper they had with them. It contained wine and many delicacies, and Cary thought they were abashed to let him see Labour leaders enjoying themselves so opulently. I *think* he told me this story at our first meeting, though I can't be sure.

It seems likely to have been in his mind, as he was already shaping the second trilogy. Did you discuss his own political views?

Cary thought of himself as a member of the Liberal party, and admired Lloyd George, though he disapproved of unsavoury aspects. I personally think that his political ideas were out of date. But Cary had normal human vanities, and liked to think of himself as more important politically than he was.

What about The Case for African Freedom? *In the enlarged edition, in 1944, he says that his argument in the 1941 edition has met with so much support in many different circles that he is glad of the chance to develop it, and to relate it to recent discussion on post-war policy.*

Perhaps *The Case for African Freedom* was more influential in England than is generally realized. He was trying hard to understand American politics when he stayed here in 1951. I think it was during the last month of his stay that I left Harper's to work with Adlai Stevenson (the political leader), and was not then in Harper's office in New York but in Springfield.

You seem to have thought his religious ideas more interesting than his politics, because you urged him to write a book on religion.

I think a book on religion would have been important.

What did you think of him in a personal way?

He was a person of a great deal of charm and quite handsome, even when I met him, when his age would have been – sixty-one. He was still somewhat military in bearing. He took good care of himself; never smoked, and drank moderately. Unlike writers generally, he didn't drink coffee constantly. He talked readily on many subjects, and would chat with my wife in the kitchen. He reminisced about his own wife, who had died at the end of '49. She was really quite ill when I was there. She was up and about, but obviously in pain, and touchy.

He talked often later about her, and even then she showed strength of character and charm, but she seemed remote from the conversation. He also talked a lot about his sons, and most about Michael. He had a harpsicord in his study made by Michael, and spoke of him as the brightest member of the family.

While I was visiting him a package of netsukes arrived from a dealer. He must have had fifty to a hundred netsukes in his study. The house was full too of African native weapons, and some of his own; also of his own paintings. It was a comfortable house in a slightly shabby, well lived-in fashion. At that time he was financially comfortable but discussed earlier difficulties. He was unduly grateful to Harper's for bringing him financial security.

Later on he stressed the importance of being able to write without poverty. Like all writers he did tend to sacrifice people to his work. Mrs Cary mentioned that she'd been worried about his health in Africa. He'd got the idea of writing by telling stories to Africans whom he could make laugh, and he liked the audience reaction. He also felt that he had wasted time and energy in teaching himself to write.

One person he became very interested in over here was Eric Hoffer. Hoffer was an orphan. And at an early age he went blind; he was blind from about seven until he was seventeen. Then he got his sight back unexpectedly, and became an insatiable reader, though he'd had little education. He became a fruit-picker, and he panned for gold, and during that time he nearly memorized Montaigne's essays. He retired only a few months ago as a longshoreman. In 1951, Joyce read Hoffer's *The True Believer* while at our house, and on his second trip he wanted to meet Hoffer. They had had some correspondence, and they did spend time together. But when I discussed Joyce with Hoffer on my last trip (it was about June '67), he said some of Joyce's accounts were not accurate. 'He's a liar,' he said. But he said this affectionately.

Joyce was fond of Edith Haggard and grateful to her as an agent,[6] and he talked of Win Davin affectionately to me.[7] The Davins walked to the Trout [Inn] with us when our family were in Oxford, in '54.

Joyce gave me the impression of being attractive to women. He made women he was talking with think they were totally interesting because he gave them all his attention. I had a hunch that he was always concentrating on character analysis.

It seems to me, from his letters and notebooks, that his understanding of women came chiefly from his wife.

It probably did. But I believe that Elizabeth Lawrence understood his work better than his wife did. I felt that he left his wife out of some of his discussion, and got the impression that she depended on him entirely. Of course she was ill then; so it's scarcely fair to judge. Elizabeth was a better fiction editor than I was. She talked for hours to Joyce on professional and technical matters.

Do you think his ideas about symbolism are evident in his own work – in his use of names, for example?

Yes. He was portraying the world in symbolic form. And all his work was didactic, I think. He said it was easy to get a plot, and this is essential to keep people reading. He discussed symbolism with me, and I know that he picked names very carefully. I remember him discussing Dickens's use of names as too obvious.

Did he ever discuss Frank Buchman[8] and Buchmanism with you?

Yes, he did. I remember that the chaplain at Lincoln College was an ardent Buchmanite, and Joyce spoke of him with some scorn.

NOTES

John Fischer (1910-1978) was an associate editor of *Harper's Magazine*, where he was editor in chief from 1953 to 1968. Before that time he was an editor of general books for Harper & Brothers, a European correspondent for United Press, and a Washington reporter with Associated Press. A graduate of the University of Oklahoma, he also attended Oxford University as a Rhodes Scholar. He was the author of many magazine articles, mainly on public affairs; his fifth and last book was the semi-autobiographical *From the High Plains*, published in the year of his death.

Publication of this interview was kindly agreed to in August 1987 by Elizabeth Fischer.

1. This publishing firm was still named Harper & Bros. in 1961, when the correspondence discussed below was given to the Bodleian for the Joyce Cary Collection; it is now named Harper & Row.

2. Cary's editor at Harper's; see item 44.

3. A discarded chapter of *the Horse's Mouth*, published as 'The Old Strife at Plant's', *Harper's Magazine*, CCI (Aug. 1950), 80-96 (S.18).

4. *Vogue* (US), CXXII (Dec. 1953), 86-87 (E.43); see items 42, 52.

5. See items 41, 42.

6. See item 47.

7. See item 67.

8. See item 18, n. 1.

41

At the Fischers' Home

Elizabeth Fischer John Fischer
Nicola Hahn [daughter]
Bernard Lubar [friend]

This discussion took place on 29 July 1967.

[*Jack*:] In 1951, Betty, Bernie, and I were working in local politics, and Joyce's visit coincided. Joyce watched TV for the first time in his life, on election night for these elections. Stevenson was shown giving a speech. Then we went to Democratic headquarters, and Joyce watched American democracy in action.

[*Bernie*:] One of the Democratic workers was explaining politics to Joyce – he was a tough Irishman, and was not content to explain American politics only, but politics generally, as if Joyce knew nothing about politics. But Joyce was a good interviewer, and wouldn't let me interrupt to explain who Joyce was.

[*Jack*:] If we couldn't find Joyce, we could usually guess that he would be talking to the drunken Irish delicatessan of the neighbourhood. He used to talk to Betty in the kitchen while she finished the dishes.

[*Betty*:] I remember that, on his second trip, the last Thursday in November was Thanksgiving Day, and on the day before I was in the kitchen preparing food. Joyce, who had walked from White Plains, came in raving about the weather and the sunset, and was dashed when I exploded that I hadn't time to think about sunsets etc. just then. On this trip he didn't engage me in conversations such as I had enjoyed the first time. I concluded he had found me uninteresting, and felt hurt.

In 1951 he didn't stay too long. But in 1953 I felt that he stayed

180

more for the convenience. I thought he was taking advantage of us to save money. Edith Haggard[1] told me that she got cross at the way Joyce would say that he would love to take her to dinner, but that she knew how he hated crowds; so couldn't they just have a chop at home. After a hard day's work she didn't feel like cooking. I felt that by the second trip he had become hard-headed.

[*Jack*:] I feel that he had the ruthlessness of all artists.

[*Betty*:] In 1954 it was arranged that we should stay with Joyce in Oxford. But when we were in Scotland with the children I got a letter saying that he'd expect us on a certain day, but on the fourth day his son and family would be coming. While we were there he did everything well. He engaged a butler, for example.

[*Nicky*:] With whom I shook hands. And then immediately realized that I'd done the wrong thing.

[*Betty*:] He quite clearly set limits for the duration of our visit beforehand. The date of our departure was set by tickets he had bought for us, to a performance of *Coriolanus* in Stratford. While we were with him, however, he was an excellent host. He had engaged the butler to serve dinner, in addition to his housekeeper, who wakened us with tea each morning, and I loved the luxury of waking up in bed, with a cup in my hand. I think we arrived on a certain day, then stayed two full days, and departed on the fourth.[2]

The children were invited to dine with us, and were brought into the conversation. One evening Lord David Cecil and his wife had dinner with us, and the conversation was wonderful. He told us that Lord David was his closest friend in Oxford, but he wasn't sure that David understood his books.

[*Bernie*:] I had plans to dramatize *The Horse's Mouth* for the stage, and Joyce seemed to like my ideas. I think the book shows unevenness of form, and in some of the characters themselves. I think Joyce anticipated the theatre of the absurd, and he knew about hippies before they happened. In my play there was to be a phone booth as a key device. You were never to see the pictures, because Gulley had to be ahead of his time.

[*Jack*:] He talked about Spinoza as the philosopher to whom he returned again and again, and said: 'I think my religion is really Jewish.' He kept saying that Spinoza embodied his own thought.

[**Betty**:] He told me that his talk at the Unitarian church was 'a gift to me.' He didn't know much about Unitarians, and called it a very Humanitarian religion. His talk was right over the heads of the congregation. Martin Wilbur (a Professor of Oriental Studies) said that Joyce didn't put it across – it wasn't a success at all.

[**Nicky**:] He understood us as children, as no other adult had done. I remember running upstairs after quarrelling with my parents, and meeting Joyce on the stairs. He showed sympathy and understanding of my trouble, but he didn't side with me. This gave me my first insight into tact.

In Oxford Joyce had several desks, one in each room, and sometimes there were more subjects than rooms. He would go as far as he could and then transfer.

[**Bernie**:] I remember that Joyce was surprised that you didn't walk two blocks instead of going in a car.

[**Jack**:] I remember that he told Elizabeth (Lawrence) he was grateful that he could prepare to die.

[*In August 1987, the following, signed Elizabeth Fischer, accompanied her agreement to the publication of the above:*]

Tribute

We had afternoon tea at the Trout Inn,
then walked home through the Oxford Meadows.
As we turned into Parks Road a telegraph boy
rode up from the other end, and stopped at
our gate. We hailed him towards us.

He handed the telegram to our host.
Joyce read the message, thanked the boy,
and said there was no reply.

Then, smiling, he passed the telegram to me.
'Nothing alarming' he commented.

I read aloud to the others, 'ALEC GUINNESS
WILL PLAY GULLEY JIMSON IN THE HORSE'S MOUTH'.

We clamoured our congratulations and delight.
Joyce said quietly, 'I'm very pleased',
still smiling.

NOTES

Elizabeth Fischer (née Wilson) is from Ayrshire, Scotland, and met John Fischer while he was at Oxford (see item 40).

She tried, unsuccessfully, to trace Bernard Lubar, with whom they had lost touch. His contribution is however appreciated.

Nicola Hahn, born in 1939, is now a professor, teaching Criminal Justice.

1. Item 47.

2. Cary's diary, MS. Cary 292/N.155, dates the Fischers' arrival on Monday, 2 Aug. '54 and departure for Stratford on 5 Aug.; 6 Aug. has 'Summer School St. Hugh's'.

42

Remembered with Pleasure

Sara Gleason

This interview took place in Boston on 22 July 1967.

Joyce Cary is one of the few adults in my childhood whom I remember with pleasure. I met him first when I was eight years old. He stayed with us at White Plains, and when he came he looked at me and my sister, and said: 'You must be Nicky and you must be Sara,' and I thought there was something about our names that he could tell by looking at us.

I was in the third grade and my teacher was interested in him as our guest. I wrote something for the school magazine about him. I quickly warmed to him, and enjoyed walking with him in the park. The road went in a circle and he would get lost- or lost in thought and just kept going round. When I (or my sister) was chided for not talking, Joyce would say, 'She'll talk when she's ready.'

We had a well in our back yard and a garage that had been a stable. I told Joyce: 'That's where they put the bad horses.' When I was told that he had put this anecdote into an article I was annoyed, and said that he should have asked my permission.[1]

While he stayed with us I had a birthday party, which included lunch at the Plaza Hotel. We also went to Central Park and I went on the merry-go-round. Then we went to Staten Island.

I went first to the Episcopalian Sunday school across the street. My mother was a Presbyterian by upbringing, but became interested in the Unitarians; so then I went to the Unitarian Sunday School. Many Liberal Jews became Unitarians.

We stayed with Joyce Cary in Oxford in 1954. He slept with a cage under the blankets to keep the weight off him. I remember that he ate oatmeal in one bowl and had the milk in another, and I though this an odd custom.

184

NOTES

Sara Gleason (née Fischer) was born in 1942, and now lives in Providence, Rhode Island, where she is employed in a Department for the Environment, and engaged in writing a book about the Lighthouses of New England.

Permission to publish this interview was kindly granted in August 1987.

1. He was with them when Sara was told, says her mother, and he said instantly, 'Yes, you are perfectly right. I should have asked your permission.' See item 52.

43

His Sense of Humour
His Philosophy of Life

Irene Wilson Laune

This item developed from a telephone conversation on 2 October 1979.

[W.C. Fields: His Follies and Fortunes[1] *is amongst Cary's books in the Bodleian Library, inscribed by him: 'from Reen Wilson / White Plains / March 1951'. On finding it, I realized that it might lead me to proof, that 'It's a Gift', as a theme phrase in Cary's writing, owed something to the film of that title starring W.C. Fields (see item 22, end). I immediately traced 'Reen Wilson'*[2] *and, though she could not give me positive proof, her story certainly makes the source more likely, besides showing another facet of Cary's personality.]*

I had recently emigrated from Britain and was living with Betty and Jack Fischer when Joyce was invited to stay with us at White Plains.

At that time I was a 32-year-old film-maker working with a documentary film company in Manhattan, and commuting to work each day on the hour's train ride from White Plains. Joyce accompanied me on the commuting train when he had to attend appointments in the city. In our spare time I took him on shopping sprees, or to the Museum of Modern Art for lunch and afterwards to showings of classical films in their cinema. We were both film buffs, relishing in particular the early comedians. (Joyce possibly saw many of the films we viewed when they were first shown in Britain in the 1930s.)

Sitting beside Joyce, I had the double pleasure of laughing at the scenes myself, and listening to his reactions. Joyce's laughter started as a loud 'HA' and dissolved into a string of merry chuckles. Charlie Chaplin's poignant brushes with life sparked our laughter and compassion. But our deepest appreciation for sheer comedy was reserved for the comic genre of W.C. Fields. His heroic portrayal of 'man against the odds' seemed to move Joyce the most. Later, on the

186

commuting train to White Plains we would re-enact the scenes. As Joyce played out the parts he seemed to say, 'That's it!'

Those commuting trips gave Joyce an opportunity to ask me things about the American scene. One night he said, 'Jack [Fischer] recommended I read *The New Your Times*, but I see you are reading *The Journal American*. Read me a story Reen.' I read of an incident summed up thus: a woman, shot by her husband, was being wheeled on a stretcher past a reporter who asked for her comment. 'I'll stand by him' she replied weakly, 'he's a good man and I love him.' Joyce gave a gleeful 'HA!' 'I must tell Jack about this paper,' he said. 'Read me more.'

I missed a rare opportunity in 1953, during Joyce's second lecture tour. By that time I was living in New York City. We arranged to be at my apartment one afternoon when a young student was to call to interview Joyce. She was working for her thesis. 'It won't take long,' said Joyce, ever the polite guest. He was so casual about the interview that I did not hook up my tape machine, and so missed Joyce Cary talking for half-an-hour on his philosophy of life and the theme of his writings.

His words escape me, but what came across was that man needs God – a religion – and an anchor. Recently I read a book about Jung that reminded me of what Joyce had said.[3] But I remember being startled by the religious basis of his theme; for I had heard Joyce make an occasional scurrilous remark on the subject of religious practitioners. When I reminded him that he had chased missionaries out of the African village he superintended he said: 'Oh I only chased the ones I thought were bogus or were interfering.'

After the interview we discussed the fate of his books in the market-place. Having written for over thirty years, he was only then having greater financial rewards and wider acclaim. He expressed his pleasure about that. Then he added wistfully, 'It would have been easier if the critics had understood, but they always seemed to get it wrong.'

Joyce acted humble when anyone tried to draw him out about characterization and plot. He appeared offhand about his knowledge and accomplishments, as though denying having made any effort. I did not attend any of his lectures, but Jack Fischer told me that Joyce jotted down notes on the back of an envelope in preparation and then pulled them out nonchalantly in front of an audience. He then proceeded to lecture on a theme that must have taken hours of preparation and was anything but encapsulated on the back of an envelope.

Joyce was entranced with the exuberance and kindness of Americans. He did not take things for granted, but wished to please and give of himself on the occasion of his visits.

'Reen,' he said, 'what can I do to make myself better?' Thinking he wanted my professional advice, and conscious of how indistinctly Englishmen came across on the airwaves, I blurted out: 'Don't speak so fast and swallow the end of your sentences.' He was not pleased. I had the feeling he would take his own time to respond to my well-meant suggestions.

NOTES

Irene Wilson Laune is from Ayrshire, Scotland, and emigrated to the United States after her sister Elizabeth had settled there as the wife of John Fischer. Her late husband, the western artist Paul Laune, illustrated John Fischer's last book, *From the High Plains*.

She has kindly agreed to the publication of the above, extracted from an unpublished article on Cary.

1. *Doctor, Lawyer, Merchant, Chief – Adrift in a Boneyard* [the title continues] by Robert Lewis Taylor (Doubleday and Company, 1949), is Cary C.709 in the Bodleian Collection.

2. Now Mrs Laune, living in Phoenix, Arizona; my book, *The Writer and His Theme*, was almost ready for publication, but I included her evidence on p. 393, n. 9.

3. Cary's notebooks reveal Jung's profound influence on him.

44

From His American Editor

Elizabeth Lawrence Kalashnikoff

This interview took place in July 1967, at Deep River, Connecticut, where Mrs Kalashnikoff then lived.

Have you a favourite amongst Joyce Cary's novels? Or do you think he had one?

Herself Surprised is the book that has captured my imagination over the years. I still believe – as Joyce surely believed – that Gulley Jimson is best introduced through the more conventional, or stable, minds of Sara and Tom Wilcher, than through the mind of the manic artist. *The Horse's Mouth* is superb, read as intended as the third volume of the trilogy. And I particularly like *To Be a Pilgrim*, *Mister Johnson*, and *A House of Children*.

I think everyone has his own novel, which is the right one by which to be sucked into the body of his work. As a judge of his work, Joyce thought very highly of Edith Haggard. I think he thought she had a shrewd sense of matters that interest people, and could put her finger on what was needed. When anyone remarked on such matters as his knowledge of women, whether in talking or in a letter, he said, 'Well, my mother was a woman, my wife was a woman.' When people spoke about Charley, he said, 'Weren't we all juvenile delinquents?' When asked what book of yours do you prefer, he'd say, 'My wife preferred *Mister Johnson*, and David Cecil *To Be a Pilgrim*.' I am sure that Joyce himself preferred the one he was working on at the time. He said once that he missed very much the world of music that his wife had opened up to him.

Perhaps it was that world in The Moonlight *that made you recommend it as Harper's first Cary publication.*

Yes, *The Moonlight*, which was the second of Joyce's novels I read, is the well-crafted story of a family, interesting if not exciting. And I

did, and do, like family novels. *Herself Surprised*, the third Cary novel
I read, excited me.

What was your first impression, when you met?

On meeting him I found there was no terrific impact. He was a tired
man when he got off that plane. There wasn't the effervescence then,
but he was comfortable, at ease, and interested. That portrait done
by Kennington prepares one for a larger man. He was not much
taller than I am. There was a sense of tension or tenseness in the
portrait, but he could be relaxed and quiet, and could be a good
listener.

His tastes were so very catholic that I asked him once if he was ever
bored. His answer was prompt: 'Oh, often.' 'When there are people
around you?' 'Never.' This responsiveness, plus a strong touch of the
Irish, constituted a charm that was warm and appealing. The human
community was both home and laboratory to him.

Joyce Cary said many times that once a writer has achieved his own
vision of life he will never run out of material to write about. By the
time I met him he was possessed of his vision; he had come to terms
with the world in a way satisfying to him. The world he viewed and
inhabited was all of a piece – not totally good or totally bad, but a
fascinating mixture with endless possibilities. He could believe in
goodness, justice, progress because he had experienced them, but he
didn't assume them to be man's inalienable right.

I think it was his ability to see the world in one piece that gave him
his special quality – a sense of wholeness. He knew who he was and
where he was going. He was no lost soul in a fragmented world,
looking to publishers, editors, critics, readers for reassurance and
guidance. He was patently pleased if there were some who would
persist to an understanding of his meaning and intention. For those
who didn't, there was always the next book, the one he was working
on, the one which promised perfection and would speak more clearly
and effectively of the drama which excited him profoundly – the
drama of free men in a free society.[1]

Did you ever discuss religion with him?

I seem to remember that he had no objection to using the word God for
the ultimate. He thought it necessary to rear children in some religion,
if only to have something to rebel against.

Joyce Cary had no feeling that he thought himself important. He
must have exerted a great deal of charm over women. But I think he

loved his wife and no one else could replace her. Of all the people I handled he stood out as a finished writer from the time I knew him. He didn't bring me his problems to solve, in life or writing.

He was a curiosity to his publishers because he seemed almost indifferent to the fate of his books as they came off the press, holding the engaging notion that it was the business of writers to write and publishers to publish. Nevertheless, about certain matters he was firm. His titles were not subject to alteration, for they were built from the beginning into the fabric of his novels. This was pointed out when our salesmen suggested that *Herself Surprised* did not have an exhilarating cash-register ring. He objected also to having each chapter begin on a new page when our designers proposed this departure from the format of his English books; he tended to build his novels in short chapters and he didn't like obtrusive breaks in the flow of his narrative. Another thing that irked him was having his novels described and the characters analysed in jacket copy. It hurt him that Rose in *the Moonlight* was called a 'tyrant in petticoats.' He saw her, with sympathy and pity, as a woman driven by an overwhelming sense of duty and obligation to family. About those problems of conformity so close to the hearts of copy editors he took a cavalier attitude. If dates and the ages of his characters failed to agree from one page to the next, as sometimes happened, he didn't want anyone tampering with his figures. He had wrestled with them and was confident that no further wrestling would better them. They were probably not important to the essential truths he was driving at.[2]

In publishing, we did a lot of photographing of his English books. The poems have not been done. At about the time I left Harper's, which was October 1964, they had just gotten to the end of his prose. But they always thought they would bring out his poems. Win Davin had an idea of getting his notebooks, letters, and autobiographical material published, but she and Curtis Brown never could agree.[3]

Do you think he would have hesitated about writing for Vogue?

No. I don't think he would have been against publishing in *Vogue*. He was so fascinated by the tabloids. Edith Haggard would have found these avenues and he wouldn't have been so precious as to scorn them. He wanted to get his ideas across.

Would you have called him a feminist?

I told him that his younger women didn't ring as true as the older ones, but he never commented on that. I wouldn't think he was a feminist. He was a great believer in women; I don't think he would have held them back.

Did you hear him lecture?

I heard him lecture at Columbia, and at YMHA [*Young Men's Hebrew Association*], where they were mobbing him. I thought him a successful lecturer. The Columbia lecture was very informal – question and answer – with students.

He was so completely at home with himself, which comes from a security – an unconscious pride, I should think. I don't think he was one given to criticism of others. If different from him a person presented a matter of interest for him to explore. I don't think that he weighed people against himself as better but saw them rather as different. He was not a formidable aristocrat, but was certainly a complete gentleman.

I picture 12 Parks Road filled with things. He commented once on my old carpets, because he found the floors these days are so uninteresting. And these are the books he gave me [*showing them to me*]: In 1948, *Castle Rackrent*, published 1782, 2nd edition, Dublin, 1801. In December 1952, *The Man of Feeling*, 3rd edition, Dublin, MDCC, LXXX. September 1953, as a wedding present, 3 volumes of *Coningsby* of 1844, London, Henry Colburn the publisher. The letter in the book reads: 'Disraeli is a far better novelist than his reputation.'

One is now left wondering whether that is true too of Cary.

NOTES

Elizabeth Lawrence Kalashnikoff joined the staff of Harper & Row (then Harper & Brothers) in 1935. She met Cary only during his American lecture tours, but a close friendship was established from the time she introduced him to Harper's, until his death, as their letters, now in the Bodleian, reveal.

In a letter of October 1987, she kindly agreed to the publication of what is here quoted.

1. The last three paragraphs are from the Introduction to the *Time* paperback edition of *The Horse's Mouth* by Elizabeth Lawrence.

2. This para. is from the Introduction, as in n. 1.

3. Mrs Davin is the Literary Editor, and Curtis Brown the Literary Agent, for Joyce Cary's estate.

45

'So nice to deal with'

Cass Canfield

This brief interview took place in Mr Canfield's New York office on 20 July 1967.

He was an extremely gentle person, who gave me the impression of saintliness. One never would guess, on knowing him rather slightly, that he was a man who had had an adventurous career. I had lunch with him in Oxford, and Lord David Cecil was there. [...]

He was one of those extraordinary authors to deal with – he was so nice to deal with. By a combination of luck we managed to build up his sales enormously. He was so extraordinarily grateful for the success we brought him. He was also leaving it entirely to our judgement how we handled his work.

The letters given by Harper to the Bodleian are a wonderful foundation for any Cary scholar to work from, and now I find that there is a great deal more material here.

You have my permission to study all our files on Cary, and to quote from them.

You are most generous. What really ensured his success in the United States, and much more of the world in consequence, was I think your choice of guests to meet him, at the party you gave at the right moment during his first American lecture tour.

[*The party was at Mr Cranfield's home, 152 East 38th Street, at 5 p.m. on 2 February 1951; the guests included several contributors to this book.*]

NOTE

Cass Canfield (1897-1986) spent virtually his entire career with Harper & Row, serving finally as house senior editor (1967-1986). His own writings include two volumes of memoirs, *The Publishing Experience* (1969) and *Up and Down and Around* (1971); and two biographies, *The Incredible Pierpont Morgan* (1974) and *The Iron Will of Jefferson Davis* (1978).

Mr Cass Canfield Jr. has kindly agreed that this item should be published.

46

'Exuberant' Describes Him

Simon Michael Bessie

This interview took place in New York on 21 July 1967.

I think *Art and Reality* marvellous, especially the insight into himself that Cary reveals in it. I used it when I was teaching at Columbia.

I was not directly concerned with him at Harper's, but I think *The Horse's Mouth* had been published there just before his first visit, in 1951. I remember that he told John Fischer and me that he sometimes had to cut out of a book some of his favourite things, as he had done with *The Horse's Mouth*. I found this remarkable, and it impressed me.

I saw him several times in Harper's office on that first visit, and I remember him at Fischers' where I took Glenway Wescott to dinner. I recall that Glenway and Joyce talked hard. Glenway has typical American mid-west originality. Exuberant describes Joyce Cary. His company was marvellous. He so burst with life and so responded to the vivacity and life-force in someone else – even someone like me, he who might seem to have got past such impressionability.

I remember talking to him about Priestley, with whom I was acquainted because my friend Jan de Hartog married Priestley's step-daughter. So Cary and I talked about Priestley, and noted his gifts, yet also the surprising absence of an overwhelming book. Cary said it was the way Priestley worked, and told me about a time when he went to stay with Priestley who, when Cary arrived, excused himself because he was not going to be able to spend as much time as he would have liked with Cary (who of course said he had plenty to do too). Priestley said he was just starting a play. About ten days later he came to supper and said, 'Well, there it is; it's done.' 'A whole play? Finished?' asked Cary. 'That's Jack's trouble,' he said. 'Too much facility. With more labour he might have produced more with his gifts.'

How do you judge Cary's novels?

As a body of work I think they are the finest collection in the English language since the eighteenth century. I would draw a line from Fielding to Cary.

He stands out as one of the most remarkable men I have ever known. He radiated intensity and an overpowering sense of intellectual and spiritual vitality. I think that the man and the work are closer in Joyce Cary than in almost any other writer. For example, Hemingway and his work are much farther apart. One of the hardest things to do in fiction, I think, is to create a character who is a painter; hard to convey in words what he painted and the kind of man he is.

When he was doing the political trilogy, I asked Joyce why there were so few really good novels having politics as their centre. He agreed that there were very few, and said the reason was that politics and people in politics have two languages: the public language of politics and the non-public language of life; and the novelist had to take seriously the language of politics intended to cover over the differences. That is, he had to define and cover over and give the sensation and impression rather than the reality.

What you say recalls the fact that judging is a central theme of Cary's political trilogy, and that the Nuremberg trials were in progress when he was writing it. Would you agree that the attitude to judgement at the Nuremberg trials illuminates the trilogy?

Having reached the age of fifty-one, I have come to realize that the last few years have been concerned with the problem of judging and being judged, and Nuremberg put the problem on the front page. It comes to most artists that they are judging themselves, not others. I think this is a subject that Joyce and I almost certainly discussed, as I am sure it attracted his attention; and also the Jewish question.

NOTE

Simon Michael Bessie (1916-) was President of Atheneum Publishers at the date of this interview. A co-founder of Atheneum in 1959, Bessie was previously Editor at Harper and again, after 1975, Senior Vice-President and Director at Harper and after 1981, publisher of Bessie Books, an Imprint of Harper & Row.

His agreement to the publication of this record was kindly given on 8 March 1988.

47

From Curtis Brown's American Magazine Agent

Edith Haggard

This record is from three conversations, between 20 and 26 July 1967, and includes extracts from letters written by Joyce Cary.

He was the greatest man I have ever known. When people met him as a famous novelist they'd say: 'He is so precisely what he ought to be' – having been generally disappointed in literary lions. He looked younger than his age – sixty-three – though his face was lined.

He was the most un-self-conscious person I have met in my life. I remember the first time he visited my flat. I was in the kitchen, and he appeared with one of the drawers from a chest, saying that the wooden knob-handle needed tightening, and that if I gave him something to do it with he would tighten them all.

That would have been on Thursday, January 25th [*1951*], when I had brought him back here to rest, before he went to dine at the Collins'. Our first meeting would have been earlier that week. (I know it was after Sinclair Lewis's death, on January 10th, and the reading of the will, on Friday 19th.) My diary shows that he came to my office on February 21st, March 23rd, and March 27th; on 28th March I stayed at home, and Joyce came between three and five. At six-thirty we went to Cheerio's for dinner.

The story recounted in Time *happened there. Would you repeat it?*

It was simply that Joyce was crossing the room to wash his hands and the music started. We waltzed together, and then he left me and continued crossing the room to wash his hands. Next day he left for England, and the plane turned back. He left on the 30th.

On his next visit, on September 13th 1953,[1] I met him at Idlewild, and took him to Fischers'. I went again to Fischers' on October 3rd, with Hal (Harrison) Smith,[2] to collect him for a party for Richard

Llewellyn. Driving back with Hal, Joyce was supposed to point out the way. But he kept describing the characteristics of the butcher and others, in shops: 'Now in that shop there is a very interesting man –.'

In 1954 I met him in London, when he came up and stayed a weekend at the Stafford during my visit.

In the spring of 1955 I got a letter, before he sent official notice, that he would have to cancel another proposed tour; he was always thoughtful for others' feelings. In the Fall I went over, and took him one of the first transistor radios. He was then using a stick, but able to walk upstairs to his study and down to the dining-room. I sailed in the Queen Mary on October 5th and arrived at Joyce's on October 10th at 9 p.m. [...] On the 15th I bought him a whistle, in case he fell and needed help, because he was shaky.

During this visit, I would have breakfast with him, and at about 10.30 I went shopping. At about 12.50 I'd come back, with packages, and Joyce would say, 'What did you buy?' I remember producing some potpourri and other things from the herb shop in the High; 'Did you get stung?' was his comment. When I produced an antique tea pot for a friend, he said: 'I've never seen a more distinguished piece of silver.' [...]

Before going over in 1955 I had told my doctor about Joyce, and he had warned me that he would be irritable. When I reported that he had not been, the doctor said that Joyce must be a really great man, and showed that a great mind can triumph over a neurological disease. During this visit, in October '55, I wrote down Joyce's account of his symptoms (of which you can take a copy [*and did*]).

For my second visit I had sailed on April 18th (1956), in the Queen Mary, which docked at 10.45 p.m. I had radioed Joyce from the ship asking what he wished, and he cabled back, on 19th, to come straight there if I wasn't too tired. I arrived at 1.30 a.m. and Mrs Lightburne was up; she said Joyce wanted to be wakened. I noticed an enormous change in him.

On the same day I think, a Monday, Win Davin and Anna called, then Rachel and David Cecil and Helen Gardner. On the Friday Tristram came for lunch and dinner. On May 1st Joyce dressed for a party, and I helped him with buttoning his shirt. Enid Starkie, Sir Oliver Franks, and Jean Banister were there, and Cecilia Dick, Alan Bullock, and A.L. Rowse came during my visit – possibly to the party. On the Monday following, at 11.15, Elizabeth Bowen and David Cecil came.

Joyce told me, on this visit, that he thought Elizabeth Bowen had made a grave mistake in keeping up her family estate. And he showed

me a letter from Graham Greene, saying that *An American Visitor* is a
very interesting book; it was written some time before *The Quiet
American*. Joyce also said: 'There's something about me that you don't
know. I wrote two or three stories for *The Saturday Evening Post*.' (This
was because Andrew Wright was working on his book about Joyce,
who thought it unfair not to tell Wright about them.) In fact there were
ten, as SEP found when their files were checked. In New York, one of
their editors had called at my office when Joyce was there, and I'd said,
'He's far too good for the likes of you!' But SEP was tough, and selling
to them then was an achievement. He couldn't sell more when his ideas
about writing changed.

Of his wife Joyce said, 'Every morning of my life I had to build
Trudy up – reassure her.' Of himself he said, 'I'm a very orderly man
who lives in chaos.' And he said of 'Success Story', 'I didn't know I was
writing a prophetic story about myself.'

Did you sell that for him?

No, that was in *Harper's Magazine*, in 1952. I remember that in '51 I
handled 'Babes in the Wood' and something for *Time* ['Romance']. *The
New Yorker* paid 2,200 dollars for 'Cromwell House', on 2 July 1956.

He must certainly have been grateful for all you did for him.

He thought I was born with good editorial judgement, and I think this
is true; I can see when something is wrong. But I can't tell you how to
put it right; so I am a destructive critic. Sinclair Lewis always thought I
should write and so did Joyce. After Joyce's death, it was arranged that
Spencer Curtis Brown should continue to act as literary agent, while
Win Davin assumed the duties of literary editor. And Michael Cary
agreed to that.

I didn't see Joyce again after May 1956. I used to 'phone every
Sunday, though he became almost impossible to understand. I thought
it was probably not worth it, but Edith Millen said that it was, as he
didn't like people to *see* him, and I couldn't. His voice was very weak
and slurred. It was rather high, and he talked very rapidly until
towards the end.

He was the only writer who seemed as interested in you as he was in
himself. Reviewers always talked about his personality as well as about
his books.

Which of them do you think the best?

I think *To Be a Pilgrim* his greatest book. But the man was greater than his work. He was great because of his awareness, perception, understanding, mental vitality, and interest in everything; his complete lack of arrogance and lack of self-consciousness. I don't think this was acquired.

Yet you did remark, when we looked at your photographs of him, that there was a different look in the eyes of the younger Joyce Cary, in photographs, and I think that is true and significant. I think it relates to the experience that he himself called a 'conversion', in his religious ideas, during the later 1930s.

I can only say that, from the moment I knew Joyce I had this feeling of a complete lack of a need to play a part; of any need for guardedness. But I loved Joyce a great deal more than he loved me. His work came first. I asked him to destroy all my letters to him. But you may copy and use his letters to me.[3]

                                                                11.8.51

[...] I think perhaps I am only a lazy man who has been fearfully lucky in his women and thoroughly spoilt by a very happy marriage. For my wife was nothing of a managing woman – far from it. She taught herself to organise out of pride and love. I know how you feel looking back on your own happiness – it is hard to say whether to have such happiness and lose it is better than never having known it at all. But one must not think of life in terms of happiness but of achievement. My only consolation in those terrible years when my wife was fighting for her life (and she adored life – no-one could be so happy) was in the thought that she had achieved so much. And in fact though she never thought of herself as having achieved anything, yet that achievement saved her because she was so occupied all the time in planning for me and for the children that she never had time to be sorry for herself. She suffered fearfully but she never despaired or ceased to be the mistress of her house and the mother of her sons. She went down fighting and I pray I may make so good and grand a death.

I have forgotten all about the numerous letters about businesses which you have written me and I have not answered. The general answer is I can't do anything about anything for a little while till the book is done [...]

21.8.51

My dear Edith,

[...] I have just been reading Tchekov's letters – how good they are and what a man comes through – quite unlike the Russian of fiction (even of his own fiction) wise, just, brave, balanced and his wit so true. It is strange that he never would admit his illness – I suppose he loved life and hated to think he might die. And then too he had his whole family to support – daresay he was frightened to think of what would happen to them if he died. Those who have family burdens get no peace from one anxiety or another and those who have none are lonely and sad – peace is too much for them. One has to choose between being harried to death, and throwing oneself in the river. [...]

Oxford. 7.4.52

My Dear Edith

The parcel has just arrived and it is going to be the greatest blessing because I have a family party for Easter and it is always a problem to feed them. [...] I am a perfect hen with my children – there must be a lot of woman hidden in me somewhere. But I have a theory that people with strong feelings and constitutions have everything on the strong side – and certainly a man like Tolstoy who had 13 children and whose sexuality was a pest to him (or so he thought with his manichee hatred of happiness and pleasure) also did some of the best portraits of women in books. And a writer can't draw the insides of people without getting or being inside himself, or having them in him. I am working on your Oxford article – it is a hard job and I am longing to get back to a story. If I were writing a story I should not find the article such a bore, I should look upon it as a holiday from the story which is always agony – but it is an agony that one endures more cheerfully because it has gleams of hope and even glory when the band begins to play – I mean the different instruments begin to make the kind of noise together which is at least something like what you dreamed up in your first frenzy. [...]

12 Parks Road, / Oxford.
30th December, 1952.

My Dear generous Edith,

It was most awfully good of you to send that parcel of butter. You couldn't have chosen a more useful present. Three of the sons were here, two of the wives (one is in hospital with a newborn baby) and three grandchildren, and all of them delighted in having as much butter as they liked for the first time in years. In fact the small children have never known such a luxury before.

And what a magnificent present the wire about Bush River. Did you keep it back on purpose for a special Christmas present? It is a great compliment that Esquire should take it when it has been published already on this side.

Do you realise that the horse in this story is the same one in Buying a Horse – my pet black Azben that carried me over about 800 miles of rough country in that war, and died of fly just before I myself was invalided?

Umaru is another story belonging to the same series, all autobiographical. [...]

                                                              27.8.54
My Dear Edith,

I'd no idea last week was your birthday but I had seen something I thought you would like, and I'd ordered it to be sent when it had been cleaned up, and it came yesterday so I'm sending it as your present. I was very glad Holiday did like that article as I'm far to busy to do anything more to it now; there's not only the book but 2 broadcasts, a review for the Nation (of Wright's book on the Gold Coast) and, hanging over all, possible film work on a treatment of the Horse's Mouth for Pinewood with Alec Guinness and Neame. Their ideas seemed quite good and I'm keen to sell the thing as it belongs to the children, who will not have to pay tax on a lump sum. Pinewood won't pay much but it is the most promising offer yet, and I've offered to do any work on it for nothing if the option is not taken up in 6 months. If it is taken up then I am to be paid [...].

                                                      Oxford. 13.9.54
                                                   24 hours and a half
Dearest Edith,

[...] I really am in the middle of the biggest rush of a not very quiet life. Neame is making the Horse's Mouth with Guinness and films wont wait for anyone except at the cost of thousands a week. I am supposed to begin doing the treatment in October and I had relied on time for the book in October before I go to France about the 20th and Sweden about the 1st of November. Meantime the book is dashing along but there are mounds of work to be done for it [...].

I am so glad you liked the little box. As soon as I saw it I said it's just the thing for Edith – so neat and small and nicely finished in the joints. Hal says you are Dresden China but the frame is steel. and Mary O[gilvie] who was there at the moment said Yes Stainless steel. [...]

28.5.55

Dearest Edith,

I saw the man in Bristol on the 24th and he changed everything again. All the specialists change things but this one appeals to me more because he has cured someone. [...]

Thank you 1000 times for the reviews. They are very nice to me though they don't have much idea of what it's all about. Yet ordinary sensible persons know there is no final solution to political conflict. It always goes on and it always will; the great thing is not to let it get to shooting and we in England and the states are fairly good at that. [...]

NOTES

Edith Zorn Haggard (1903-) was born in New York City; married to a lawyer (1921-27); on 4 Aug. 1927 she married Sewell Haggard, a magazine editor, who died on 3 Jan. 1928. Her professional career began as a magazine editor in 1928, and in April 1937 she joined Curtis Brown as manager of the magazine department; she retired on 3 March 1963.

This record was kindly checked and approved for publication by Edith Haggard on 24 January 1988.

1. In *Joyce Cary: The Writer and His Theme*, p. 353, the date is given as Aug. 10; I apologize for any confusion caused by this.

2. Harrison Smith, publisher and assistant editor of *The Saturday Review*, had died shortly before I visited New York in 1967; but his secretary, Miss K. Gildersleeve, gave me access to his file on Joyce Cary, and agreed that it could be given to the Bodleian, where it now is. Cary's letters, beginning 'My Dear Hal', reveal his affection, and his eagerness to respond to Harrison Smith's interest in his ideas.

3. I have photocopies of the letters, and the extracts below exemplify their interest.

48

Links with *Time* Magazine

T.S. Matthews

This interview took place in London on 15 September 1967, and was updated by correspondence in March 1988.

I met Joyce Cary through Jack Fischer, who had been developing him for Harper's. He persuaded me to do a cover story of Cary, and I bought two stories, though *Time* didn't run fiction; but I bought them, and managed to find suitable space, indicating it was educational. I was always *nagging* Cary to publish a book of short stories, but he was always finishing his novel. I was very keen on *Not Honour More*, the book about Jim, who interested me most as a character. My former wife (a writer) thought Cary a dull conversationalist. But I thought he was giving nothing away, and storing everything up. If he thought I did much for him, it was that I helped to spread knowledge of him in America.

I thought him *charming* for a writer; they tend not to be nice people. His personality was like warming one's hands before a fire; he radiated life and vitality. He stayed with me in Princeton, when I was living there, in 1953. Then, after I retired from *Time*, in 1953, and came to England, I visited him several times in Oxford.

Which of his books, besides Not Honour More, *did you particularly like?*

I think his African novels are probably greater than the others – especially *An American Visitor*, which is a wonderful book. I didn't think much of *The Drunken Sailor*. But I thought *Mister Johnson* nearly perfect. I didn't think him so hot on theory, but marvellous on creating a wide range of characters, especially rascals. I didn't think all that theory behind the novels of much interest.

I didn't think of him as an aristocrat, but I felt very much aware of his Irish background. I never knew his sons, and often wondered what they were like. As a much younger man when I met him, I was openly full of admiration, and Joyce was amused by this. I thought him so unconcerned for himself; he had passed over his money to his sons, and was working away for very little money. He was not worried about his health.

[*What followed in the interview appears thus in his latest book,* Angels Unawares, *which I have Mr Matthews' permission to quote:*]

I went to see him at the hospital at Stoke Mandeville. He was thinner but as lively as ever. In the two weeks he had been in the hospital, he told me, he had written four stories – 'three of them quite good!' When there was nothing more the doctors could do, he went home. Everyone knew, and he knew, that he was dying, but he continued to carry on his normal life as well as he could, yielding little by little to the inroads of the disease.

[...] He had been pleased by my enthusiasm over his short stories (the best, I said, since Chekhov) and had agreed to collect them in a book. On one of my last visits he apologized for postponing this job and explained that he was very keen on finishing a novel first.

Funerals are seldom cheerful affairs, but his was. The church, St. Giles's, was crowded with his friends and family - you could see the Cary nose, the Cary cheekbones, the Cary head, all around you. A family affair, the service was straightforward Church of England, with no frills, and the hymns were good old thumpers that everyone knew and sang with a will.'[1]

NOTES

Thomas Stanley Matthews (1901-), born in Cincinnati, Ohio, son of Bishop Paul Clement Matthews, is a BA of Princeton University (1922) and of Oxford (1924), MA (1968); his career in journalism began as assistant editor, then associate editor for *New Republic* (1925-29), and continued with *Time* as books editor (1929-37), assistant managing editor (1937-42), executive editor (1942), managing editor (1943-49), editor (1949-53). He now lives in England, at Cavendish Hall, Cavendish, Suffolk.

Noteworthy amongst his prolific writings are his autobiography, *Name & Address* (1960), and *Great Tom: Notes towards the Definition of T.S. Eliot* (1974). His kind agreement to the publication of this interview was given with his permission to quote from his last book (see n.1).

1. *Angels Unawares: Twentieth-Century Portraits* (Ticknor & Fields, 1985), p. 241.

49

From *Time* Magazine's then Book Review Editor

Max Gissen

This letter was written on 14 June 1968, in reply to an enquiry of 11 August 1967.

I owe you an apology and I offer it now. I have not been a laggard in the matter of Joyce Cary: it is simply that a ludicrous failure in *Time*'s infallible system has made me somewhat useless for your purposes. A few months ago, all the Cary files disappeared from the 'morgue'. [...] Perhaps someone else is doing a book on Cary. [...]

My own first meeting with Cary was arranged by Tom Matthews. He came to me one day (I was then the Book Review editor at *Time*) and took me to lunch at the Century Club. He was in a nice state of excitement about a writer named Joyce Cary. Had I read *The Horse's Mouth*? Tom's enthusiasm rather amused me for several reasons at the time. In the first place, I had read all of Cary then published. Tom confessed that he knew only *The Horse's Mouth*. And what he seemed to have forgotten was that when I reviewed *Mister Johnson* for *Time* and called it the best novel yet written about Africa (or something to that effect), he wondered if we should go that far. He was, of course, the managing editor of *Time* and could have edited me down, but he let it stand. I have since read basketsful of novels about Africa and my opinion still stands (I am not forgetting Evelyn Waugh and the many 'native' novelists who have come along in recent years).

Tom wondered if I would like to write a 'cover' story on Cary. Now, these are hazardous matters because there is never enough space; there are the *Time* requirements of interesting (but not important) blather and so on. But I jumped at the chance because I thought we had skipped him for too long. (I did not know him at the time.) Since you want information, I should tell you that Tom's enthusiasm led to quite a bit of editing on his part. The first two columns of the *Time* story are almost entirely his.

[...] Tom arranged a dinner for Cary when he was next in the US.

205

There were only six or eight of us and though we met at the River House in New York (Henry Luce's home), Harry was not there. Jack Fischer was and so was Louis Kronenberger, who was our drama critic. (To my horror, as we left the place, Kronenberger confided to me that Cary was the dullest man he had ever met.) Well, no comment about Louis. I found Cary wholly fascinating. I sat on his right, opposite Tom. I wanted to know about his African experience and he wanted to know about my dreary walk from Normandy to Czechoslovakia as an infantry lieutenant in the second World War. It was not until I read his little book about the Balkan war he got into (was it 1912?) that I realized how deep his interest was. Kronenberger, a great liberal fighter through the mouth and on typewriter, but who would have screamed like a girl if he'd heard a shot fired, naturally thought that Cary was dull. He wasn't at all. He was quick and vivacious all evening, painfully modest about his writing, but what I remember most clearly is that he wanted to talk about the substance of his books and not the writing itself. I got him onto *Mister Johnson* and there he was little short of enchanting. He began to sound like the book itself and for a while there was noone in the room but the two of us. No one else, it turned out, had read the book. He talked with near excitement about his duties as judge and administrator in Africa, the tact it all required, the great joy he derived from understanding, finally, the people and their problems. Had Mr Johnson danced into the room, I wouldn't have been the least surprised. This was the wonderful kind of talk that Louis Kronenberger found boring.

Well, what else? Cary rather embarrassed both me and Tom at some point when he was lecturing in the US. He was at the University of Buffalo and the morning following his lecture we got an exciteable wire from our local 'stringer'. I had asked him to cover Cary's lecture on the off chance that he might say something quotable to run in the magazine. At the end of his talk there was a 'question and answer' period and one of the students asked him if he had met any interesting Americans during his stay. He had indeed, he said, and named Tom and me. Perhaps *Time* can supply you with a copy of the dispatch but it certainly doesn't matter for your purposes and Tom had the good taste to throw it in the waste basket. What it did say to me was that the many more 'important' people he must have met were probably stuffy as hell and he chose to name Americans to whom he could speak in that delightful way that made our dinner at the River Club so memorable for me. [...]

NOTES

Max Gissen (1909?-1984) was born in Kiev, Russia (now USSR); after an apprenticeship at the *New Republic* and distinguished military service during World War II, he began reviewing books for *Time* magazine; during the next twenty years, he became the chief reviewer and editor of the *Time* book section, which came to be regarded as one of the leading review pages in the United States. He retired in 1967 – before writing this letter, which suggests, by its warmth, that he would have agreed to its publication. It was written from Ladder Hill Road, North Weston, Connecticut.

50

A Totally Religious Author

Harry Sions

This interview took place in New York on 20 July 1967.

I first met Joyce Cary in 1951 at Edith Haggard's. But his first article in *Holiday* was not published until 1953 – the one on Oxford.[1] He called *Holiday* his American magazine. In correspondence we described the sort of article we wanted, but what he sent wasn't quite right. There was a lack of communication – he didn't understand what was required, and the article lacked form. I was apprehensive of writing to tell him this, but was touched and pleased by his reaction. He was anxious for direction, and he appreciated the professional viewpoint of another professional.

The trouble was that he hadn't grasped the requirements of our magazine. He forgot that he was writing for an American audience, so that his references were directed to fellow-Englishmen. They were too private. I had to point out that his audience had to understand what he was talking about; he couldn't take the audience for granted. He was trying to bring Oxford to life.

We published 'Switzerland' in 1954, and 'the Heart of England' in 1955. But the last, 'Westminster Abbey' [*1956*] was the best article he did for *Holiday*. Not a comma was changed. He had learnt our style, and the specifications were clear.

He told me that he regarded himself as a totally religious author; to go to church was unnecessary for him, though he agreed that it was probably necessary for some people. In fact, I think he was probably the most religious man I have ever known.

I saw him about two months before he died and he struck me as the most spiritually serene person I had ever seen. My wife and I drove to Oxford with Curtis Brown, and we got there for tea. He had two girls there who were nervous and dropping things, and he was saying, 'Now my dear', etc., with such patience and good-humour. Both his arms were in traction, and it was heartbreaking to see him meeting his commitment, even though he was about to die. Such cheerfulness was unbelievable.

He was most worried about 'this dreadful man Nixon' in the 1956 election. 'Nixon is ethically outrageous,' I said, and Cary agreed. He was absolutely interested – there was no pretence. He talked about his disease but with no self-pity. He kept on talking about his disease!

At about five to five-thirty we left, and in saying good-bye my wife kissed him and kept under control, but she wept bitterly afterwards in the car. Curtis Brown and I too were deeply affected at the sight of this dear sweet great man.

Do you think of him as a great writer?

I believe he was a greater man than he was a writer. But I have found that the major writers are easier and more considerate than others. Faulkner re-wrote for me, just as Joyce Cary did. Cary said he respected the judgement of a professional.

In New York we went to the 21 Club. I never went there, normally. But Ted Patrick was a devotee of it, and he wanted to take us there because the proprietor and his wife were great admirers of Joyce Cary. Our table was very noisy and Cary talked non-stop. We couldn't hear him, partly because of his English voice, and partly because of the noise. In fact, even when there wasn't noise he was often hard to follow, because he talked too fast. I didn't really enjoy myself, and I don't think he did either.

But he was fascinated by American politics – the presidential elections – even though he didn't understand them very well. He did understand the situation in Africa, and I find some of his books, like *Mister Johnson*, prophetic. [...]

Joyce Cary struck me as an aristocratic in the best sense of the word. He had an inner gentility that glowed out of him. He had the instincts, sympathy and warmth, that made him react to people. He had a sense of their weaknesses. He refused to be called a Christian. And I, who regularly see signs of anti-Semitism in most British authors (for example Agatha Christie), saw none of it in him. I think he was incapable of bigotry, because he saw people as people.

NOTES

Harry Sions (1906-1974) was born in Philadelphia; served during World War II with AUS. (1942-45); became an editor with *Holiday* magazine, finally editorial director (1946-65); then senior editor for Little, Brown and Co. (1965-74). I trust that the publication of this interview will be approved of by relatives.

1. 'The Oxford Scholar', 1953 (E.41).

51

'Myth of the Mass Mind'

Charles W. Ferguson

This letter was written on 25 September 1967, in reply to a letter of 8 August 1967.

[...] Alas, there is nothing in the [*Readers Digest*] office file about the article of the February 1953 issue, 'The Myth of the Mass Mind'. Our files do not go back that far. All I have to go on is my recollection, seeing that any correspondence that may have taken place was probably between Edith Haggard and me. I recall only that I discussed the subject with Cary on one of my visits with him in Oxford. He brought out convincingly in conversation the point that it was nonsense to think that we are all standardized in a mass society. He cited one or two odd creatures around Oxford in support of his view. His view struck me as fresh, as all his views did, but it seemed to me also that he might have the basis of an essay for a mass magazine. I encouraged him to write it and he did. The article was not accepted as a Digest original – that is, one that we would purchase direct. Edith sold it to Harper's and later, as is occasionally the way with us, we used it from Harper's.[1]

Surely this bit of incidental information is of little use to you in such a big project on which you are launched – and with commendable zeal, Edith tells me. I can recall nothing else that might be of interest except for a telling remark Cary made to me when we were discussing religion or matters relating to religion. He said, 'If you believe in altruism, you believe in God.' It's a statement and text that has lingered with me and one that occurs to me often. If I got the import of it properly, a mechanistic universe leaves no room for freedom of individual impulse, much less action, and that one's wish to aid another or his fellows is an expression of direct and practical belief in the personal nature of the Cosmos.

My best wishes go with these inadequate lines.

[...] *Such 'incidental information', as you call it, is valuable to me, as it helps to confirm my opinion that Cary's influence has been greater than is generally realized. His religious views, which were to him all-*

*important, seem to have impressed many intelligent minds in the sort
of way you mention, and who knows how far-reaching such thoughts
eventually are? [...].*[2]

NOTES

Charles W. Ferguson (1901-1987) was a Methodist minister (1923-25); associate editor
of The Bookman and religious editor for Doubleday, Doran & Co. (1926-30). He joined
Readers Digest in 1939, and was senior editor (1940-68); the last of his eleven books was
Organizing to Beat the Devil: Methodists and the Making of America (1971).

Mrs Hugh Ferguson, who is herself 'a true Joyce Cary fan', is sure that her
father-in-law would have been pleased to have the letter published.

1. 'The Mass Mind: Our Favourite Folly', *Harper's Magazine*, CCIV (March 1952),
25-27; see E.29.

2. From B. Fisher's reply of 2 October 1967.

52

Contributions to *Vogue*

Allene Talmey

This interview took place in New York on 26 July 1967.

I lunched with Joyce Cary and Edith Haggard in September 1953, and probably in 1951 too. His first article for *Vogue* was published during his first visit to the United States.

That was 'The Revolution of the Women', published on 15 March 1951, and actually written during that visit, as his manuscripts show.

Yes. As always, I had made it my business to know his work, and to suggest a topic on which he could write. This is the secret of my job. I gave him the subject, the title, and the length required.

From what you say, he might never have thought of writing about 'The Revolution of the Women' (which he called the greatest social revolution in the true sense that the world has seen), if you had not given him the title. Like me, you apparently found the subject implicit in his writing, and challenged him, as it were, to write about it. What of 'A Child's Religion'? As it was published in December '53, I assume that you suggested that title too, when you lunched together on his second visit. It is centred on the story of John Fischer's daughter Sara,[1] and I see how you cleverly caught him to write it while that incident, and the child herself, were fresh in his mind. What of his stories?

I remember the trouble we had with one of them. There were five or six children in a family, whose ages were about five months apart.

That would be 'Out of Hand'. I've been reading through his letters to Edith Haggard, and he apologized in one for having done such a careless job on a story for you. I'm glad that you got him to write the article, 'Last Look at His Worlds'. It does read like a very sincere and personal last reflection.

212

Yes. I visited him in Oxford in August 1955, when I learned that he would not be coming back to the States, as we'd expected. He could still just manage to walk. He came down once a day and then went upstairs for good. We had lunch, and then he took me upstairs and showed me his books – his own books, which he had illustrated, as I remember.

How then do you remember him?

I found him a very gentle and amused man.

NOTES

Allene Talmey Plaut (1903-1986), known professionally as Allene Talmey, worked at *Vogue* magazine from 1936 (as a columnist) until 1971, when she retired as associate editor; she also wrote film reviews for *Time*, and her book, *Doug and Mary, and Others*, concerned film stars.
1. See item 42.

53

'You worried for him'

Harvey Breit

This interview took place in New York on 26 July 1967.

I had an interview with him on 29 November 1953, which you will find in my collection of interviews, *The Writer Observed*. I asked him then if he would like a party, to meet people he might not ordinarily run into. He said he would like to meet the Trillings and Monroe Wheeler, and that the 4th or 6th following would be a suitable date for him.

He'd said at our interview, 'I'm tough you know.' But you worried for him; you thought he didn't have the strength for that kind of vitality.

You make me wonder whether what you observed about his vitality had anything to do with his final illness. Doctors apparently do not know the cause of that disease.

When we met I thought him nice but felt sorry for him. There was a fragility in him, and as you got to know him you thought him not strong except morally. Beneath the strength there was too much sensitivity, and that worried me.

But one immediately liked him, and was immediately impressed. At our first meeting I felt affection and respect, and at the second, when he came early to the flat with Edith Haggard, I felt a love for him and thought: 'this is how a man of sixty-five should be.'

At the party he gave about a forty-five minute monologue. He talked about Africa too, and anecdote and ideas wove together. At the end I wanted to applaud. I got a unique feeling, as if I had been listening to Mozart. I don't usually respond in this way, and I have known many great men. I had in fact been nervous of his ability to keep pace with people like Trilling. But I believe he would have had a similar effect on others there – that is, of greatness. I think nobody left without thinking they had been close to a great man.

I didn't think of him as saintly. On the contrary, he made me feel

214

that, given ideal conditions, a man could grow into this. He did strike
one as a profoundly honest man.

What of his writing?

I enjoyed the first trilogy, but it didn't intrigue,or make me want to
read more. There wasn't enough mystery in him for me to want to read
every word he wrote. With what I found in Joyce Cary I felt I knew it
and loved it so well I didn't need to know any more. I would call the
novels moral and metaphysical. I know he wrote several at once.
Hemingway wrote three or four novels at the same time, and they
tended to be contrapuntal.

The question is, in terms of contemporary criticism, why aren't
there dozens of essays, as on Kafka, Yeats, Pound, Faulkner? I think
perhaps Cary lacked a special contemporary quality because he has
universality. As with Tolstoy, there seems nothing more to be said –
whereas with Dostoevsky, for example, there is more to take apart.

At the party people felt it was a great party because Cary was there.
Trilling had a good time. But as you got fond of him you worried!

NOTES

Harvey Breit (1909-1968), born and educated in New York City, became a journalist,
with *Time* (1933), and with the *New York Times* (1943-57); besides *The Writer Observed*
(1956), his books include poems, a novel, and (in collaboration) two plays and an edition,
the Selected Letters of Malcolm Lowry (1965).

54

Remembered by a Critic – and as Friends

James Stern   Tania Stern

This interview took place at the Sterns' home in Wiltshire in April 1966.

[*James*:] I first learned of Joyce Cary from Pamela Hansford-Johnson, who was enthusing over him and also C.P. Snow.[1] But we didn't meet him until 1953, when Harvey Breit was renting our flat in New York, and we gave a party for him.

Within five minutes of meeting him I felt that Joyce and I understood each other; we could have gone on talking together for hours. It was our similar Irish background that explained our affinity, I'm sure. He was delighted to discover that I was from Northern Ireland, and that we had a 'mutual' friend in Londonderry. His talk was full of the initiative, drive and ambition of the Northern Irish people, or at least of this friend, and he said more than once of him, 'He got things done. He wasn't afraid to do things.' This idea of Northern Ireland struck me as odd at the time, and even ludicrous when I myself returned there twelve years later, in 1965 - after 50 years away from it! I longed to know the basis of Cary's notions, and thought that perhaps he admired power.

Power in Men, *as the title of his first political treatise, urges us to see 'the right use of power' as the central idea in his writing.[2] As a writer, he was of course obsessed with the power of the word, and the two reviews you wrote about him nicely reveal this, not least in the fact that they both appear on the front page of* The New York Times Book Review. *Their very position in the newspaper illustrates the power of the critic and journalist to make or break a novelist – or any other kind of preacher. This is clearly the message of his last novel,* The Captive and the Free *with regard to the journalist Hooper, who seeks power for himself by manipulating the preachers Syson and Preedy, and you draw attention to it very well, I think, by heading your review 'Two Rogues in Pursuit of Power'.[3] A similar idea seems to underlie*

216

your review of Not Honour More, *which you have called 'Portrait of a Corrupted Idealist',*[4] *by whom you mean Nimmo, (the political preacher and narrator of the second book of Cary's second trilogy). But a key message of the book for its narrator, Jim, is the power of journalists, as 'wanglers', to present his story in the papers in the way that suits them. I think your first impression of Cary was even more right than you realized.*

I had a letter from him thanking me for that review of *Not Honour More.* Talking of it reminds me that in some ways Cary seems to belong to Devon rather than to Ireland.

He makes the reader aware of the Irish links with Devon in his novel Castle Corner.

I greatly regret not having got to know him better. And I certainly think that the thing to concentrate on with Cary – or any author for that matter – is not so much to find the hole in which the pigeon fits, nor whether he is a 'great' or 'major' novelist, as to put one's finger on where his *uniqueness* lies. For unique he certainly is.

If he hadn't been an artist of some kind, I think he might well have been, have become a General – perhaps a Major General! Born among and surrounded for years by army men, I have never been a great admirer of them as men – except for *Generals*, for whom I have always felt a special affection!

Lord Montgomery (one-time Major General?), was the person of whom Cary reminded Walter Allen.[5] *Being Anglo-Irish, from the same part of Ireland, could have something to do with that likeness. Have you any thoughts about his method of writing?*

[*Tania:*] He was all too ready to talk about his technique. I remember the phrase 'the jam-jar'; you put all in and shake up.

[*James:*] I recall Joyce's description of writing sketches and then putting them together to see how they fit.

Perhaps those were ways of saying that he presented his sub-conscious with a problem to sort out. He explains it best in Art and Reality, *which he worked so hard on, to finish before he died.*

[*Tania:*] I was struck by his *serenity*, when we saw him in 1956, and he was already ill.

NOTES

James Andrew Stern (1904-) born in Co. Meath, Ireland, is a writer of short stories (three volumes) and memoirs (not yet in book form); also author of a volume on Germany in 1945, *The Hidden Damage*, Harcourt Bruce, 1947.

Tania Stern (1904-), born in Breslau, Silesia, has made translations from German into English with her husband.

In January 1988 Mr and Mrs Stern kindly checked this record and agreed to its publication.

1. Her reviews and articles on Cary include 'Three Novelists and the Drawing of Character: C.P. Snow, Joyce Cary, and Ivy Compton-Burnett', *Essays and Studies by Members of the English Association*, n.s. vol. III (1950), 82-99; she was herself a novelist, and married C.P. Snow.

2. See MS. Cary 268/S.10.De, Cary's synopsis of *Castle Corner*, which illustrates *Power in Men*.

3. *New York Times Book Review* (New York, 25 Jan. 1959) 1, 45; in the review Stern recalls his first meeting with Cary, as described above, and names the friend as 'a highly successful farmer'.

4. *The New York Times Book Review* (New York, 29 May 1985), p.1.

5. See item 28; also 5.

55

Joyce Cary in Sweden
Some Remarks

Birgit Bramsbäck

This interview of 23 December 1987, in London, was completed by correspondence.

Joyce Cary gave lectures in Sweden during December 1954, and I heard him at Uppsala University. The title of the lecture was, as far as I recall, 'The Novel as Truth', but my strongest recollection of him, and of the occasion, is his answer to my question, if he considered himself British or Irish.

'I am Irish,' he said, 'oh yes, I am Irish, born in the North of Ireland.' Of course, I was very pleased because I had insisted on his being Irish, although my colleagues at the time in the Department of English, all without any exception, had insisted that Cary was British, and that his books should be placed among British authors, not among the Irish ones.

He was extremely kind and very interesting to talk to, and I remember him as of medium height and build. However, Herbert Tingsten describes him as slender, and 'the ideal type of an English gentleman.' This is in an article published on 15 August 1954 in *Dagens Nyheter*,[1] 'Joyce Cary's ideer' ('Joyce Cary's Ideas'). There, among other things, he mentions that Joyce Cary has often been suggested for the Nobel Prize for Literature, but he does not say by whom.

In his 1954 article Tingsten states that it is only in the early 50s that Joyce Cary has become famous, although his first book appeared in 1932 and had a motif from Nigeria. From 1941 his more important novels start to appear, Tingsten says, and every book has meant a step forward until by 1954 Cary is world famous. He has been translated into many languages and discussed in many periodicals and biographies and recognized as one of Britain's three or four foremost novelists. Tingsten calls him an advocate of Protestantism against the Catholicism of, for example, Graham Greene and Mauriac. He writes

219

about Cary's undogmatic belief in god and his belief in man, his belief in liberty and the inner light of man.

His 'pilgrim' trilogy has been translated into Swedish, and also other novels.[2]

NOTES

Prof. Birgit M.H. Bramsbäck (Bjersby), Ph.D., D.Litt., received a Gold Medal for long and meritorious service to the State (1979), and two honorary D.Litt. Degrees, one from the National University of Ireland (1981),and one from the Marquis Guiseppe Scicluna International University Foundation (1987).

She has taught at University College Dublin and at Uppsala University, where she was appointed professor in 1979. She has been in charge of the Irish Institute and the Celtic Section of the Dept of English. Her publications include *The Interpretation of the Cuchulain Legend in the Works of W.B. Yeats* (1950), *James Stephens: A Bibliographical and Literary Study* (1959), and *Folklore and W.B. Yeats* (1984).

Professor Bramsbäck's kind consent to the publication of this interview was received on 24 March 1988.

1. Of which Tingsten was editor; see item 39.

2. A Swedish critical study that deserves mention is by Ingvar Soderskog, *Joyce Cary's "Hard Conceptual Labour": A Structural Analysis of* To Be a Pilgrim, Goteborg: Aeta Universitatis Gothoburgensis, 1977.

56

The *Horse's Mouth* film

Alec Guinness

This item is compiled from letters of 1967 and 1988 (see notes).

[...] *Several people seem to think that you had discussed the part of Gulley Jimson with Joyce Cary, when a film of* The Horse's Mouth *was under consideration, shortly before his death. If this were so, I should be most interested to know anything you can recall, of the man and more particularly of his ideas.*[1]

[...] Unfortunately I never met Joyce Cary and by the time I had completed the script of 'The Horse's Mouth' and was very anxious to talk to him, he was really too ill and I felt he should not be bothered by people like me. So you see there is no information I can give you?[2]

[...] *I have wondered why the film is different from the book at the end. Can you say anything about the way it ended?*[3]

The ending of the film of 'The Horse's Mouth' was not quite as I had written it. I had wished to see the ramshackle boat floating down the lower reaches of the Thames and there cut to Gulley inside the wheel house drawing, very painstakingly, on a small piece of paper. The last shot would have been of what he was working at – an exquisitive, academic, drawing of a flower. I had hoped that this would establish him as an acceptable artist to the larger world. The producer, however, wanted it to go out with a bang.[4]

NOTES

Alec Guinness (1914-), Kt. 1959; CBE 1955; Hon. D.Litt. Oxon. 1977, was educated at Pembroke Lodge Southbourne and Roborough Eastbourne. He began his acting career in 1933 and, following war service from 1939-45, resumed it with the Old Vic in 1946; he received Oscar awards for the best actor of the year (1957) and for his contribution to film (1979), and the BAFTA award (1980, 1983). His autobiography, *Blessings in Disguise*, appeared in 1985.

1. From a letter sent by B. Fisher on 6 Oct. 1967.
2. Sir Alec's letter is dated 13 October 1967.
3. In this letter of 4 Jan. 1988, permission to quote Sir Alec's previous letter was requested.
5. Writing on 6 Jan. 1988, Sir Alex kindly agreed that I might use both letters for this book.

57

Belief in the Good

Iris Murdoch

This discussion was developed by correspondence in December 1987.

I know from our previous conversations that you went regularly to the Sunday evening gatherings at Joyce Cary's Oxford home during the 1950s. You have been quoted as saying of them: ' "One felt if one wanted to stay all night, one could without being noticed." '[1] *I wonder whether, from your own Anglo-Irish background, you might have thought that Cary was re-creating, consciously or unconsciously, something of the relaxed atmosphere of a typical Irish 'big house'?*

I would not compare the atmosphere with that of a 'big house' (though actually it's not a bad idea, now I come to think of it) – it was rather more for me like the atmosphere of a writers' pub in London! A step outside the Oxford world. Dan Davin's gatherings,[2] which are somewhat similar to Joyces's, take place in pubs. I like pubs.

Do you recall anything of your discussion of Under the Net, *of which Cary saw the manuscript, you have said?*

I don't think Joyce liked *Under the Net* much, though he praised it a bit, and he certainly encouraged me! He said, in criticism, that it was 'picaresque', a series of unconnected episodes, and so lacked a central theme. This was not my view of it.

Your central character, Jake Donaghue, interests me as an Irishman who grew up in east London, as in fact Cary's Gulley Jimson was also – and indeed Cary himself. I am not suggesting that Joyce Cary influenced you; rather that whatever quality made French critics regard Cary as an Existentialist is recognizable in this novel of yours also. A discussion of Gulley's origins led Cary to declare – 'Suddenly', as his interviewers said:

223

The French seem to take me for an Existentialist in Sartre's sense of the word. But I'm not. I am influenced by the solitude of men's minds, but equally by the unity of their fundamental character and feelings, their sympathies which bring them together. I believe that there is such a thing as unselfish love and beauty. I am obliged to believe in God as a person. [...] Of course, if you say I am an Existentialist in the school of Kierkegaard, that is more reasonable. But Existentialism without a God is nonsense – it atomises a world which is plainly a unity. It produces merely frustration and defeat.[3]

Do you recall discussing Existentialism with Cary in these, or any other, terms?

I've never been an Existentialist (though I wrote on Sartre) but of course Existentialism was much in the air, and lots of writers were accused of it! Jake Donaghue was connected with Pierrot in Queneau's book *Pierrot Mon Ami*, and Murphy in Beckett's *Murphy*. I don't recall discussing Existentialism with Joyce. I agree with him that Sartre's Existentialism excludes love and sympathy.

Cary's insistence on learning from the unique and particular real is something that you seem also to stress from the first. I take the key point in Under the Net *to come when Jake asks: ' "What about the search for God?" ' and Hugo replies: ' "God is a task. God is detail. It all lies close to your hand." ' That seems to follow directly from the words with which Hugo (as Annandine) gives the book its title: ' "All theorizing is flight. We must be ruled by the situation itself and this is unutterably particular. Indeed it is something to which we can never get close enough, however hard we may try as it were to crawl under the net." ' Am I right in thinking that your second novel developed directly from those words: ' "All theorizing is flight" '?*

No, the 'flight from the enchanter' is the flight from a god or demon. Hugo's words reflect an earlier and more radical kind of philosophical thought with which I still live. I wrote a philosophical (*Aristotelian Society*) paper in the 1950s called 'Nostalgia for the Particular'.

Are theories of race and nationality amongst those in your mind in this statement? Your London characters in these two novels, by their very names, strike one as non-English, and I am reminded of Cary's last essays, in which he reveals clearly what it means to him to be an Anglo-Irishman, but stresses the fact that nationalism is 'the idea that now dominates all political thinking and most propaganda. And it is tearing civilization to pieces.'[4]

I have some Irish characters. Jake has an Irish name. No special nationality planning in the books. *I* certainly feel Irish – but my characters vary.

Did you by any chance give Joyce Cary copies of Under the Net *and* The Flight from the Enchanter?

I think I gave him a copy of *Under the Net* and probably of the other as well.

You may be interested to know that he annotated his copies of both. In Under the Net, *'good' in various forms appears in chapters Two to Five, culminating with 'good notion' in Fourteen, beside Jake's reaction, when Breteuil wins the Goncourt prize, so making Jake's judgement of Breteuil's writing seem wrong; Cary felt sympathy for Breteuil, perhaps. But his chief enthusiasm was for chapter Six, where he has marked the passage containing your title (quoted above), and noted:* 'quite true see Blake'. *Of the dialogue he notes:* 'great fun but too obviously the reason for the book – philosophy wrapped up in paper.' *Yet he marked the third paragraph further on (which begins* 'What the piece of dialogue had been trying to remind me of'*):* 'all original interesting and important.'

However, there are adverse comments, which have prompted Molly Mahood to conclude (of you as this book's author): 'He regarded it as outrageous and absurd that she should have adopted a male persona.'[5] *This judgement invites reflection on* The Flight from the Enchanter, *where his annotations (on the back fly-leaf) are brief, yet show that he read it with attention. He noted* 'the young girl', *of Mischa's account of young girls who dream of saving men;*[6] *one wonders whether that might have influenced his creation of Alice in his last novel. Of page 255 of your novel, he notes:* 'Hunter also a girl'. *Here your attitude to the female in human nature seems to interest him – as that of a woman, I presume. Do you recall discussing the creation of characters of the opposite sex from one's own?*

I don't recall such a discussion. I have never felt any problem or difficulty here. (Dan Davin said of Jake Donaghue, 'He never shaves.')

I know that you have said, ' "His ways were not my ways." '[7] *In your method and technique, in conveying your view of the world, above all perhaps in the way you arrived at it, you are different, I am quite aware. Yet*

I feel that the world as conceived by each of you is very similar. A highly significant similarity is that you too, as I have read, reject belief in an after-life; and that is a starting-point for any other belief, Cary shows in notes. Did you ever discuss this?

I don't know exactly what his religious views were – rejection of after life is, and was then, fairly common, and compatible with various attitudes. He certainly seemed to me to be a religious man, in a high, undogmatic sense.

Did you ever hear him speak of a trial title, which appears in his notebooks from the mid-thirties, and was to have been the title of his last novel, if he had written his last book as a trilogy. This title is 'Boiling Down to Heaven', *and I'd very much like to know whether you can cast light on its source and meaning.*

Trial title. No. The word 'boiling' might connect with Eckhart (God pictured as 'boiling over') – but I've no idea if Joyce read or was influenced by Eckhart.

My belief is that it relates to Dostoevsky, who chiefly inspired his last novel (Cary's notes show). Do you recall any discussion with Cary of Dostoevsky, Tolstoy, or anyone else whom he acknowledged as an influence?

Tolstoy and Dostoevsky; yes, I love them too, and we may well have talked about them.

Regarding his powers of characterization, Walter Allen echoed Coleridge's description of Shakespeare by saying of Cary (in 1953): 'pre-eminently he is "the one Proteus" of the English novel today.'[8] *Since much has been said about the influence of Shakespeare on you, could this be taken as a point of resemblance between you?*

Well – I would *very much like* to be influenced by Shakespeare – I don't know if I've managed it!

Essentially, however, what I feel most strongly that you share with Joyce Cary is a profound belief in the Good – which, to judge from what you have both written about it, owed much to your understanding of Plato's influence regarding it. Did the substance of The Fire and the Sun *ever enter your discussions? And would you agree with what Cary says in* Power in Men: 'In the last resort, Plato's guardian philosophers are simply himself and the idea of the good is Plato's idea of the good. He belongs to the great class of religious and political theorists who have said in all ages, "I know inside me what is good for men, and they must do it (p. 41)."'

Platonism, yes. I like what you quote of his. And the sense of him as having such views, yes: a belief, which I share, of the absolutely central and fundamental place of goodness, and of the struggle between good and evil, in human life. How to express this philosophically is another matter.

Though not trained, as you are, to refute professional philosophers in their own language, Cary does end Art and Reality *(which he fought death to complete), with a challenge that I feel accords with yours:* 'If every born child has power to love, then goodness is a natural thing, as natural as hydrogen gas, and we belong to a world of personal value.' *Would you comment on that message, in relation to your own?*

I think good impulses, as well as bad ones, are instinctive and 'natural', and that our personal world is everywhere coloured by value. Perception is evaluation. But I may be more of a pessimist. I believe (leaving philosophical questions and presentation aside) in the reality of Good in a Platonic sense. But the problem is how to overcome the very powerful forces of egoism. (As Plato also indicated.)

Is there anything that you would like to add regarding Joyce Cary, as man or writer – as an Anglo-Irish writer, perhaps, or as the man in whose home friends gathered, over thirty years ago?

I don't know whether one can speak of Anglo-Irish writers as a group with something in common. The IRA have certainly given the Anglo-Irish a sense of identity! But that's another matter. Joyce was a universal writer and a moralist in the best sense. We (the people who came to those gatherings) all regarded him as a wise good man, and were very fond of him.

NOTES

Iris Murdoch was born in Dublin of Anglo-Irish parents. She went to Badminton School, Bristol, and read classics at Somerville College, Oxford. During the war she was an Assistant Principal at the Treasury, and then worked with UNRRA in London, Belgium and Austria. She held a studentship in philosophy at Newnham College, Cambridge, for a year, and in 1948 returned to Oxford where she became a Fellow and philosophy tutor at St Anne's College. In 1956 she married John Bayley, teacher and critic.

Miss Murdoch kindly agreed, in December 1987, that this discussion might be published.

1. Malcolm Foster, *A Biography*, p. 462.
2. See item 67.
3. See 'An Interview with Joyce Cary' (Q.7).
4. 'Joyce Cary's Last Look at his Worlds' (E.76).
5. See item 65.
6. *The Flight from the Enchanter* (London: Chatto and Windus, 1955), p. 142; Cary's copy, published in April, 1956, is Cary B.158 in the Bodleian.
7. Foster, *A Biography*, p. 462.
8. See item 28, n. 3.

58

His Home in Later Years

Nora Lightburne

This interview took place in Oxford on 28 September 1968.

Lady Ogilvie had wanted a house lady, and this fell through; so she asked if I would go to her brother-in-law. I was taken aback, as I had never worked, having grown up in Switzerland, and married at twenty; I had just become a widow. Before me he'd had a young girl of about eighteen (whom Lady Ogilvie had also found, I think); but she was leaving to go to the University. That was in October 1954. When I was engaged he was gentlemanly, polite, not too friendly (just right). I admired him very much. He wanted everyone to be happy. He always came out and thanked me after every meal. I lived in all the time and couldn't really leave him. I went to Scotland for one month, but they didn't like the person who relieved me. Mr Cary allowed my daughter to come and stay. He never interfered in my life, and I had my own sitting-room. A woman came in daily to clean.

What was the layout of the house?

In the basement was the kitchen and a beautiful dining-room, with a beautiful oblong table and sideboard, and my sitting-room. On the ground-floor there was a big sitting-room in front, with a piano; a tiny room which was Mr Cary's sitting-room and had been Mrs Cary's; then his bedroom and bathroom which he'd had made. He slept in a huge four-poster. The first floor had a very large bedroom, with a four-poster, for guests; another with two beds, and a small bedroom which I had, and a toilet. There were basins in the bedrooms. On the top floor he had his study and above that was the attic, full of junk. There were also a smaller and a bigger bedroom on the top floor, and a bathroom.

The house was very inconvenient, and it struck me as odd that they had lived there so long. I supposed that he'd come from a family house, and he said that they'd run it with four maids before the war. His study

229

had been the children's nursery. The plumbing was very inconvenient, and all went up the cold side of the house, so that the water
outlet therefore froze.[1] People who did repairs all liked him. They
had been coming for years.

Later he had all his meals in his room, but at first he had them all
in the dining-room. For breakfast he would have prunes, toast, and
coffee. The only things he didn't eat were chocolate and coconut.
For dinner he liked candles and the best silverware on the table, and
so did I; so that was no trouble. He would have just one glass of wine
each night. His favourite was called Châteauneuf du Pape.

Regarding drink, he told me that many officers took to it in Africa
in lonely places, but he did not, because his writing had kept him
happy. Regarding the silverware, he wanted it all plated before he
died, so that everything left to the sons would be worthy. He
admired his wife so much, and never forgot that she practically kept
them and always helped him, and this was a way of making up to
her.

When he engaged me I was told that he would have a dinner party
about once a month, but these soon faded out. He had little idea
about food, and always said 'A crown of lamb' when I asked what
meat to order. He would get a butler from one of the colleges.

The visitors who stayed were mostly family. The brother and
sister from Somerset stayed, and for the first two Christmases [*in '54
and '55*] he had the whole family there, just as they did when Mrs
Cary was alive. But only Michael and Lucius came on the last
Christmas. I went and cooked the dinner at night. The children at
the end worried him, because he could not control them touching
things, or falling over. But previously he had loved them to come to
his bedroom in the mornings for example. Michael's daughter Kate
was the first girl in the Cary family for fifty years, he said. Peter and
his wife probably stayed more than the others at the end, as they
were freer to come.

Edith Haggard came twice to stay, and was devoted. It irked Mr
Cary that she spent money on him – it embarrassed him; for
example, she gave me money for flowers, and I would spend about
three pounds at a time. I told him that he should accept the gift as it
was intended – to do something when she couldn't come to see him.
He got me to get a Georgian coffee pot to send her in return.

His wife would every now and then enter his conversation – of
what she had meant to him; he was still in love with her, and could
not therefore love anyone else. He told me what a wonderful pianist
she had been, and the people next door spoke of her wonderful

music, but said she had been very shy. These neighbours were Sir Donald and Lady Hurst, who now live off the Banbury Road, and were friends of Mr Cary.

He was very fond of the Davin girls, who came on Wednesday afternoons after school and on Sundays, at about four o' clock. I would put tea ready and then Mrs Davin took over. Lucius also came on Sundays, from the Dragon School. They were all keen to hear the next instalment of the serial story which he invented for them week by week; Anna [*the eldest Davin girl*] came too. David Cecil would come for a few minutes every evening at six and also on Sundays. Enid Starkie came on Sundays, but I don't recall her at other times. However, visitors didn't ring. The front door was left open for visitors to come in to save me having to answer the door; so I didn't always know who called. While Andrew Wright was there he came in the mornings, and by then Mr Cary was in his sitting-room.

He was visited regularly by a circle of literary friends. After he was confined to bed, they would take it in turns to go in to see him, one at a time, while the others continued their discussion over drinks in the drawing-room. He kept a cabinet for whisky, gin, etc., for visitors which I kept stocked while Milly paid the bills. Milly was Mr Cary's name for Miss Millen, his secretary and nurse who came in the mornings at first, then all day and then finally lived in.[2]

Mrs Haggard gave him champagne. He didn't smoke, but had cigarettes for guests. When I went there he had no flowers in the house, and I asked if he liked them. He said yes, but Robina (the housekeeper girl before me) wasn't keen. He loved flowers, and I took over the garden, because the gardener had ceased to come. Mr Cary offered to pay me what he'd paid the gardener. He gave me housekeeping money for incidentals, which I was supposed to enter in a book that he gave me. But he never looked at it, and Milly paid the accounts.

He was so considerate. He rarely rang, even though he couldn't get out of his chair. But gradually Milly was doing everything, working up to ten o'clock at night. An Australian nurse was engaged as night nurse but she was not congenial; then a local nurse from Kidlington, separated from her husband and more Mr Cary's type, used to come when Milly was out. For about two months at the end there was a night nurse.

I sometimes helped Milly to turn him (to avoid bedsores) at the end, during the last fortnight. He never spoke at these times. He was writing until the last fortnight, eating soft food. But he could eat less and less and I think that he really died of starvation. He got worried earlier about losing his voice so that he couldn't dictate. His throat muscles were paralysed. I was out shopping when he died.

After he died Michael and Tristram made a bonfire of junk, like old chairs. Mr Cary never threw anything away. Once I found a scholar's gown green with age which he said a grandson would be proud to wear. But he had cupboards full of beautiful clothes – shoes galore. I think Tristram got his evening cape, but otherwise his clothes didn't fit any of his family.

He never went out socially after I went there, which I thought odd, as he could have gone and come back in a taxi. He went only once, that I remember, to give a lecture. At first he went into the garden after lunch, but as it got cold, towards the end of '55, he ceased and never went out again. At first I had helped him to go down into the basement. But once, at night, after I had gone to bed, he fell. Fortunately he had the whistle (which Edith Haggard had given him), and I went to find him bleeding at the head. But he refused to let me call the doctor, though the next day it was discovered that he had broken a rib too. After that he never went up and down stairs.

At the funeral there were a lot of relatives, and Michael took charge. The service was in St Giles. The parson had kept wanting to see Mr Cary, as he was in his parish, but he had seen him only once. Mr Cary kept asking me to keep him away, because he felt uncomfortable with him. I found it difficult to offend the man. He was an elderly man. The funeral was in the morning, and then they had a buffet lunch, which I had had to slip away to prepare. There were about twenty people at the lunch. Then they retired to open the will. But only the relatives were there then, I think.

NOTES

Mrs Nora Lightburne (1898-) née Munch, daughter of a Swiss architect, married (1920) Revd H.R.H. Lightburne in Canterbury;, she has four daughters, and now lives in St. Andrews, Scotland.

She kindly checked this record of our interview, and agreed on 24 January 1988 to its publication.

1. In a letter of 10.2.54 to Edith Haggard, Cary wrote: 'I have been flooded out and had to tear up floors and tear down hoardings to get at the bursts which were pouring into my drawing room and ruining the carpets. Now I have to put everything back again just when I am most anxious to get on with the book which is giving me trouble.'

2. See item 61.

59

'Beloved grown-up of my childhood'

Delia Davin

This interview took place on 7 November 1987 at the Davins' home in Oxford, where Joyce Cary had visited them.

Joyce was certainly the most beloved grown-up of my childhood, except for my parents. I think, too, we liked him even more than those of my parents' friends we were fond of and who were fond of us, because he wasn't part of the pub culture they otherwise belonged to. So instead of constantly taking them away from us by taking them to the pub as their other friends did, he was the one who would stay here and say, 'No, I don't think so,' when my father said, 'shall we go to the Vicky [*Victoria Arms*] now?' My father would go off, but my mother would usually stay here to keep him company; so he was somebody who made us see more of our parents.

Did he give you the notion that he was Anglo-Irish?

Yes. We knew that we were all from the same country, but he was different in some way. In some way we felt we were real Irish and he wasn't quite.

How old were you when you first met him?

I know that he knew our family from 1949 onwards, when I would have been five. And I have the impression that we became much closer to him when his wife died and left a family gap. I think we filled that gap.

Were you aware that you were doing that?

No. We knew his wife was dead because he occasionally spoke of her. He always carried an old five pound note, which you'll remember was a

233

large sheet of white paper. He had originally carried it so that if Trudy saw something in a shop which she liked, he would be able to go in and buy it for her immediately. He taught us to pick-pocket it. I don't know why, but he liked to see children able to pick-pocket without grown-ups noticing. So one of my pieces of knowledge about his wife was that they had this relationship where he liked to be able to indulge her impulses. He also wore a fob-watch in his waistcoat pocket; that was another thing we used to pick-pocket.

We had a very close relationship in that sort of way. He would sit in that chair and his right knee was my knee and his left knee was Brigid's, and we would sit on his knee while he told us stories. At his house we learnt to pick-pocket him in the big sofa. When his arthritis got very bad we used to take a hand each and massage the knuckles; and at the beginning of the afternoon his hands might be closed up, and we would take pride in opening them up as much as possible. We would compete to see whose hand was straightened more. A lot of people would find the very close attentions of children for all that time rather irritating, but he didn't.

I remember when Graham Greene's novel *The Quiet American* first arrived at his house. I was eleven or twelve, and this one copy was passing from hand to hand. We had had tea at Joyce's before people started arriving for drinks, and I had booked this book to borrow it next. I can remember several grown-ups were annoyed at this, but Joyce said, 'I'd promised her, so she gets it next, and that's it.'

Which is your favourite book of Joyce Cary's?

I probably like *A House of Children* best. I was interested in the Irish link; and later I was sent to Gaelic College in Donegal. And also, I was enchanted that there was a character in it called Delia; Joyce used to tell us stories about Delia. The American edition was the first book of his that Joyce ever gave to us – a signed copy each.

Then he gave us a copy each of *Not Honour More*, which he dedicated to his six godchildren. We were jealous that other children had godparents and we didn't, because we hadn't been baptized; so we asked Joyce, 'Can we adopt you as our godfather?' He said, 'Yes, but you don't believe in God.' He was always a little troubled that we hadn't been brought up to believe in God. So we said, 'We adopt you as our non-godfather,' and he said to our mother: 'Winnie, I can't really dedicate the book to my three godchildren and my three adopted godchildren. Can I put them all in the same category?' She laughed and said, 'Of course.' You knew he was being very careful about the scruples he felt she might have and in fact didn't have at all.

Are you interested in his non-fiction?

No. I read *Art and Reality* when it was published, but I don't think I related to it very much, because I was twelve when he died, and the Joyce I knew was a friend of my childhood and was a wonderful story-teller. I knew that we were politically different, because he voted liberal, and I think that he had made me quite conscious that he was Anglo-Irish and we were not. Perhaps I didn't expect to like his theoretical side. I probably feared to read something I disagreed with, from someone I loved so much. I didn't read any other non-fiction except *Memoir of the Bobotes*, years and years later, because Winnie was closely involved in its production. But it's story-telling again. We thought of Joyce as a wonderful and adorable person who also happened to be a writer. I read his books because I loved him. I had read all his novels by the time I was thirteen or fourteen, within a year or so of his death.

Have you ever re-read them?

I've re-read some of them, but I find it quite painful. For a long time it was such a painful area of life that I didn't think about him too much. But now I talk about Joyce with my family when we meet again. When I was at school, and I thought I was going to have an uncontrollable fit of giggles, I used to think of Joyce, to quell them by making myself sad. Recently I found out that my sister, Brigid, used to do the same. We had evolved this peculiar technique independently. His having died, his not being there any more, was so upsetting that it controlled anything. However hysterical we were, we just thought of that, and that blanket came down over the world.

If at night I couldn't sleep I would go over happy memories of having been with him, like our holiday in Northumberland together, in 1955. We stayed in a castle called Barmoor, near Lowick, belonging to someone who had been at Balliol with my father (Bill Sitwell, who was a cousin of Osbert and Edith). We went for wonderful long walks with Joyce. Once we went to a disused mine where the ghosts of two miners were rumoured to be fighting at the bottom of a pitshaft. Bill Sitwell, who was very superstitious, told us to stay away from it, and Joyce laughed and said: 'You don't really believe in ghosts, do you?' and began to jump up and down on the timber covering the mine head. We all shrieked at him to come off, because we were afraid the timber was very rotten and he would go through. We did rather believe in ghosts, too, living in this ghostly castle. I thought it funny that he was rational about ghosts when he believed in God.

His influence seems still to persist strongly in you – thirty-two years later.

He is still very important to me. I have his self-portrait hanging in my study, looking down on me. That's how I remember him, in the last months, when we went so much to his house. We used to go there straight from school, because my mother was always there then. We used to go to the drawing-room and do our homework, and when we were told that Joyce wasn't too tired we would go in and spend time, however long he wanted. I made the tea and carried it up. The Indian tea which we drank was always in the stainless-steel teapot, and the China tea which he drank was always in a very beautiful silver teapot, that must have come down from his or Trudy's family.

What about the cliff-hanging stories he told you? Can you remember any of them?

I remember the one where I had six tigers very well.

Were the stories always about you?

The last and longest serial was, and whenever we had child visitors, they would be put in it for the occasion too. My father had given me a little gold crucifix which his mother had given him. In the story a man with a six-shooter tried to shoot me and all the shots bounced off this little cross. But one episode ended with this man pointing his six-shooter at me, and we had to wait until the next week to know how I would be saved. He knew so well the things that children would like.

He never carried pennies or halfpennies because he said they make holes in your trouser pockets. He shuffled them off into what he called his copper drawer. And once a year, before St Giles' Fair, we would be allowed to empty his copper-drawer and share it out between the three of us. When his grandson Lucius was at the Dragon School and came with us, we would sort it out into four. That would be our spending money for one of our visits to the Fair. But at another visit Joyce would take us and he would pay for everything.

For the last Fair he visited before his death, when he was very ill, we got a wheelchair to take him in. I think it was our idea. I certainly remember that Anna and Brigid and I went up to the Red Cross and borrowed it, feeling very adventurous, taking this initiative. Up to that point, he had been very reluctant to get one, but we begged him to come to the Fair, and he said, 'All right, but I'll need a chair.' So we took him. We pushed him and were very proud about it. I suppose he was very trusting to be pushed by us. I remember we got to the Big Wheel and he said: 'I'm coming on the Big Wheel with you.' And my mother said, 'You can't Joyce.' And he said, 'I am.' And he got up and we supported him one under each arm, and sort of helped him to the Big Wheel. You know how those benches take three people. He lived life to the full. [...]

He always trusted us. For example he had a beautiful collection of netsukes of which he was very proud, and he always got us to clean them.[1] He believed in the abilities of children and also believed in never discouraging them. In that *Life* Magazine interview, when he's asked whether we tell him stories, his answer is that none of them are any good. Yet I have a memory, which perhaps I invented, that he said: 'I couldn't have said that. I never said that. I said some of them are very good.'[2] That certainly would have been much more like Joyce. He always encouraged us to write and to draw and to believe that we could do things; and as I didn't do very well at school at that age, that was important to me. He'd laugh and say: 'Oh well, I got a fourth. It doesn't matter what teachers think of you.' [...]

I don't know whether I have invented some of these childhood memories. Actually, when I think about Joyce, I'm amazed how much I can remember, because there are other areas of my childhood which are totally blank. Yet I could describe his house exactly – what furniture was where – and I can see the secret drawers of his desk in my mind's eye. I think it is because his home was our second home, and he was like family. You see, outside our parents, we didn't have any family in England. We looked forward to meeting relatives some day, but they weren't a real presence. Other people at school stayed with and went to tea with their relatives. So Joyce had filled that gap for us.

We loved his recklessness and his naughtiness. He had a bicycle with a very bent wheel, and when we first knew him he cycled to tea here every Wednesday on it. Everybody was always telling him that it was dangerous, and he would laugh. He told us very dare-devil stories of how he dived for money when he was a child. He was a great diver as a kid and really loved diving, but at some point he burst an ear-drum and was told he must never dive again, and that was a great sadness to him. When we were small we used to skate on Port Meadow and he was a beautiful skater. He was very proud of being able to skate backwards and execute various turns and he knew the technical names for them. There had been an ice rink in Oxford when he was a student here.

He had loved being active. He talked a lot about his polo in Africa and his horses and swimming the river with his most beloved horse.[3] You got the impression of somebody who had never grown up in the sense of becoming very careful. And he was so generous with us. I remember when I fell and cut my knee coming home across the University Parks from a friend's in Marston. It was the first time I had walked so far on my own, and I went to his house because it was near. He immediately broke off working, did my knee up, gave me a bar of chocolate and rang Winnie; he took care of me in a way unusual in a man then.

Do you think he wished he'd had a daughter?

Perhaps. He had great affection for his daughters-in-law. He was always glad that we had long hair, and he liked to see us brushing our hair. I remember that we were sitting with him when he drew that picture in *The Old Strife at Plant's* where she's brushing her hair.[4] He was looking at our hair and talking about the way light comes off hair etc. And he told us he was upset when Trudy cut her hair; he described how she had flicked her plaits back across the bed-posts when she lay down in bed at night. That was obviously important to him. Strange that he liked to talk to us children about it.

People often unburden themselves of things that matter to them to people whom others would think unimportant – especially children.

Maybe. He hated make-up. He would tell us he hated it and then he would suddenly remember that my mother wore it and he would look worried that he had been tactless.

It was always very clear to us that he felt very easy with women. He kept boxes of chocolates and of nylons in the bottom drawer of his desk so that he would always have presents for women on their birthdays. In fact I now have a drawer where I keep presents. That's one thing I learnt from Joyce; it's a very sensible habit.

Do you think you could have formed so close a relationship if you had been three boys?

I really don't know, because I knew him as a child, not as an older person would have known him. I know that I felt very odd at the funeral, because I realized suddenly that the family were the main mourners; that Isabel was in charge of the hospitality etc. When we used to go to tea with him, it was normally his housekeeper's time off. Cakes would have been made and that sort of thing put ready, but it was my job to set the trays and make the tea, and everything always had to be very nice. I had felt important to be doing all that, and I suddenly had the sense of loss. The house was going, everything had gone. We saw him in his coffin, and I'm very glad I did. In the Irish tradition you did see but my mother asked us if we wanted to and said that we shouldn't feel bad if we didn't, but I never regretted it. It did help me to accept that he was dead.

What is your memory of him then?

His skin looked almost plastic, waxy; he was pale and calm and gone away – taken away from us.

Were you at the Sunday evening parties that went on to the very end?

Yes, always. We poured the drinks for the guests – gin and orange or whatever. He had quite a good wine cellar, which he stocked through Enid Starkie, because she ran the Somerville wine cellar. Enid took a great pride that she had built up a cellar as good as those of the men's colleges; so by buying from her rather than from his own old college Joyce was boosting a women's college as well as a friend. It must have been good wine, because it always arrived wrapped in the straw jackets; we used to take the straw off the bottles when we were having a bonfire on Guy Fawkes' night. It was Joyce's suggestion that we should.

I don't remember him telling us not to do anything. We used to go and explore in his attic and go through his boxes and things. I just don't remember him giving us the feeling that there were things we shouldn't touch. When I think of it now it seems extraordinary to me, the freedom we had to do as we wanted. We used to play with the crane that loaded him into his bath and took him out of it when he was ill.

Can you think of anything else of significance?

He talked to us a lot about faith-healing, when he was receiving all those letters about it. He told us that he was going to give up all the ways of trying to be healed, whether medical or faith, but he felt he must

write nice letters back to these people. It was awful, because he wanted
to get on with his work and not waste time having to write nice letters.

I remember being upset when *The New Yorker* brought out a story
about a marriage between a black man and a white woman, and Joyce
said that if he'd had a daughter he wouldn't have liked her to marry a
black man. I admired Joyce so much that I didn't expect him to have
any fundamental principled attitude that I disagreed with.

*At least he was being honest. I remember an Indian girl in London (daughter
of a diplomat, I think) who said, when the question arose: 'My father would
never allow me to marry a white man.' The feeling relates to something
fundamental in the human species, perhaps – of fathers for daughters?*

I think now that he was probably thinking about the prejudice that
existed in society that makes life difficult for people in such a situation.
More so than now. But it shocked me then.

Have you any other adverse memory of him?

None at all.

How did you feel towards his grandchildren?

We got on very well with Lucius, who is the only one we really knew.
He went to the Dragon School, and we used to collect him and bring
him to Parks Road for tea on Sundays.

NOTES

Delia Davin (1944-) was educated at the Oxford High School for Girls and Leeds
University, where her first degree was in Chinese, and her doctorate in Chinese social
history. She is a University lecturer, mainly in Chinese studies, and her publications
include *Letter from Peking*; *Woman-work in China*, and *Chinese Lives* (translated in
collaboration, 1988).
She has three children and lives in Leeds.
    In January 1988 she kindly agreed to publication of this interview.
    1. Cf. the last pages of chapters 16 and 17 of *The Horse's Mouth*, where Gulley admires
and steals Hickson's netsukes.
    2. See Q.11; the interview was based on Cary's answers to questions sent in Dec.
1956, which could have been wrongly copied, in Oxford or New York, and seen and
discussed by Cary and Delia in a proof copy before he died.
    3. See item 47, his letter of 30 Dec. 1952.
    4. Opp. p. 9, in the Bodleian edn; see S.18.

60

Memories of My Grandfather

Lucius Cary

This interview took place at Huntswood House on 14 December 1987.

What are your first memories of your grandparents, and of 12 Parks Road?

That's hard. I don't remember Trudy. But I can certainly remember going downstairs to eat at Parks Road, when I was very young. It had a very distinctive smell, Parks Road – a smell of floor polish, probably. It had a wonderful maroon red stair carpet, and also a very good gramaphone, which used to play *The Barber of Seville* and *Figaro*. When I was there, of course, what was being played would reflect more the taste of his sons. They'd always done a concert for him every year when Trudy was alive, and they kept it up; 'Prepare Thyself Zion' was always a great performance, and this tradition meant a great deal to Joyce.

What do you remember best about him?

I remember when I was at the Dragon School, I used to go on Sundays across the Parks and have tea with Joyce. And every Sunday he would tell us a serial, which was about the Davins, particularly Delia and Brigid; the story used to concern the three of us. It always ended at an exciting climax, and lots of other people used to listen. There'd be Enid Starkie and other people listening, and then he would carry on the week after, where he'd left off.

How often did this happen?

I should say five or six times. It would have been during the latter part of 1956. In one of these stories, I remember, Brigid and I were walking down Banbury Road, and we were picked up by a man in a car, and we got in the car and the car then had wings and a propellor and it took off and became an aeroplane. We ended up, in that episode, in a little boat

241

in the channel, and we were about to be run down by a ship. The next week, one of the mines (or a big cake of gunpowder, that had been left from the Spanish Armada) blew up under the boat, and it blew us into space. But we separated on either side of the bows of this ship, so that Brigid ended up in one bit of space and I ended up in another bit of space.

You must certainly have found it exciting, to have remembered it so clearly after thirty years. Do you remember anything else about those visits?

I remember, one rainy day, we were painting the illustrations for *The Old Strife at Plant's*. There was a great big pile of them. They hadn't been bound at this point, but they'd all been printed, and they all needed colouring in. They were all hand-coloured before they were bound. I did the tigers – not all of them; I wouldn't have had enough patience for that. I don't suppose I'd have been let loose on more than half a dozen, but I can remember sitting there with a pot of paint, painting tigers.

What else do you remember?

Christmas was always quite a ritual, in that we used to be banished from the drawing-room at Parks Road on Christmas Eve, and then all the holly was put behind pictures and on the Christmas tree. On Christmas Day we used to have a Christmas lunch, and after it all the children got sent to bed to rest, until about three. Then there were three bells: the first bell meant that you could get up and put your shoes on; the second meant that you could go to the top of the stairs; at the third bell you'd come down the stairs and go into the drawing-room where the grand piano was. There'd be a carol, 'While Shepherds Watch', with the candles, which had been lit, on the Christmas tree. All the presents would be there, and then they would be opened.

On Boxing Day there was the pantomime. We always used to sit in the same place, which was in the front row of the dress circle. I thoroughly enjoyed it, and always thought that Joyce did; but I've since learned that he didn't, from my mother. What he enjoyed was seeing how the children enjoyed it, she says.

Can you remember his last Christmas?

Yes. I was sent in to sing 'O Little Town of Bethlehem' by his bed, because he couldn't get up, and Tristram was playing the accompaniment. And we got out of sync[hronization], because Tris. couldn't hear me; so I then sang it unaccompanied.

It was on Christmas Eve, and it was the one time that Joyce Cary broke down, according to Dan Davin.[1] *Do you remember that?*

I think I do. I think I remember asking Daddy why it was, and he said it was because Joyce wouldn't see another Christmas.

What age were you? And can you remember when you last saw him?

I knew he was ill. I was nine then, and ten when he died, and I saw him again after Christmas, I think. I certainly remember when he had that strap, and could hardly hold anything in his hands, and his hands were held up on that writing machine.

I have a copy of a letter that I am sure will mean a lot to you. It was given to me by Thomas Higham, to whom it was written by your father. It is dated 2nd April, 1957, and it ends: 'I am beginning to realize only now how much I shall miss him. I take comfort from the fact that it could have been so much worse. He had a fear that he might have lived on for weeks and even months in a state of complete helplessness; and as it was he died peacefully in his sleep, and had been able to recognize and to smile at Lucius only the evening before.'

NOTES

John Lucius Arthur Cary is Michael Cary's eldest son and the first grandchild of Joyce. He was educated at the Dragon School, Eton, Trinity College Oxford, and Harvard Business School. He founded Venture Capital report in 1978, and published *VCR Guide to Venture Capital in the U.K.*, 1st edition 1983, 2nd edition 1983, 3rd edition 1987. He married Joanna Pamela Monica Sheppard in 1985; Eleanor Elizabeth Ewbank Cary was born in June 1986.

On 6 January 1988 he kindly agree to the publication of this interview.

1. See pp. 119-20 of *Closing Times*, (item 67, n.1).

61

From His Secretary

Edith Millen Stapleton

This interview took place on 14 July 1967 at Mrs Stapleton's home, in Bozeman, Montana.

It was the most interesting job I had ever had. I started in July 1955, and was rather awestruck at going. He was very formal at the time; I was just a typist. I worked upstairs at the top of the house, in a room overlooking the back garden. The first thing I typed was 'You're Only Young Once', a story about St Giles's Fair.[1] He was working on *The Captive and the Free* at the same time. At first I went in the afternoons, and he had finished writing in the mornings. (Later, for a time, I worked for a pathologist in the afternoons, and for him in the mornings.) Where I couldn't read what he'd written I was to leave blanks, which he would fill in. His manuscripts were hard to decipher, but he didn't like to dictate. Then, with 'The Tunnel', when he was bedridden, I typed it as he dictated.[2]

When I went to him his second trilogy had already been published, and he thought more highly of it than of the first, I think. There were negotiations for a film of *The Horse's Mouth*, but he didn't really *want* them to make a film. He might have agreed if they'd offered a really high sum.[3]

He was really eager for praise. If I said I liked something, he reflected. I became interested in his theories, after reading 'The Split Mind of the West',[4] and he asked me to sit down and talk with him about them. Then there was the interview with Nathan Cohen, which was recorded, and I remember it clearly.[5] Cohen first raised the question of censorship, and Cary said there was no case for it whatever. He had written to *The Times* saying that logically Boccaccio is censorable.[6] But to ask members of a jury whether they would allow their daughters to read a certain book was a plea to old-fashioned sex prejudice. Then Cohen asked whether Cary had experienced a return to a quest for religion, and he said he had returned to religion 'pretty early on'. Once accepted, God dominates the world, he said; that is, he accepted the world as a character which is fixed and limited. He said Catholicism is a religion, and Protestantism is a faith, and what he needed was a faith. But he found it by re-educating himself, discovering his own ignorance, and discovering his own world.

Writing is absolutely easy, he said; the difficulty is to choose. He wrote about a world of creative freedom and power. Dostoevsky could never make up his mind, and he talked of him as an example of the split mind. 'Praise matters a lot,' he admitted to Cohen, because every writer is an evangelist. And he wanted to be understood.

Do you think he enjoyed giving inteviews and lectures?

Yes, he did. But he hated the sentimentality of some of the journalistic articles about him. He especially enjoyed seeing students who were writing theses. He was always willing to talk to them. He was also very meticulous about replying to all letters, however mad. He had a file of 'bug' letters, and would say, 'Send him a copy of the "bug" letter' – or ' "b.b." letter.' He would dictate replies to important letters.

He stuck to a routine for as long as possible, of working in the mornings, and reading or seeing people in the afternoon, while I typed. He re-read a lot of books, which he talked about, and quoted – mainly Dostoevsky, Tolstoy, Hardy, and Conrad.

He was very proud of, and fond of, his sons. He was fond of George's wife, and spoke about her belief in an after-life.

Would you say something now about his illness?

I remember he told me that when he was in Greece, early in '55, he had tried to open a door with his left hand and found that he couldn't; that was the first indication he had of paralysis. He had already had treatment in Stoke Mandeville hospital before I worked for him, but it hadn't done any good. He had been sent there by Ritchie Russell, the neurologist, whom I knew because I had worked in his ward as a sister in the Churchill hospital.

Joyce Cary was certainly fortunate in finding a secretary who was also a trained nurse. When did he go to Bristol for treatment?

In November '55. I drove down there in a taxi with him to a hospital – really a nursing home, but I didn't bring him back. He was back in Oxford for Christmas, but I was away until a day or two after Christmas. I also had a holiday, for about two weeks, in June '56, and he had to get a nurse and a secretary in while I was away. He hadn't wanted me to go, but he was understanding,and unwilling to give trouble. He was less self-centred than most people in such a position.

He was still walking a little during the summer of '56, with a stick. We got a wheelchair from the Red Cross in the late summer of '56, and then got a better one. He never went downstairs after that. I went to live at 12 Parks Road in September '56. I would go down at about 7.30 and we had tea together and read the papers. He read *The Times* and a Liberal paper that has since ceased publication [*The News Chronicle?*] He was very interested in current events. After breakfast I would help him bath and dress and get into a wheel chair in the study. He would dictate letters and I would type them while he wrote. He worked on until lunch time, when he had a tray in his study on a folding-table for lunch on his own. He was getting up until after Christmas, but then he couldn't sit in a chair – he would slip down – and so he stayed in bed, and we had to feed him.

He loved flowers, and Edith Haggard sent money to Mrs Lightburne to buy them every week. I always remember he said that Edith Haggard and he each had a hole inside them left by the death of someone close and loved. His hearing remained good to the end, and his sight, and loving care did make a difference. There was only one time in that whole period that he ever said, 'Oh my god. I just can't stand this.' But it didn't last long. What was important was to be able to communicate thoughts. He never gave evidence of wanting to hasten his death. Even the doctor commented on this. He wouldn't take sedatives because he wanted to have a clear mind. It was only during the last two to three weeks that he couldn't write, and only in the last couple of weeks that he was kept under phenobarbital. He had periods of being uncomfortable and so was given some sedatives. He had something to help him sleep.

For perhaps the last two months he had a night nurse, who came from an agency. Shortly after Christmas I'd had some sort of collapse, and couldn't cope. I'd had to get up at nights to him, and there was a certain mental strain, as I was very fond of him. I thought it the worst death I had ever seen – he was so completely clear in his mind. He died very quietly. Because he was restless he'd had an injection of a sedative drug from the night nurse in the early hours of the morning, and he was in an unconscious state. I was shaving him. I'd shaved one side of his face and never finished. I was suddenly aware that he wasn't breathing. I went up and told Peter, who was staying there, and I phoned the doctor and Win Davin. Then I went away – that day – for a few days.

I stayed on in the house until around the end of May – for about two more months. I worked on the manuscript of *The Captive and the Free*. Michael was in France, and this possibly explained why they kept on the house. He left Win, Mrs Lightburne and me £200 each, and he sent Edith Haggard a watch belonging to his father or grandfather. He also sent her a garnet brooch and a punch ladle.

Those were the most memorable, valuable years of my life – in some ways the happiest but also the saddest. It was a turning point in my life because he made me see things as I never had before. I admired and loved him as a friend and as a father. I never felt jealous except when another nurse filled my role (satisfactorily).

NOTES

In a letter of November 1967 Mrs Stapleton wrote that their plans were to leave Bozeman, but she did not have an address to give me at that time, and I have not heard from her since. I can give no further details of her life, but believe that she would agree to the publication of this interview. I should be most grateful if she, or anyone reading this, could tell me where I might now get in touch with her.

1. S.38.
2. S.43; Cary's letter of 9 Sept '56 to Edith Haggard describes this new method.
3. Cf. item 47, his letters of 27 Aug. and 13 Sept. 1954; also item 56.
4. MS. Cary 247, a long, unpublished essay.
5. It took place in Sept. 1956, was broadcast on the CBC programme 'Anthology' in Jan 1957, and published in the *Tamarack Review*, no. 3 (Spring 1957), 5-15.
6. On 2 Aug. 1954 (L.4).

62

Such a Brave Patient

Ritchie Russell

This interview took place at the Churchill Hospital, Oxford, on 2 November 1967.

I am afraid that I have a bad memory, and have not considered Joyce Cary at all as a writer. I never discussed his books or philosophy with him. I did not attend him regularly. His medical file will show the occasions.[1]

There was no problem about diagnosis. The disease was recognized about a hundred years ago, as a disease. There is still absolutely nothing known of its cause or cure. At my hospital we get about twenty cases a year. It is properly called amyotrophic lateral sclerosis, of a type sometimes called progressive muscular atrophy (PMA for quick reference); another name used is motor neuron disease. It usually takes about four years – so that Joyce Cary's was rather quicker than the average. What happens is that the nerve cells in the spinal cord disappear, and this causes the muscles to waste. There is no pain with it. Research in Guam, where there is much incidence, suggests that there is some sort of inherited liability there; but there is no evidence that it is so here.

The treatments tried for Joyce Cary are no longer used. Snake venom was a dead loss, and might have made him rather worse. The disease was fairly well developed when I saw him, but I sent him to Sir Charles Symonds because he wanted confirmation.

He was a very good patient, and a very likable person, with a most charming personality. It was always a pleasure to go and see him. I was very impressed with the way he continued to work, and with his absolute self-reliance, though he understood his situation. If he ever broke down, it would have been from frustration rather than from fear. You will see from the file that he felt he must have lead poisoning. I was afraid of his breathing being affected. It is a dreadful, horrible disease, and he was such a brave patient.

Do you think he might have wanted to set an example? Facing death as a theme recurs in his writing, and 'The Firing Line', as an early trial title, reappears towards the end.[2] *Tolstoy attracted much public notice in the manner of his death, and Cary was always absorbed with everything about Tolstoy – the man as well as the writer.*

I have no doubt that Cary had faced up to death long before, and I agree that he might have set himself to be an example. Many people think their behaviour is on trial when dying, and do set this sort of example. It certainly becomes more likely if it had been an abiding theme in his writing, and I find what you say about Tolstoy interesting.

His nurse, Edith Millen, thought Cary's the worst death she had ever seen.

I agree that it was dreadful to see a fine mind incarcerated in a lifeless body. But I would debate whether it was not even worse to see the deterioration of a formerly great mind.

Do you know whether Cary knew Lord Brain?

If he had I think he would have seen him professionally. I used to see Brain two or three times a year, and I have no recollection of Brain's mentioning Cary.

I ask because Lord Brain spoke of Cary in his book The Nature of Experience,[3] *showing that he had found inspiration concerning the imagination in Cary's* Art and Reality, *which had been published shortly before. People might think more deeply about Cary's ideas, I feel, if they realized that someone like Lord Brain had already done so.*

You should see Dr Whitty, who helped with the nursing hoists for Cary. He is interested in literature, too.

NOTES

Professor Ritchie Russell was educated at Edinburgh University and worked in Oxford at the Military Hospital for Head Injuries during the last war, after which he became consultant neurologist to the Oxford Hospitals and University lecturer in neurology. He became the first holder of the Chair of Clinical Neurology at Oxford in 1966, and his work for the disabled is marked in the naming of Ritchie Russell House, the special unit for the Handicapped at the Churchill Hospital, opened in 1979. He died in December 1980, aged 77, leaving a widow and two children.

   In January 1988 Mrs Russell kindly agreed to the publication of this interview.

   1. I was given this for perusal, with permission to pass it on to the Bodleian, where it can be seen when the authorities agree.

   2. Cf. MSS. Cary 251/P.3 (fol. 28), and 296/P.172.

   3. (London, 1959), p. 72.

63

' "I want to finish this book," he said'

C.W.M. Whitty

This interview took place at the Department of Neurology, the Radcliffe Infirmary, Oxford, in January 1968.

I knew Joyce Cary for about a year only, at the end of his life. I do regret that I didn't discuss his books or philosophy with him. But my feeling is that a doctor should not take advantage of someone who is a captive because of his illness, and might feel compelled to talk if the doctor wanted him to. Sometimes the opposite occurs: the patient wants to talk but needs encouragement to do so. I don't think that applied here. I wish I had talked to him more though – for example about Clifton, where we both went. But we talked only about the weather, or his illness.

Do you remember him vividly, and do you think you would, if he had not been a famous man?

Yes, I'm sure he would have stood out in my memory, because of his remarkable stoicism, fortitude, and bravery. He faced this illness, which he knew to be fatal, with considerable stoicism. 'Whatever happens, I want to finish this book,' he said. He never complained, and didn't want to be doped, as he wanted to give everything he could to his writing. It was unusual, and very helpful, to have a patient who did not need consolation and possible glossing over the truth, but who would say, 'I've noticed this, and so we must get round it in this way.' We fitted springs to his fingers by gloves, to help the movement. Then he began to use a thicker pen, because it was easier to hold.

Do you see any significance in his ability to use the thumb and forefinger of his writing hand to the end?

Of course there was nothing mystical or unnatural in it. But it can happen that the demands of the environment enable someone to do what ordinarily he could not. I remember the case of a victim of Parkinson's disease, who was caught in a fire, and managed to move quite normally in order to escape, though afterwards he returned to his former state. That is, there are ways in which impulses can force their way down channels they don't normally use, and I agree that Cary's compelling need to write could have forced power into his right hand, while the left became infinitely weaker.

The disease is a purely motor condition; it is very organic. There was a diagnosis of possible polio in 1951, and that may in fact have been an early stage of the sclerosis.

Do you think he was conscious of facing death in an exemplary way? Journalists' reports of interviews stressed the fact.[1]

I'd never have thought of it. He just struck me as a very integrated chap who was facing the situation realistically and with great courage. But it *is* rare to find a person who can behave as he did. I didn't know about the newspaper articles.

Did you ever see him break down?

No. And I must say that anything in his final novel would be significant, I'm sure, if it bore at all on his illness.

It centres on belief in miracles, which a faith-healer tries to prove by treating a young girl and an old woman, both of whom die. A younger woman, Nona Clench, appears to be cured, but as Cary said many times that God would be denying his own nature if He performed a miracle, he must intend us to see her cure as working – somewhat in the way you have just described, perhaps. The book does reveal the faith that sustained Cary himself, I believe.

NOTES

Dr Charles Whitty (1913-) was born in Tunbridge Wells and educated at Clifton; graduated in medicine at Oxford and St Thomas's; after service in North Africa, returned to Oxford and was appointed NHS consultant neurologist in 1948; studied long-term effects of local brain wounds with Ritchie Russell. In January 1988 Dr Whitty kindly checked and agreed to the publication of this interview.
    1. Merrick Winn's (Q.8) was one, much quoted.

64

From the Author of
The First Book on Joyce Cary

Andrew Wright

The following is a record of discussions on two occasions during the summer of 1967.

I met Cary in 1953, when my University, where he was to give a lecture, asked me to look after him. I met him at the airport, and spent most of the next two or three days with him.

I was then at Columbus, Ohio State University, and I thought him intense, rather harried by his lecture tour, but immediately sympathetic. We went to an academic lunch, and then to a 'coffee hour', where I introduced him. The room was full – about fifty to sixty undergraduates, as it was just after *The Horse's Mouth* had been published in the USA. Joyce was quick on his feet and went over well. In the evening, there was a dinner and then a formal lecture, in which he talked about *Anna Karenina* etc. I'm not sure that the audience was up to what he had to say – they were too well-fed. (It was a private club.)

Does anything in particular about that time live in your memory, to suggest why you decided to write a book about him?

I had loved *The Horse's Mouth*, then read as many of the others as I could lay my hands on. The man was in the novels; I responded strongly to his warmth, magnanimity, and also courage.

What makes you the authority with whom every later scholar should begin is clear from your Foreword to Joyce Cary: A Preface to His Novels: *that, in 1956, you worked daily for six months in his house, with ready access to all material now in the Bodleian, and Cary himself there, willing to answer your questions without reservations. Have you then memories and impressions that your book omits (and that time now perhaps makes easier to discuss), regarding, for example, how he felt towards his father?*

252

I don't think Joyce had great admiration for his father. He emancipated himself from the family early. I think he had been persuaded by his family to read law [*for his Oxford degree*].
But I didn't press him on the details of his private life – I simply listened to what he chose to say.

Did he ever speak of his mother?

Not to me.

What impression did you get from him of his wife, and of his relations with her family?

He really loved his wife and he was desolate when she died.
All his wife's family were at him to get what they felt would be a proper job. But his wife steadfastly defended him. I got the strong impression that he was looked down on in Oxford even after he became a success as a novelist.
   Helen Gardner said – and told me recently [*in 1967*] that she stuck by it – that all Cary's women are facets of Trudy.

That is certainly something for critics to ponder upon. What of Middleton Murry?

Cary gave Murry money for *Rhythm*, but Murry never thought Cary much good, and gave him no encouragement; Murry never mentioned Cary until his article about London.[1] Their reunion in the summer of 1956 was warm, but the discouragement of Murry had been very strongly felt in the early years: Cary took it to heart. When they met in 1956 Murry was very regretful that he was known only as a critic; he felt that he had failed.

In early letters to his wife, when Murry the critic was gaining great influence, Cary wrote of him as a 'scamp' and a 'rascal', who should now pay back his debts to him (as he apparently never did). Did Cary ever talk in that vein to you?

Never. He was too generous-minded to say such a thing, to me.

Was the advance of Cary's illness very apparent during the months you knew him in Oxford?

Yes. In April 1956 he could still go upstairs, though he was walking with a stick. But his condition deteriorated rapidly. He had walls altered downstairs to make a bathroom; and he had to have the pen tied to his hand and write with a scroll by September.

Which visitors do you particularly remember?

Murry's visit was the highlight. It was a great reconciliation. He stayed for a day. In the spring some Professors of English at Moscow came – the first such visitors to England since 1917. David Craig came to dinner. But Cary gave the impression that he thought him a dour Scot who had been corrupted by Leavis at Cambridge. Certainly Craig's ideas had altered since he wrote his essay on Cary, and he became contemptuous.

That was sad, since Cary had thought so highly of it.[2]

Herbert Davis came every day, and Helen Gardner came often. I don't think she greatly admired Cary as a novelist; she was very conventional in such matters, and high-minded. T.S. Eliot, as you know, was the object of her particular literary devotion.

The way his unorthodox belief enabled him to face death must at least have impressed her.

I am sure it did. She liked him as a man. As my wife said, he didn't seem saintly, but very lusty of life – surrounded by adoring women and loving it. I'm sure he knew himself attractive to women, and enjoyed it.

Can you suggest why he was attractive to women?

I'll try: he was masculine, lively, and tender.

Was he aware of Helen Gardner's opinion of his work, and were there others amongst his friends in Oxford who shared it?

You will have noticed that David Cecil's preface to *The Captive and the Free* gives no opinion of him as a novelist. Cary was certainly plain spoken about the Master of Trinity, who had no use for him. He had a sense of being isolated from respectable opinion, and this he shared with Gulley Jimson.

Did you discuss the background of The Horse's Mouth? *The importance of Spinoza, for example?*

I don't recall his mentioning Spinoza. But he did say that I was making too much of the influence of Blake. 'I love Blake but he is not my master,' he said.

I have always thought the Nuremberg trials highly significant to the second trilogy; did you and Cary ever discuss them?

Only that he thought them frightful.

What of his political writing generally, and regarding Africa in particular?

C.K. Allen – Warden of Rhodes House – was of the old Empire building type, and thought Cary wrong about Africa. But they got on well.

Do you think history may be lending weight to Cary's ideas?

Certainly.

Did he discuss his religious ideas, around which he was writing The Captive and the Free *while you were in Oxford?*

He was interested in Billy Graham as magic-tongued – corrupted by his own tongue which was powerful and god-given. He was interested in the Mormons, and wrote to MRA.[3]

His attitude to MRA (Buchmanism as he always called it), and also Billy Graham, is quite clear in The Captive and the Free. *When writing this book, was he actually using a notebook with a red-blue marbled cover and brown binding, which he'd begun using in 1913?*[4]

I remember it still at his side in September 1956.

I have wondered whether it was a kind of talisman for him. Most striking is the way names are grouped in that notebook, even for the last novel. Did he discuss his use of names with you?

I remember he said that he'd used the name *Goodman* instead of *Godman* for a character in *The Horse's Mouth*, because it was less obvious, though *Godman* was the meaning he intended. He made much of names and altered them frequently in the course of composition.

Your own notebooks show how systematically you worked, and students will be glad to know that they are also in the Joyce Cary Collection in the Bodleian.

What advice now would you now offer, regarding Cary's, and therefore his manuscripts', ultimate worth?

They repay study. They are indispensable to a full understanding of Cary. Your own work with them is of enormous value, and I'd like to say so with much gratitude.

NOTES

Andrew Howell Wright (1923-) was educated at Harvard University, and Ohio State University, where he took his MA in 1948 and Ph.D. in 1951. He was Professor of English at Ohio State University from 1955-1963, and has been Professor of English at the University of California, San Diego, since 1963. His chief publications are *Jane Austen's Novels: A Study in Structure*, 1953; *Joyce Cary: A Preface to His Novels*, 1958; (Co-Author) *Selective Bibliography for the Study of English and American Literature*, 1960; *Henry Fielding: Mask and Feast*, 1965; *Blake's Job: A Commentary*, 1972; *Anthony Trollope: Dream and Art*, 1982.

In December 1987 Professor Wright kindly checked this record of our discussions and agreed to its publication.

1. 'Coming to London', *London Magazine* III (1956), 30-37.

2. It is in the Bodleian, and was published as 'Idea and Imagination: A Study of Joyce Cary', *Fox* [c. 1954] pp. 3-10; Cary had said that Craig was the one critic who had taught him anything about himself.

3. See item 19, n. 2.

4. The notebook has the shelfmark 253/N.14.

65

From the Author of
Joyce Cary's Africa

M.M. Mahood

The following discussion was begun in Oxford on 21 November 1987, and completed by correspondence.

Joyce Cary's Africa reveals how well-qualified you are to comment upon his African writing. Would you say first what attracted you to Nigeria, where you spent nine years as Professor of English at Ibadan University?

I knew next to nothing about Nigeria in 1954 when I took up a post in Ibadan. I had become interested in African education after two visits to South Africa, the second of them spent teaching in the only black university, Fort Hare. On my way home from this second visit I stopped over for a few nights in Ghana. I fell in love with the country, largely on the rebound from South Africa: the charm and beauty of the people, the absence of racial tensions, the idea of starting a university that was to be of the same standard as a British residential university, all encouraged me to apply for a job there. I did not get it, but two years later I was offered one at Ibadan. Nigeria was less like Ghana than I had realised, though all the points I've made about Ghana applied, and in some ways it was even more stimulating.

When did you decide to write a book about Joyce Cary?

The idea of a book on Joyce Cary did not occur to me until after his death, when Mrs Davin drew my attention to his letters from Nigeria. That must have been shortly after all Cary's papers were given to the Bodleian – perhaps 1958?

How well did you know him? Was he helpful regarding material?

Though Cary was an honorary member of the English Faculty at Oxford when I was teaching at St Hugh's, 1947-54, I haven't any recollection of meeting him in that period nor of reading any of his novels other than *The Horse's Mouth*; I remember remarking to an undergraduate how good I thought it and she retorted 'I've been telling you to read it for years.' I didn't discover the 'Nigerian' novels till I was actually working in Nigeria. Then I thought it would be wonderful to have him out in Ibadan as a sort of writer-in-residence and early in 1955 I wrote to suggest this. But by then he must have begun to feel the bad effects of the aircraft accident which triggered off his final illness,[1] and he had to refuse. I went to see him in the Long Vacation, when I always returned to Oxford. We had tea in the garden, but he was probably not feeling good or found me dull and I remember being disappointed by remarks like 'the average Nigerian is a very good sort of chap, isn't he?'. I think I saw him the following year, but by then he was largely confined to his bed. (I'm afraid this is a disappointing non-memoir. I have always been overawed by writers and unable to ask them questions.)

How did you discover facts about the local scene?

From holiday jaunts inside Nigeria I knew some of the places in which Cary passed his first tour. I paid a special visit to Borgu and explored the filing cabinets in the District Office, turning out some of the manuscript records I made use of in my book. Others I read in the Archives at Kaduna and in Ibadan. And of course I tracked down as many of Cary's contemporaries in the Nigerian Service as were still alive.

You have concluded with a chapter entitled 'The Comedy of Freedom'. Would you say something about that title, in relation to Cary's work, and to your assessment of it?

I think I've said somewhere in *Joyce Cary's Africa* that although Cary wanted to give the title of 'The Comedy of Freedom' to his whole oeuvre, it fully applies only to the novels from *Mister Johnson* onwards. From then on he conceives of life as a comedy in the Dantean sense: just as the Divine Comedy is God's inventiveness and creativity overcoming evil, so the individual in struggling to make his own life is part of that creative process. Johnson's death is creation, not destruction, because in making Rudbeck shoot him he makes him part of his vision of the two friends who together beat the system; indeed he liberates Rudbeck. Further comedy, in the ordinary sense of the word, comes from the way our separate creativities clash – young against old, man against woman, etc. In the novels before *Mister Johnson* this theme makes itself felt, but in an inchoate way, perhaps because Cary was still very much under the influence of Conrad, who was deeply distrustful of individualism, who put his trust in codes of practice and social conditioning; who for all his deep scepticism is the born Catholic in contrast to the born Protestant, Cary.

You write that 'an African setting for his first few novels helped him to clarify his fundamental ideas.' Do you think they equally clarify his ideas for his readers (if read with sufficient attention), and should therefore not be ignored by serious scholars?

I think the serious scholar needs to look very closely at all Cary's early manuscripts, whether the story in question has an African setting or not: his struggles with his first novel, *Aissa Saved*, are particularly interesting since his attempt to contrast the responsible initiatives of Ali with the emotional self-abandon of Aissa to the latter's disadvantage breaks down as Cary comes to understand the affirmative strength of Aissa's behaviour.

In his prefatory essay for The African Witch, *Cary answered those who assumed from it* 'that the Empire had failed to educate the African, and that this was the worst of its crimes.' *His answer was that education would* 'open the whole country to the agitator', *and is not* 'a natural and "obvious" right of mankind', *since belief in education* 'belongs to metaphysics, to a view of the world as the realm of spirit. The real reason why Africa shold be educated is that it is the duty, the religious duty, if you like, for all of us to desire enlightenment for all men, for all God's souls.' *Do you think that such remarks deserve more attention from his critics than they have received?*

In view of the time that the prefatory essay to *The African Witch* was written, Cary seems to be addressing himself to left-wing critics of colonial stagnation and criticises their two assumptions that education will make everyone happy (it will in fact spread discontent) and that it is a natural right (he maintains it is a supernatural one). Very characteristically, Cary conceives education in terms of the awakening of vision rather than the transmission of skills. For that alone I'd like to see more attention given to his ideas on education. But as far as Africa is concerned, it has to be admitted that he was bound by his own zeitgeist in being hopelessly paternalistic – thinking of education as something given to the poor deprived Aficans by the colonial power. (Though to be fair there are indications that he is well aware of the value of

traditional 'tribal' education.) In a notebook he talks about giving a full
European civilization to Africa. It's true he adds that this won't swamp
'African culture'. But there is a strange nineteen-forties cocksureness
here that European civilization is the highest good. Equally dated is the
élitism of the assumption that one gives a tip top education to the
selected few who are to be leaders of their people. I suffered from both
illusions when I went to Africa, and it took a lot of disillusioning
experience and the written words of Fanon and others to shake me out
of them.

Chapter XII of The Case for African Freedom *is entitled 'Importance of
Women's Education', where Cary says:* 'The adult education of women
is not only the most urgent part of the whole problem in Africa, it is one
of special difficulty.' *Would you comment on his views in this regard?*

Cary was certainly right about the importance of education for African
women (the often repeated truism of the time was that if you educate a
woman you educate a family) but the special difficulties were I think
exaggerated by him because of his limited African experience. Women
in Southern Nigeria or places like Ghana, South Africa and many other
areas (as he admits in the last paragraph of this chapter of *The Case for
African Freedom*) have a strong and in many ways an independent
position in the economy and in the social structure. It is in many ways a
separate position, which makes it necessary, as Cary stresses, for
women's education to be a thing on its own.

*Cary said that the revolution of the women is the greatest social revolution, in
the true sense, that the world has seen. In view of social developments since
his death, is this also an aspect of his theme that deserves attention at this
date?*

I think what Cary says about women's emancipation and indeed what
he says about women is the least satisfactory part of his work. He was
committed by his literary and intellectual affiliations to cheer on the
emancipation of women, but he was brought up in an almost all-male
environment to distrust everything feminine as potentially effeminate.
One of the most revealing things in the Cary Collection is his marginalia
to Iris Murdoch's first book. He regarded it as outrageous and absurd
that she should have adopted a male persona. I don't think he ever rid
himself of the Edwardian certainty that men and women have totally
different mental processes. Blake's horror of Female Domination was
very congenial to him – he makes great play with it in the relationship of

Sara and Gulley. I personally find his attempts to get inside a woman's mind in Sara and Nina the weakest thing about his writing.

How do you think he deserves to be remembered, and what chance do you think there is of that happening?

I think Cary deserves to be remembered for the springiness, the élan, the vitality of his writing; for the coherence of his philosophy of life and for the seriousness with which he treated the novel as an art form in making his own novels the vehicles for that philosophy; for adding a whole important area of neneteenth- and twentieth-century experience to the novel's scope, in choosing to write about West Africa; for the courage of his stylistic and formal experiments; for his ability to surprise us with joy. Inevitably he is out of fashion at the present, but he will I think, in a couple of generations's time, be recognized as in say the top ten of English novelists of the first half of the present century.

NOTES

Professor Molly Maureen Mahood writes of herself: 'born 1919, ran away to Nigeria after several years as an Oxford don. Went on to Tanzania. Twelve years at University of Kent, where I helped launch African and Caribbean Studies. Retired, took a degree in biology, then settled down to being a Shakespearean critic. Best book: *The Colonial Encounter*, 1977, if you can find it.'

On 4 February 1988, Professor Mahood kindly agreed to the publication of this discussion.

1. On 16 Jan. 1955 (see 'Outline', above).

66

The Bodleian Bequest

James Osborn

This interview took place on 24 July 1967 in New Haven, Connecticut, at the Osborns' home; Mrs Osborn – Marie Louise – shared her husband's memories of Cary.

Did you meet Joyce Cary during the 1930s? His cousin Lionel Stevenson thought that he might have introduced you, when he too was in Oxford, working for a B.Litt. degree.

No. I met him once only, shortly before he died, when Win and Dan Davin took us – Marie Louise and me – to visit him. The way he played the genial host, in spite of his physical difficulties, was unforgettable. We especially remember how he chuckled as he asked us: 'Have you heard Oxford described as a hotbed of cold feet?' He was a man whose sense of humour stayed with him, and a sense of the incongruity of mankind. He was most impressive.

When he died, Win asked my advice about his manuscripts. She knew of me as one of the most active collectors, although my interest really stops at about 1820. (The only other instance of my collecting anything more recent is a piece of African sculpture, which I shall show you after lunch.)

At first I suggested that the collection should go to Sothebys, and then I had a second thought; that this was a chance to keep the manuscripts together, and this would be unique. I therefore wrote to Bodley, saying that if they would accept them and keep them together, I would give the collection. Bodley agreed. Andrew Wright had already arranged for Ohio State University to buy the books of Cary's library (those not wanted by his sons); so he had to say that the deal had been superseded.

It is practically unique to have everything together in this way. No modern creative writer of Joyce Cary's status has been associated with Oxford. Yeats was considered a fool in Oxford. He was not appreciated. When seated next to a dowager, and asked 'And what is your speciality, Mr Yeats?' he answered, 'Astrology.' So I thought:

'Oxford didn't appreciate Yeats. Let us see what Oxford makes of Joyce Cary.'

When I saw an article on Joyce Cary (by someone with a name like Little, or Liddell), which I thought offhand about the Cary Collection, I mentioned this to Robert Shackleton *[Bodley's Librarian, then]*. And I said that Win Davin should be the person to give permission to use the Collection.

NOTE

Dr James Marshall Osborn (1906-1976) was an alumnus of Yale University, who came up to St Catherine's College Oxford in 1937 to take a B.Litt. His previous notable gift to the Bodleian had been the hitherto unknown autobiography of Thomas Wythorne, the Elizabethan musician. His gift of Cary's books and manuscripts was made through Bodley's American Friends, which had recently been formed, largely through his efforts. Most of the manuscripts were given between 1959 and 1966, the remainder being given in 1972 and 1975 by his two sons.

67

Closing Recollections

Winifred Davin   Dan Davin

This discussion took place at the Davins' home in Oxford on 16 November 1987.

This book would be incomplete without a few words from you both, though you must feel that you have said and shown all that should be expected from you. Your essay in Closing Times, *Dan, is by far the best portrait of Cary from every viewpoint, including that of a fellow novelist.*[1] *And no-one can begin to study his manuscripts in the Bodleian, without realizing that you, Win, performed tasks that ensured his immortality, but could so easily have been left undone. Would you tell again, because it deserves a permanent record, what was involved in clearing all that the James Osborn Collection comprised from 12 Parks Road, and arranging for its transfer to the Bodleian?*

[**Win**:] Most of Joyce's manuscripts were stored in a box for each novel, and all of these were up in the loft of his house. You climbed up a ladder, and it was one of those absolutely fascinating lofts where there were still elephant-hair bracelets that he had brought from Africa – all kinds of things. There were two beautiful dresses from an eighteenth-century wedding in his family; he got our children [Delia and Brigid] to put them on.[2] They had already become very well acquainted with the loft, because he couldn't move off the ground-floor for the last eighteen months of his life; and he used to send the children up and tell them to find this or that, because he knew how they adored adventuring up there and finding things. [...]

Even before we heard that Jim Osborn was going to give the manuscripts to Bodley, we had started to clean them. Everything had to be electroluxed first because, although the boxes were lidded and wrapped in paper, the dust had infiltrated. They had been there for years – each one went up after the novel was finished. I'm sure that Trudy had organized it all in the old days, and it had been kept up. There were a couple of boxes which weren't sorted, as you know.

Well, then we sorted them into files, which Bodley sent along, and all this took, I suppose, a couple of months altogether. The children used to come in after school and help, and Edith and I did a lot of it together – Edith Millen, Joyce's secretary, because she stayed on for a while. She was enormously helpful, especially with 'The Captive and the Free' which, as you know, has got a lot of different versions and so on, but also with the other posthumous publications, *Memoir of the Bobotes*, *Art and Reality*, and *Spring Song*. Then all went to Bodley.

A few months later I had a quick letter from Jim Osborn, saying, 'My manuscript dealer, who lives in New Haven, Lawrence Witten, is coming to England and can spend a couple of days in Oxford, if you will kindly take him to Bodley and show him the Collection. You know that I bought a pig in a poke, on your recommendation. I would like to know what I've got.' Actually, it wasn't quite a pig in a poke, because I had written a quick description. However, the dealer came, and it was very interesting to me to see a book-man assess a literary collection.

He said, 'I don't know anything about literary merit or literary prestige or rank or anything like that.' And at the end he said, 'It doesn't really matter what this man's literary status is, because in sheer bulk this is the second greatest collection of a writer's work that exists in Europe.' And I said, 'Who is first?' And he said, 'Balzac. Of course you know that there is a special museum in which all his things are. It's been existing for – I don't know how long he said, eighty years or something like that – and they still haven't managed to catalogue it all yet.'

Apart from the sheer magnitude of his literary remains, can Cary be compared in any way with Balzac, do you think?

[**Win**:] Balzac was obviously one of the writers he liked; I don't remember that he thought Balzac had a great influence on him. But he always had a very great interest in France and Paris.

I ask because I wonder whether you would link 'The Comedy of Freedom', as Cary's considered over-all title for his novel series, with Balzac's Comédie Humaine? You may remember an early letter to his wife, where he regrets that he hasn't 'racketed about' in London more, because he 'would like to be London's Balzac and make a new Comédie Humaine.' He calls the novels 'the finest sort of history as well as interesting novels.'[3]

[**Dan**:] What you have quoted is the sort of frame of reference in which Joyce would conduct any literary discussion with anyone quite casually. I've no memory at all of it, but I'd be very surprised if Balzac hadn't come up more than once when we talked. As to the *Comédie Humaine*, my guess is that, if Cary was thinking of 'The Comedy of Freedom' as a collective title, he would find there were echoes of Dante there as well, which would be at least as obvious a point of reference as Balzac's.

I'm sure you are right. But, as author of The Horse's Mouth, *Cary may have something of 'London's Balzac' about him too, I think. And that leads to another question. I remember your saying this, Dan:* 'I think he had never quite lost the sense that only cads go into pubs. At least the once or twice that he came into one I never felt him to be comfortable. All the more surprising then, that his own description of pubs, in *The Horse's Mouth* for example, are so completely convincing.'

Do you think that, perhaps, his marriage developed that attitude in him, so that his discomfort was a kind of subconscious guilt?

[**Dan**:] I rather think he did always have that attitude to pubs. You suggest that it was an attitude developed during marriage. I imagine it was probably confirmed during marriage. I think his first impression of pubs would have been formed when he was a child in Ireland, and then only the book-makers and horsy chaps around the place would use pubs. A gentleman would drink his sherry or whatever at home in the drawing room or in the conservatory or wherever he smoked. And I guess Joyce would have been conditioned very much by that. I don't think he had any explicit prejudice against them, but you could feel instinctively that this was not his scene. It really wasn't for men of his generation in general.

[**Win**:] He never went to a pub.

My question was related to what you say in Closing Times, *Dan:* 'And after Trudy's death he liked to talk of the world of his young manhood, the world before 1914, and how beautiful its beautiful women were' (*p. 110*). *His son Michael said that his father liked to talk of that world, but his mother disapproved. Apart from the women in them, were places like the Café d'Harcourt, which he frequented in Paris, so very different from an English pub?*

[**Dan**:] Quite different. A café, or a brothel for that matter, is of a different order of being from a pub.

[**Win**:] You see, when he was up at Oxford, no undergraduate was allowed to go to a pub. Then he went to Africa, and I'm sure he never drank in a bar in Africa. In fact, he was in a Muslim state, so there were no bars. All of this must have confirmed that attitude.

[**Dan**:] I don't think it was a very strong prejudice, it was an unconscious attitude of his generation. C.S. Lewis and his chums drank in the Eagle and Child, and people still think it's worth recording, whereas on the whole I would have taken it for granted.

Could we talk now of change in the attitude to women? Cary strongly upheld women's causes in his writing, and also in life, I believe. Can you recall any examples?

[**Dan**:] Joyce was particularly at home with people like Enid Starkie and Helen Gardner, who were obvious examples of women's having an independent career and being able to take it for granted that they were thought of as on the same intellectual and other levels as people like Joyce himself. But it was easier to take it for granted with someone else who takes it for granted. And in this case the man certainly did.

[**Win**:] One evening Joyce was here, and Enid Starkie; Helen wasn't, Jean Banister was (who was tutor at Somerville in physiology), and various others – about a dozen people. And Enid, who loved to tease Joyce, said: 'Joyce, I can't understand how, when you write a novel with a woman in it, you always make her one of those dreary characters who's always polishing the table and that's what she likes – that's the way she lives her life. I can't understand it. All your friends are intellectual women. Why don't you put them in your novels? You haven't got one! You haven't got one that could be mistress of Somerville, for example.' And Jean said: 'Oh yes, there's one.' And Joyce said, 'Jean, is there? Who is it?' She said, '*The African Witch*.'

In fact, intellectual women appear quite a lot in his work.
Helen Gardner told of a letter she cherished particularly, because he wrote it with great difficulty when he was dying; it concerned an occasion when he thought she'd been unfairly treated just because she was a woman.[4]

[**Dan**:] That would have been when she didn't get the Chair of English. That's when Bowra said: 'I'm sorry you didn't get the Chair, Helen. Of course, you're trouble is that you're a woman.'

[*Win*:] 'You're the wrong sex,' he said, and gave her a slap on the back. She said it nearly made her fall down the steps. But she did get it the next time round.

By then Joyce Cary was dead, of course. I do like what Helen Gardner says, in relation to the letter I've just mentioned, regarding his view of women's emancipation, as the most profound social revolution he had lived through, which 'went happily along' *with his sympathetic view of women as embodying the values of family love –* 'life itself', *as she quotes that he said. Her understanding of his view of women clearly differs from Enid Starkie's – and Molly Mahood's [above].*

Regarding injustice towards women, do you think Jim Latter's failure to marry Nina a key point of the second trilogy, in relation to his theme of honour? In Closing Times *you say, Dan:* 'The great European novelists of the nineteenth century were those he read and re-read, though he would sometimes say that Conrad was the only novelist who had influenced him.'

[*Win*:] I heard him say that too. I remember it because Graham Greene as a novelist is obviously influenced by Conrad, and Graham and Joyce are miles apart. Yet each of them was influenced by Conrad, who isn't *the* one you would think of immediately.

I wonder whether Cary made the remark you remember when he was creating Jim Latter, and at the same time preparing his lectures 'The Novel as Truth', in which he shows that for him Conrad's Lord Jim is unconvincing.[5] *Did he hope Jim Latter would be more convincing, perhaps?*

[*Dan*:] I doubt if he thought like that really. There was no book Joyce ever read, that he wouldn't reconstruct – he would say that a writer had missed an opportunity here or he ought to have done that there; something of the sort. So in some such context he might easily have been a bit critical of *Lord Jim*.

[*Win*:] He considered Jim Latter to be a fascist character, more or less, whereas Chester Nimmo is a kind of Lloyd George character. And he always said, 'Chester's my man.'

[*Dan*:] I wonder whether he had in mind, when he was creating Chester, the Latin *nimis* for too much – Chester Nimmo! He always defended Chester as the better character – not necessarily more convincing, but as a better man.

[**Win**:] In real life I don't think he would have chosen him for a bosom friend.

I feel that Jim is much more him.

[**Win**:] He didn't.

[**Dan**:] He didn't. He'd repudiate that, but that isn't to say that it wasn't to some extent true.

[**Win**:] There was an African colonial administrator whom Joyce disliked very much, and he'd attributed everything he disliked about him to Jim.

Did you ever discuss Frank Buchman, from whom Brightman, the real mischief-maker of Not Honour More, *seems to be drawn?*

[**Win**:] Joyce was terribly interested in the Oxford Group [founded by Buchman].

[**Dan**:] The name was later changed to Moral Rearmament.

[**Win**:] Joyce was frightfully interested in any strange religion, and when he was writing *The Captive and the Free*, he used to get Edith Millen to send away to all sorts of people, and religious groups, to send him their pamphlets. He had a drawer full of them and was fascinated by it all.

In his notebooks, Cary seems always to have referred to Buchman and his followers as 'The Buchmanites'. And he seems to be remembering an actual meeting he had attended in Oxford, when he ridicules them in The Captive and the Free.

[**Dan**:] They were often called Buchmanites, and I remember telling him about a Buchmanite meeting in Otago (New Zealand).

Would you say something, Win, about this last novel, which we would not have unless you had edited it for publication. Had he discussed it with you much?

[**Win**:] Not really.

Did he think you might edit it, if he could not finish it, do you suppose?

[**Win**:] It was never discussed.

[**Dan**:] He hung on to it as long as he conceivably could – long after I thought he wasn't going to finish it.

[**Win**:] I don't think he himself knew how near he was to finishing it. When he began the novel, he intended it to be a trilogy, but the inexorable advance of his illness made him change from that plan, to a single volume novel. However, Joyce did not write a novel by beginning at the beginning and progressing towards the end. He had a set of shelves to hold twelve files, one for each part of the novel he was writing, and he might work on any section of it, from day to day. A consequence of this method (which was rather like an artist's in painting a picture) was that a great deal of work had to be done in the last stages of the novel – he called the process 'jointing-up', and he often discarded whole sections – the famous example is *The Old Strife at Plant's* – and he rewrote passages to bridge the gaps. The manuscript of *The Captive and the Free*, which I edited, was in many sections of course, and my aim was to reveal the nearest I could to a final version. But the novel, although it has an ending, is unfinished as a painting might be – detail, relation of parts, high and low relief are imperfect, and there are some gaps in the narrative line.

[**Dan**:] I think, towards the end, he liked to do things where he did see the end. So he wrote those last stories.

Who in Oxford, besides yourselves, regarded him as a great novelist, do you think?

[**Win**:] I don't think people go round saying, for instance, 'Iris is a great novelist.'

Dan says in Closing Times *that you said it of Cary.*

[**Dan**:] Yes, you said it in Bristol in 1943. I hadn't heard of him before then. But I remember C.K. Allen [Warden of Rhodes House] saying how remarkably interesting this chap Cary was. They had done Air-Raid duty together.

But did he read his novels? Did many Oxford people like, or even know, his novels, do you think?

[**Dan**:] You have to remember that people in Oxford have a lifetime habit of picking holes in things. Someone only has to make a statement for it at once to be contradicted or queried. And the Oxford nature is a bit like that. However much they may like a person or his product, they will first of all concentrate on what they consider to be its faults. So nobody is less perfect than somebody in Oxford is.

What about the description of Oxford as a hotbed of cold feet?

[**Dan**:] I'd never heard it before Joyce said it, but that doesn't mean that it couldn't be a proverbial expression.

But it's equally likely that it was originally his?

[**Dan**:] I'd be very surprised if it were in *The Oxford Dictionary of Proverbs*.

So would I.[6] *But I think it's a perfect description of the place.*

[**Dan**:] Yes, it is.

Might he have felt himself to be an Irishman in Oxford and an Englishman in Ireland, and could that explain his conflicting accounts of his own nationality? In Memoir of the Bobotes, *he is explicitly Irish; in 'Speaking for Myself', in 1950, and in late essays like 'Cromwell House', he seems eager to show himself as Anglo-Irish. But also, as you say in* Closing Times, *Dan:* 'There were times when he seemed to speak as an Irishman but, after Ireland became a republic and perhaps before, he considered himself an Englishman whose family had happened to live in Ireland for three hundred years.'
What do you think is the significance of this remark?

[**Dan**:] I would have thought it was quite a neat way of putting a state of affairs. By then the political distinction had become apparent and explicit.
   I would have said though that in a way the same problem probably existed in the nineteenth century: that Anglo-Irishmen coming to London to represent Ireland in Parliament would sometimes feel English; at other times, because of the behaviour of the Englishmen

towards them, they would feel themselves Irish. I'd be surprised if you couldn't find in memoirs more or less explicit statements to that effect.

That is the feeling I am suggesting Cary might have had about himself in Oxford. Some contributors to this book thought him more Irish than English, and he and his brother were apparently ridiculed because of their Irish accents, when they first attended school in England. The feeling that, as an Anglo-Irishman, he was both English and Irish, is the real point, I think, of his late essay, 'The Meaning of England'.[7]

[**Dan**:] It's rather like being a New Zealander living in England (provided you aren't Irish) or vice versa.

Do you think that the way history and ideas have developed in recent years will make him better understood than he was in his lifetime, and appreciated in the way he had hoped?

[**Dan**:] I think every writer who survives is permanently misunderstood, but in different ways for every generation. I think they are all misunderstood. But I think he'll survive. That kind of vitality invariably breaks through in the end, because it's the best kind of art. You can feel the life pulsing in it.

Do you think his centenary a wholly appropriate time for a reassessment of his work?

[**Dan**:] I think any time is time for reassessment. But there is always something about the topical which hooks attention, and what we all would like to see is Joyce getting more attention. He certainly deserves it, even though the fashion for the moment has passed him by.

NOTES

Winifred Davin (née Gonley), of Irish parentage, was born and educated in New Zealand. She has lived in England since 1937, in Oxford except for the war years, when she was a social worker in Bristol University Settlement. Her work has been mainly editing (including Joyce Cary's posthumous publications), and lexicography. She acts as literary executor at the request of the Executors of the Joyce Cary estate.

Dan Davin was born in New Zealand in 1913, of Irish parents, and educated at the University of Otago and Oxford, where he became a Fellow of Balliol. In the Second World War he served in the British Army, and after 1940 as an officer in the New Zealand Division, in Greece, Crete, North Africa, and Italy. Besides *Closing Times* (quoted above), he has written seven novels, two volumes of short stories, and a military history, *Crete* (1953). He was Deputy Chief Executive and Academic Publisher for the Delegates of the OUP in his late years at OUP. (He was at the Press from 1945-1978). In 1987 he was awarded a CBE for services to New Zealand literature.

In January 1988, Mr and Mrs Davin kindly agreed to the publication of this discussion.

1. 'Five Windows Darken', one of seven biographical essays in *Closing Times* (London: Oxford University Press, 1975). pp. 93-120.

2. Lady Cary has them now; she says they are eighteenth-century bridesmaids' dresses, but have disintegrated; the wedding was between a Chichester and a Cary, Win Davin thinks; another possibility is that they came from his maternal grandmother's family, the Hacketts.

3. From a letter of 21 Oct. 1916, to his wife; there are 13 novels by Balzac amongst Cary's books in Bodley, some having been bought on his honeymoon; the wish expressed in that letter might have been formed by then.

4. 'Foreword', *Selected Essays*, p. xi.

5. See MS. Cary 239 *a*, typescript notes for '1st night', page numbered 7.

6. I have not found it in any such dictionary.

7. *Holiday*, 1958, (E.79).